Guardians of the Gate

A Military History of the
MOHYAL FIGHTING BRAHMINS

Guardians of the Gate

A Military History of the
MOHYAL FIGHTING BRAHMINS

Maj Gen (Dr) GD Bakshi, SM, VSM (Retd)

KW
KNOWLEDGE WORLD

KW Publishers Pvt Ltd
New Delhi

ISBN   978-93-86288-77-6   Paperback
ISBN   978-93-86288-78-3   ebook

Published in India by Kalpana Shukla

KWV
KNOWLEDGE WORLD

KW Publishers Pvt Ltd
4676/21, First Floor, Ansari Road, Daryaganj, New Delhi 110002
Phone: +91 11 23263498/43528107
Email: kw@kwpub.com • www.kwpub.com

Printed and bound in India.

Contents

Dedicated

to

My father and mother

Dr S P Bakshi

Mrs Kshama Bakshi

And my ancestors

Foreword

The Mohyal Community is celebrating the 125th founding anniversary of its General Mohyal Sabha (GMS) on 12th March 2017 with a grand concourse at the Talkatora Stadium at New Delhi. This is an apt occasion to reflect upon our history and antecedents. Where we are going depends a lot on where we come from and hence it is important that we record and learn from our History.

I would like to compliment Maj Gen (Dr) G D Bakshi SM, VSM (retd), a true blooded Mohyal scholar- warrior for taking out this invaluable document on the Military History of the Mohyals. The Mohyal Brahmins have been warriors of great renown and it was essential to record their Military History to inspire our future generations. The Mohyals have also excelled in many other fields as academics, bureaucrats, doctors, scholars, scientists, engineers, cinema artists, business leaders and men of letters. This community has not just a great past – it has an equally bright future. On the 125th founding anniversary of the GMS, I am happy to note that Maj Gen Bakshi and his son Aditya Bakshi have taken out two documentaries- one on the 'History of Mohyals' and the other on the 'History of the General Mohyal Sabha.' I commend their dedication to the cause of their community and hope this book will encourage our people and scholars to further research the history and exploits of a very unique people.

Rzd B D Bali
President
General Mohyal Sabha New Delhi
March 2017

Introductory Note

This is a well recorded military history of a fascinating people who have fought every invader who crossed our borders – right from Alexander to the Arabs, the Turko-Mongols, Pathans, Uzbeks and all others. It forms a fascinating history of these invasions and especially throws light on a glorious period of Indian Military History – the repelling of the Arab invasions by the Hindu Mohyal kings of Afghanistan. The world-conquering Arab armies had spread through the Middle East, Persia, Central Asia and North Africa and even conquered Spain. The first time they were checked and thrown back was by the Hindu kings – the Rutbils and Shahis of Kandahar and Kabul. They held the Arabs at bay for 300 years. This is a meticulously researched document and throws new light on Alexander's invasion and retreat, as also the often misrepresented Arab invasion of Sindh.

It also throws new light on the Afghan invasions of Mehmud Ghazni and Muhammad Ghori and the rise of the Sikhs as a military brotherhood. An Indian Military Revival had taken place under the Sikh Gurus, and the Mohyals played a leading part in this Renaissance.

I have known Maj Gen (Dr) G D Bakshi since the time he was a 2nd Lieutenant in the Sixth Battalion of the Jammu and Kashmir Rifles. As his Colonel of the Regiment I watched the progress of his career progression with great interest. He is a combat veteran and a dedicated military historian who compiled the history of his Regiment, as also that of the National Defence Academy and the National Defence College of India. As such he was uniquely qualified to attempt the military history of the Mohyal – Fighting Brahmins. This is a work of great scholarship and meticulous research and I commend him for this service.

He has pointed out how vibrant and alive the Mohyal Military tradition still is. This small community of some 6-7 lakh people has produced three Governors, six Army Commanders and equivalents in the Army and Airforce, 10 Corps Commanders and equivalent in the Army and Navy, 15 Major Generals, 21 Brigadiers, 5 Air Vice Marshal and 2 Air Commodore. Above all it has won one Ashok Chakra (Posthumous), 4 Maha Vir Chakras and 4 Vir Chakras – an impressive tally for so miniscule a community. I am certain this well researched book will prompt many more scholars to study the subject of the many military invasions of India and the lessons to be learnt therefrom.

The primary lesson is about our tragic lack of unity that has cost us so dearly in the past.

Lt Gen **G L Bakshi** PVSM (Retd)
Vice President GMS

1

Prologue

A Paradigm Shift in Indology:
From the Indus to the Saraswati

Rivers of Identity

The Ganga is the most sacred stream of the Indian Civilization. It flows not only through space but also through time. In the Indian tradition, each night this river is worshipped by a *'Ganga Aarti'* – a ritual liturgy in which the priests wave the lamps of light (*diyas*) in the honour of this most sacred stream of the Indian consciousness. When you stand amongst the ecstatic throngs that gravitate to this river each evening for the *aarti*, you partake in a ritual that is as old as the millenniums. As you stand among the reverent throngs, you are deeply touched by the power of the ritual. Rituals tie us to our origins. It reflects the essence of the spectacular cultural continuity of this civilization that has been empirically carbon dated to 7,000 years of age and antiquity. The relics of Mehragarh in Baluchistan and the undersea artifacts extracted from the historical port city of Dwarka have been carbon dated to 7,000 years of age.

Standing amongst the throngs of people attending the *Aarti* ritual on the banks of the Ganga River, one gets deeply struck by the amazing cultural continuity of the Indian civilization – the continuity of rituals, practices, ways of thought and worship across the millenniums of history. You sit by the banks of the Ganga and watch the garlands of golden and brown marigolds pulled along by its current. Each one of us would like to retrace our roots – to come to terms with our own identity. What were our origins? Who are we as a people? Where did we come from? Did we come from the faraway steppes of Central Asia? Or did we go outwards from India to distant lands? Where are we headed today, as a nation and as a people? These are seminal questions that we have to ask at one time or the other.

This book is about such questions. It is about my personal quest for my identity and my people.

The key to our quest for identity is locked up in these sacred streams of India. These *rivers flow not only through space – they also flow through time.* These are not just water bodies. They are the sacred repositories of our spiritual traditions. They are the streams that bind us with our origins. In India, the rivers are deemed to be not just physical bodies of water but sacred streams of our collective consciousness. Numerous sages have sat on the banks of these civilizational streams and have meditated deeply. The conscious energies of their meditations have charged these flowing streams of waters and rendered them incredibly sacred. These bodies of water get energized by our deep meditations and powerful streams of thought. It is water that holds this charge in a remarkable fashion. This civilization therefore regards these rivers as the most sacred symbols of our cultural continuity down the vast vistas of space and time.

The '*Nadi Sukta*' of the Rig Veda lists these sacred streams as the *Sapt Sindhva* – the land of the seven sacred streams. Surprisingly this Sukta begins – not with the Ganga – now the holiest of all Indian rivers, but with the mythical stream of the Saraswati. In Vedic times this river was considered the most sacred of all the rivers of India. In fact, the name of this most sacred stream occurs some 50 times in the Rig Veda. It was supposed to symbolize the Goddess of wisdom, learning and intuition. Clearly, it must have been a mighty river – whose memory has been preserved with such astonishing clarity, by our oral tradition. When you go to the *Sangam* (Confluence) at Prayag (Allahabad) – the boatman takes you to the point where the sacred streams of the Ganga and Yamuna meet. The two streams merge here, he announce, but there is a third stream — which is invisible now. For it has gone underground. This is the legendary Saraswati.

For long, people considered this river to be just a myth. The story of a long lost river, people felt, was just a fairy tale. Then we saw the remarkable satellite photos taken by the Indian Space Research Organization (ISRO) in the first decade of this century. These depict in clear and astonishing detail the dried out tract of a mighty river that once flowed from the Himalayas to the Arabian Sea. It was a perennial snow-fed stream – well supplied by the melting glaciers of the mountains. Its dry, sandy bed even today measures 6-8 kms wide. It was indeed a mighty river – so much mightier and bigger than the Ganga and regarded with deep reverence by the Vedic Aryans. The Yamuna and the Satluj rivers both used to merge with the powerful flow of the Saraswati. It flowed along the town of Kurukshetra in Haryana and then near Fort Abbas, before entering into the area which is now arid desert in Pakistan, and flowed down to the Gulf of Kutch. Sixty percent of the sites of the Indus valley civilization have been found along the course of this ancient stream and only 40 percent are along the Indus river per se.

The Indus valley civilization therefore, is not the real cradle and mother civilization of our people. The Arabs, the Greeks, the British have all got it wrong. They termed us as Hindus as we all supposedly lived first along the banks of the Sindhu Nadi (the Indus). The word 'India' itself can be traced back to the Greek word Indica that owed its origin to the Indus river.

Satellite imagery however, has now confirmed beyond an iota of doubt that the most sacred stream of the Indian civilization was not really the Ganga nor even the Indus, but the Saraswati. That was the mightiest river of the Indian civilization. That was the real cradle of the Indian civilization. Terracotta dolls found in these settlements have the traditional *bindi* on the foreheads of the women. Indian married women still sport these *bindis*. There are toy bullock carts which are so remarkably similar to the bullock carts still in use in rural India. There are seals depicting a God seated in the classical Yogic posture of *Padamasana* and surrounded by animals – the classical image of Pashupatinath or Shiva – the lord of animals. There are seals of a Mother Goddess. All appear to be testimonials to the amazing cultural continuity that sets this civilization apart from most others. In fact, no other civilization on this earth (except perhaps the Chinese) can lay claim to this degree of cultural continuity and antiquity. Our origins lie really along the banks of this sacred Saraswati – regarded as the Goddess of Learning and Intuition in the Vedic pantheon.

The Death of the River. So what happened to the Saraswati? Historians and geologists tell us that in 2900 BCE, a massive earthquake shook Northern India. As a consequence, the region south of the Shivaliks rose. This tectonic plate shift caused the Yamuna and Satluj rivers to suddenly change course. The Yamuna now moved eastwards and joined the Ganga. The Satluj shifted westwards and became a tributary of the Indus River. The mighty Saraswati now lost its perennial source of ice-melted water from the Himalayas. Over the next few decades, the river gradually died out and was reduced to a seasonal stream, then isolated pools and patches of water which finally disappeared altogether. Parts of the paleochannel water went underground. Mughal emperor Akbar's cavalry knew of the tract of this ancient river bed and used to thunder down its length for rapid North to South movements of their horses. Fresh drinking water was readily available along this dry river bed just a few feet below the surface.

The memory of a mighty river that once flowed from the Himalayas to the sea was thus preserved in the oral tradition and collective racial memory of an ancient people. Even when this water course disappeared, by sheer force of tradition and habit Hindus still went to Kurukshetra (where this river once flowed) to offer *"Pind Daan"* to their ancestors. Thus a mighty river simply vanished over the course of a century. A vast civilization situated on its banks was forced to migrate east and settle along the Ganga-Yamuna doaba. A part of these people migrated westwards to Iran and the Middle-East. Vedic Gods appear in the treaties signed between the Assyrian and the Mittani. The Kurds, the Armenians, the Persians as also the Yazdi carried with them their sacred memories, legends and myths. We are struck today by the strong parallels between some of the myths of the Middle-East, Anatolia, Greece and even Europe with the myths of India. There is the myth of a Great Flood that is common to many cultures. There is the myth of Hercules – a God who lifted up the earth, and a God in India called Krishna, who lifted up a mountain called 'Govardhan'. There is Achilles – a Greek hero who was vulnerable in his heel – there is Krishna who dies of an arrow wound in his heel. There is the most beautiful Sita and the Helen of Troy, who are both abducted

Satellite Imagery of the dried up course of the Saraswati River and vast armies clash to rescue these paragons of beauty. There is the Siege of Lanka and there is the Seige of Troy. So which way did these migrations and memories flow – East to West or West to East?

All subsequent migrations have come from the cold and arid steppes of Central Asia to the warm, lush and fertile plains of India. The invaders from the arid desert wastes of Arabia and Iraq came to loot and plunder. So did the Greeks, the Sakas, the Scythians, the Huns, Mongols, Turko-Mongols and Pathans. Many of then settled down in this land and were absorbed seamlessly. Some others tried to proselytize and convert by the sword. Surprisingly, despite being under Muslim rule for a thousand years – virtually 80% of the Indian population remained Hindu. This was in sharp contrast to what had happened earlier in Iraq, Syria, Iran, Egypt, Central Asia and Afghanistan. These ancient civilizations had been completely converted to Islam – entire populations had been terrified into changing their faith and way of life. Their conquest and subjugation was not just physical but equally – ideological and transformational. The breaks from their civilizational past were complete and total.

But far back in 2,900 BCE, a great mother river had simply dried out and caused a civilizational catastrophe in India. That could equally well have forced masses of people to migrate from India to the west or east. As they migrated to new lands, they took with them their Vedic Gods – Indra, Mitra and Varuna, their myths and memories of a very sacred river – in a one-time migration caused by the drying out of their life-giving river. The amazing fact is how the racial memory of a mighty river has been preserved in oral tradition for thousands of years.

It is time therefore to jettison the fiction of Mortimer Wheeler and other British historians who sold us the story that the Aryan hordes on horseback had burst out from a Central Asian homeland to burn, loot and destroy the original Indus valley civilization of India. This British piece of colonial fiction has been held on to so trenchantly by the foot soldiers of the colonial historical tradition – the Romilla Thapars, Ramchandra Guhas and Bipin Chandras – the court historians who took upon themselves to ensure that the propagandist fiction of the Raj era was sustained forever, to distort Indian history and reduce it to a pathetic caricature to suit the colonial narrative. Today, the empirical discovery of the lost Saraswati River however has revived Indology. The fresh evidence makes nonsense of the colonial constructs of Indian history – designed to tell a subject people that they were the left over litter of invasion after invasion, from Europe, Middle East or Central Asia. Being subjects and slaves was their perennial destiny. They were unfit to rule themselves and needed the British overlords to impose Imperial Justice upon the warring tribes and squabbling castes of India. And after the departure of the British they needed Anglophile rulers as some sort of a rearguard of British colonialism to see that the natives stayed in line and did not stray too far from the laid down narrative.

Genetic studies have now clearly revealed no distinction whatsoever between the DNA of North and South Indians. Yet the colonial rearguard of court historians and toadies of this empire continue to dutifully peddle the fiction of their erstwhile colonial masters. For them it is sacrilege indeed to transcend the narrative dictated to us by our former British masters. How can the Brown people disown the history that was written down for them by the British? Empirical evidence from satellite photos however, now demands that there be a paradigm shift in the basal assumptions of Indology. This shift of paradigm is long overdue. We have to rescue our history from the clutches of trenchant Anglophiles and collaborators of the Raj era – the pathetic rearguard of the empire who are a strange anachronism on the Indian scene today. Seventy years after the British left these camp followers who constitute the baggage of the empire, wish to dictate to us what our history should be and how we should organize our literary festivals and view ourselves as a people.

A Personal Quest for Identity: The Mohyal Brahmins

The people who lived on the banks of the sacred Saraswati River (especially the twice-born Brahmins) called themselves the Saraswats – dwellers of the land of the Saraswati. That sacred geography was their primal inheritance. One conversation that I had with my father when I was merely a boy of around 10, is sharply etched in my memory forever.

"Who are we?" I had asked my father as a child. "Who are the Bakshis?"

"That son is the historic title conferred on our family in Mughal times. Actually we are Mohyal Brahmins – a part of the larger clan of Saraswat Brahmins who lived along the tract of the sacred Saraswati River – the Saraswati that once stretched from the Himalayas to the sea. The Fighting Brahmins who lived on its banks thus were directly in the path of every invasion of our country – whether it came from across the Hindukush, across Baluchistan and Sindh or even across the seas. We are the Guardians of the Gateways to India. We are the defenders of our ancient and most sacred civilization. We are the defenders of a faith and a tradition. We fought the Greeks, the Sakas, Huns and Scythians, the Arabs, the Turko-Mongols and later, even the Pathans. No invader could cross into India without battling the trenchant bulldogs of the border".

"But we are Brahmins – people who traditionally engaged in prayer and meditation. We were supposed to be priests who presided over religious ceremonies and lived on alms.

How and when did we become warriors? How was it that we became the Guardians of the Gate? Wasn't that traditionally the duty of the *Kshatriyas* – the warrior class?" I asked him.

My father told me with great pride, "Son, we are the direct descendants of the greatest Warrior Sages – Parshuram from your father's side and Guru Dronacharya from your mother's side. These were the greatest warriors of ancient India who taught the Art of War to the Kings and Princes and all renowned warrior races of that era. Parshuram is said to be an incarnation of Vishnu – the God who periodically descends to Mother Earth to revive and resuscitate our civilization in its periods of anarchy and decline. It is said that before the era of the Ramayan – there was an emperor called Krityavir Arjun who ruled over North India. He was a terrible tyrant – much worse than the mythical Kans of the Mahabharatan era. He was a cruel and oppressive ruler – who took what he wanted and was ruthless with those who dared to oppose him. He was a mighty warrior and people were terrified of him. He had unleashed a reign of terror. In that era the great sage Jamadagni Rishi had his hermitage on the banks of the Renuka River near modern-day Jalandhar and Phagwara. Legend had it that he owned the mythical Kamdhenu (wish-fulfilling) cow. Krityavir Arjun happened to visit his hermitage along with a huge army. Rishi Jamadagni welcomed him and treated the King and his retinue with the help of Kamdhenu. The king was surprised at the sage's ability to feed an entire army. He enquired how he did it. He was shown Kamdhenu. The greedy king now demanded that this cow be handed over to him. Rishi Jamadagni refused point blank. The cow was needed for the performance of rituals he said. Krityavir Arjun flew into a rage. He drew out his sword and killed the sage. The Rishi's eldest son Parshuram was then away in the forest, chopping wood. He heard the cries of his father and rushed back. By then Krityavir Arjun had left with his retinue and taken Kamdhenu with him. Parshuram came upon his slain father's dead body and his wailing mother. He flew into a terrible rage and swore revenge. Parshuram was a great warrior. He was famous for wielding his huge battle axe. He assembled an army of Brahmins and waged war against the Krityavir Arjun and his hosts. He led 21 military campaigns against this tyrannical ruler and ultimately slaughtered him, his clans and his evil hosts. He conquered Krityavir Arjun's entire kingdom and in fact fashioned a new empire in North India. He distributed these captured lands amongst his Brahmin warriors – who now metamorphosed from priests and savants to owners of lands and tillers of the soil. Thus they became the Fighting Brahmins who later went on to become the Guardians of the Gateways into India.

The word Mohyal comes from the Sanskrit *Mahipal* or owners of land. The successors of Parshuram became the Mohyal fighting Brahmins – as also the subsequent Bhumihars of Bihar and Uttar Pradesh (who initially formed some 60% of the East India Company's armies) and the Tyagis and other fighting Brahmin races. This is how the Brahmins were transformed from pious priests and savants into warriors, who defended the land and tilled the soil. In fact, Swami Shajananada Saraswati, in his history of the Bhumiar Brahmins, divides Brahmins into two broad categories—the Shalins and the Yayavars. The Shalins were the masters of land and even soldiers and kings, while the

Yayavars made their living solely by practicing their traditional priestly vocation. Parshuram's campaigns against the tyrannical rulers of India had transformed the Brahmins into owners of land and into weapon-wielding warriors who gave up their priestly vocations to become the defenders of the Indian civilization and its values.

Their very geography placed them squarely in the path of each and every invader who attacked India. It started with the Greek phalanxes of Alexander – the world-conquering commander from Macedonia. He got a stiff fight from a Mohyal King of Jhelum called Puru (Paurva) or the world famous Porus. Though he lost the battle narrowly, being badly outnumbered, his 200 war elephants had thoroughly shaken up the Greeks. After the battle, the homesick Greek army refused to go any further into India. Alexander was a great orator. He harangued his soldiers for hours on end to enthuse them onwards in his mission of global conquest, but they would not budge. Finally, he went into a great sulk for three days. He then erected seven fire alters on the banks of the Beas River at a place called Tibor (modern Tibri in Punjab?) to mark the farthest point of his advance. He then started his retreat along the course of the Indus River. Homeward bound at last, his Greek phalanxes now fought with a rare ferocity. They encountered many kingdoms and clan republics on their way to the sea. Keen to get home with their plundered loot, the Greeks carried out savage massacres along the way to clear their path and terrify the people into giving them safe passage.

They got their toughest fight at Multan. This was a kingdom of Mohyal Fighting Brahmins. The Greeks called them the Malloi. They put up fierce resistance. They specifically targeted the Greek generals and leadership and felled many of them. They shot a one meter long arrow which penetrated Alexander's armour and wounded him badly. He fell from his horse and fainted. His enraged soldiers now began to massacre every single man, woman and child in the kingdom of Multan. Alexander regained consciousness. He was aghast at the massacre. "These are the finest soldiers we have met on any battlefield", he said, "don't kill them; take them with you." And so it was that the Greeks took with them many clans of Mohyal Brahmins as they retreated along the banks of the Indus.

On reaching mouth of the river near Karachi and the Makran coast, they built a huge fleet of ships. The invading army now divided itself into two parts – Alexander retreated along the Makran coast, while the bulk of his forces now traveled by sea along with the loot. After many privations, Alexander's forces reached Egypt. In Alexandria, the world famous conqueror died. He had never really recovered from the wounds that the Mohyals of Multan had given him. Alexander died due to the wounds inflicted by the Saraswat fighting Brahmins. Some of the Mohyal clans that Alexander had taken along now migrated and settled down in Saudi Arabia and Iraq, where they would later take part in the Karbala War – the primal conflict between the Shias and Sunnis, much later in the 7th Century A.D.

The Bhumihar Brahmins

Meanwhile back home, Chanakya (the legendary Kautilya) went up and down the Indus in the wake of Alexander's most savage and brutal invasion. Shocked and appalled at the massacres, he exhorted the warrior Brahmins of the Indus region to join the Mauryan Army and unite India under one single political authority. India had been till then a civilizational entity that had great cultural unity but was badly fractured and divided politically into so many squabbling kingdoms and clan republics that they could never present a united front to any foreign invader. Even as Porus had bravely fought Alexander on the banks of the Jhelum, his neighbour, Ambhi Raj of Taxila had shamelessly joined the Greek invader.

The need was to unify India into one political and military entity that could defend the land from such rapacious foreign invaders. The massacres that Alexander and his Greek phalanxes had carried out in India were truly horrifying. These amounted to genocide. It is noteworthy that when Alexander's invasion had taken place, Kautilya had gone to the court of Mahapdma Nanda in Patliputra. Nanda then had the biggest army in the whole of India and Kautilya asked him to do his civilizational duty and come up and face Alexander. Nanda had refused contemptuously. Kautilya was caught by the tuft of his hair and thrown out unceremoniously for his pains. He was furious.

"You are unfit to rule", he had told the Nanda monarch and vowed revenge. Angry and disheartened Kautilya then returned to the Punjab. Rallying again he exhorted the people here to join the Mauryan Army that he and Chandragupta were raising and unite India so that it could stand up to such external invasions and not think in petty terms of local kingdoms. The ravaged people of the old Saraswati and Indus tracts needed very little persuasion. They joined the Mauryan army in droves. Amongst them were a large number of Saraswat Mohyal Brahmins who had suffered the most. The fighting Saraswat Brahmins flocked to the banner of the Mauryan army under Chandragupta. These were then amongst the best fighting ethnicities in India. They had suffered terribly at the hands of the invaders and were determined to prevent any such disaster from repeating itself. Joining Maurya's army they marched on to Magadh in an attempt to unify India. They routed the armies of Mahapadma Nanda and established the vast Mauryan Empire. Around 300BC they had helped unify the whole of India – stretching from Afghanistan to Kamrup (Assam) in the East and down south to Karnataka. They settled down mostly in present day provinces of Bihar and Uttar Pradesh .

Many of the warrior Brahmins from the Indus river valley now became the Bhumihar Brahmins of Uttar Pradesh and Bihar and were the main constituents of the Imperial Mauryan Army. The Mauryan Empire was the first empire to politically unify the whole of India. Its splendour lasted almost for 150 years. Emperor Ashoka took this empire to the zenith of its glory. However, after the massacre of the Kalinga War, he had a sudden change of heart and became a Buddhist. He now turned from military conquest to Dharma Vijay (conquest of hearts and minds). An army of saffron-clad Buddhist monks now fanned out to all corners of Asia to spread the message of the *Tathagat* – a message of peace and *Ahimsa* (non-violence). Instead of projecting military power by overland and sea-borne invasions, Ashoka offered to spread the soft power of India to all corners of Asia.

The onset of pacifism however corroded the military power of the Mauryan Empire. The Greek satraps now began to resume their invasions and intrigues. The last ruler of the Mauryan Empire Brihadrath proved to be weak and effeminate. He tried to conclude a treaty with the Greek satraps who had almost come back right up to Patliputra. This crass and craven surrender to Greek power enraged his Brahmin Military Commander-in-Chief, Pushyamitra Sunga (a Bhumihar). He staged a coup and overthrew the effete Brihadrath, who became the last Mauryan emperor. The Sunga dynasty, established by Pushyamitra, now ruled now ruled for another 150 years. Pushyamitra Sunga drove the Greeks back – all the way to Afghanistan and beyond and re-established a mighty empire. He performed the *Ashwamedha* and *Rajsuya Yagyas* (sacrifices) and reinforced India's political unity and cohesion for a century and a half. The Satvahanas (another set of Brahmin rulers) were now on the rise in the South. The Indian polity fractured again.

Muslim Invasion

By the 6th century A.D. a Brahamin kingdom had emerged in Afghanistan and Sindh. The Arab invasions began in the 7th century but were held at bay for almost three centuries by the Mohyal Brahmin rulers of the Shahi dynasty of Afghanistan. This was for the first time that the triumphant Arab armies of Islam had been halted and driven back. When the cruel Hajjaj—the Caliph's governor in Iraq drove these armies back to invade Afghanistan again- they mutinied. There was civil war in the Caliphate for four years and the Islamic spree of conquest came to a grinding halt. Arab folklore to this day speaks of an end of time battle in Khorasan and the final Gazwa-e Hind (war for the conquest of India) which the Arabs had failed to do in the 7th and 8th centuries. Frustrated by his failure in Afghanistan – the Hajjaj turned to attack from the south and targeted Sindh. Chach, the Mohyal Brahmin ruler of Sindh had expanded his kingdom to the borders of Kashmir. However, his descendant Dahir, drove back many Arab excursions but finally succumbed to the Arab onslaught in 712 A.D. Thus while the Shahi Mohyal rulers of Afghanistan successfully held off Arab military power and invasions for almost three centuries, the resistance in Sindh crumbled suddenly. Heroic resistance however was offered by the Mohyal rulers of Afghanistan. These included the likes of Samant Dewa and his son Kalvarman and finally Bhimdeva, who ruled till 964 A.D. Bhimdeva did not leave behind a male heir and his kingdom in Kabul was merged with the Vaid (Mohyal) kingdom in Punjab and Jayapala (the fifth ruler of the Vaid Mohyal dynasty of Punjab) now became the sovereign of a vast kingdom that stretched from Kabul to Sirhind. This loss of local Hindu Afghan leadership at such a critical juncture was a great tragedy for India. The Hindu ruler of Zabul (Kandahar) also known as Rutbil, was now getting highly apprehensive about the buildup of Muslim military power in the form of the Sultanate of Ghazni to his north. He decided to launch a pre-emptive attack. He was however invited for negotiations and killed treacherously. Unlike his predecessors, he failed to exploit the defensive potential of the formidable Hindukush Range and lost the fight due to his impetuous nature which led him to mount Balcalava style charges in the mountains which so greatly favour the defender. The way to Afghanistan and India now lay open. The Brahmin Hindu Shais in Kabul continued to resist for another century more. Unfortunately, as Bhimadeva the valiant Shahi king had no male heirs, the Afghan kingdom now came under the Mohyal king of Lahore, who lacked knowledge about the local terrain and also because his capital was far too removed from the scene of fighting. This loss of local Afghan Hindu leadership proved tragic at this critical juncture. Finally the Turko- Mongols use of superior – fighting tactics of inciting the enemy to attack and then using skilled archers to cause heavy losses and exploit the disorder caused by Mongol-style cavalry, finally won the day. The Turko-Mongol converts to Islam succeeded where the Arabs themselves had failed.

Sultan Mehmood Ghaznavi now set his eyes on mainland India. He began his invasion via the Khyber Pass. Anandpala (son of Jayapala) moved up with his army to give battle. It was a very fierce encounter that lasted the whole day. As per Muslim historian Ferishta – the Mohyal forces were close to being victorious. The Pathans now adopted their favourite tactic. They fired flaming naphtha arrows at the elephants on which the Mohyal King Anandapala was mounted. The elephant turned unruly and fled. The elephant had been the mainstay of the Indian armies right through the epic period of the Mahabharata and later, the Mauryan empire. Unfortunately, the use of naphtha flaming arrows neutralized the war elephants of India and made them a liability on the battlefield. The Indian tragedy was their failure to learn and realign their tactics and fighting techniques. The Mohyals lost this crucial battle. Mehmood Ghaznavi attacked again in 1014 and forced the Marigala Pass near Rawalpindi. There was a fierce battle but the combination of swift Afghan cavalry and the fire and naphtha arrows proved decisive. Ghaznavi captured the hill fort and capital at Nandana – located near Katasraj in the Salt Range.

Ghaznavi now advanced towards Kashmir and won the battle on the banks of the River Tausi. In 1021 A.D. Ghaznavi marched on to Lahore and captured the whole of Punjab, ending the rule of the Vaid-Mohyal dynasty there. They had held off Arabs and then Turkic invasions for almost over three centuries (from the 8th to the 10th centuries). Unfortunately, Indian rulers of that era continued to squabble and fight amongst themselves. There was then the tripartite struggle between the Mohyal Kings of Kabul and Punjab, the Gurjar Prathiharas of Central India (Kannauj) and the Rashtrkutas. They failed to unite and present a common front to the invaders. Ghaznavi thus overcame them single-handedly, and one by one they fell. The Mohyal Vaid kings held on tenaciously but the use of Turkic cavalry and the naphtha fire arrows proved to be a decisive innovation. The elephants became the biggest liability when fire arrows were used in war.

The Hindu Holocaust and Survival

Much has been said and written about the Jewish Holocaust. Frankly it pales into insignificance when compared with the holocaust of the Hindus in Northern India since the 10th century. Once again, the invaders were even more brutal and rapacious. Over the successive centuries there were horrible massacres of the Hindu population. Entire cities were sacked and burnt, temples destroyed, women raped and enslaved, and horrific massacres perpetrated. There are no accurate historical records of these slaughters of the indigenous Indian population, but the horrible carnage and casualties run into millions. In fact one estimate puts total Hindu casualties over successive invasions, slaughters and Hindu holocausts, at a mind – numbing 100 million. A series of Muslim invasions later enslaved India. They had initially come to loot, rape and plunder, but now stayed back to rule and establish empires in an India that was so badly fractured and fragmented – that it could not even put up a cohesive or unified defense.

The amazing fact however is that unlike Iran and in many other countries, the Islamic invaders failed to destroy the Hindu civilization. Despite such comprehensive military defeat and subjugation, amazingly, the Indian society was able to put up a dogged resistance to mass conversions. There were no complete conversions of the entire population as had taken place in Iran and Egypt. The Iranian civilization had been overwhelmed – even as the ancient Egyptian civilization had been overrun and had vanished without a trace, after the Muslim conquest. The Hindu civilization survived this terrible onslaught – this most horrific holocaust. The seminal question is HOW?

Strangely, India proved to be a weak state but a strong society. The Hindu ethnicity per se was preserved by splintering the four main castes (Brahmins-Kshatriya-Vaishya-Shudra) into a series of sub-castes and exogamous and endogamous *biradaries (clans)*. These biradaries enforced compliance with traditions and preservation of genetic pools and strains through inter-marriage within a set of sub-castes (but never within one's own Gotra – or patrilineal descent lineage). This was the time when the Mohyals divided themselves into seven sub-castes or biradaries of Chibber, Datt, Bali, Mohan, Mehta, Vaid, Lau and Bhimwal. These were exogamous to the extent that they would not marry within their own clan but chose brides from any of the six other clans (endogamous). These cohesive and well-knit biradaries paradoxically provided local support systems that helped sustain customs and traditions and preserve genetic purity. These local support systems of biradaries had amazing strength and tenacity. They preserved local identities and cultures in a period of terrible flux, change and political upheaval. In such uncertain times – people clung with amazing tenacity to their smaller clan *biradaries* as local support systems. The very threat of ex-communication from these small clan groupings kept people in line and helped Hindu identity survive this holocaust. It may be noted that Buddhism had done away with caste and clan groupings. They also had Monastries and the sangha-an order of saffron clad monks who could be easily targeted and destroyed. Buddhism and to a large extent, Jainism therefore, did not survive the Muslim invasions. Hinduism was so amorphous, it had an open architecture and accommodated such a variety and range of beliefs that it could not be destroyed merely by the destruction of its temples. The Muslims did target the Brahmin community in particular – as they were the thought leaders of the Hindu civilization. What helped them survive were these smaller, tightly knit clans and biradari groupings. These not only provided social and psychological support systems and anchors of identity in such a time of crisis but served as last ditch defense mechanism that stepped in to hold Hindu society together once the Hindu political states had collapsed. The greatest threat that these smaller clan biradaries held out was the threat of ex-communication – the stoppage of social relationships – of partaking food together or offering brides in marriage. Hindus clung tenaciously to these biradari support systems for their survival in times of the Hindu holocaust caused by the Muslim invasions.

And thus it was that though the Muslims ruled India for almost 1,000 years – some 80 percent Indians did not convert to Islam. They clung on to their Hindu faith and culture. This had not happened anywhere else in the world. India had proved to be a very weak state but a very strong society, which could resist outside cultural penetration – even when defeated militarily. Another factor that helped India was the sheer size and space of the Indic civilization. There were portions of it that remained unconquered – especially in the southern expanses, which preserved their centres of learning and culture till the very end.

Akbar's Tolerance and Aurangzeb's Persecution
The simple fact is that India's plurality was also preserved to an extent by the secular and tolerant ethos of one of its greatest empire builders – Mughal emperor Muhammad Jalaluddin Akbar. Akbar was inherently tolerant and secular. He ushered in a relatively liberal and tolerant rule and tried to cobble together an inclusivist faith (*Din-e-Elahi*). He encouraged the Hindus to participate in the governance of the country. He created marriage alliances with the

Rajput Princesses and employed Hindu scholars and economists in his court. This was the time when the Mohyal Brahmins mastered Persian and Arabic and were employed as commissariat officials, book-keepers and paymasters by the Mughals. Many Mohyals rose to high positions and were given titles like Mehta, Bakshi, Raizada, Dewan and even Khan and Sultan. Despite the military defeat – their tactical skills, intelligence and talents were recognized by the new Uzbek rulers and thus they prospered, even under alien rule and managed to preserve their unique culture and identity through this period of flux and change.

The Indian Military Revival

Akbar's secular consensus however began to unravel after just one century of Mughal rule. There were signs of a backlash of Islamic fundamentalism that began to reappear in the time of Jehangir and Shahjahan. By and large however, both these emperors preserved Akbar's secular consensus and culture of tolerance. Shahjahan's eldest son Dara Shikoh was highly liberal and tolerant and had Hindu scriptures like Ramayan, Mahabharat and the Upanishads translated into Persian. His brother Aurangzeb however staged a palace coup, at the behest of fanatical elements in the Mughal court and the ulemas. He imprisoned his father and ruthlessly slaughtered his brothers. He now became a fanatical tyrant and a most oppressive ruler. He reimposed the hated Jazia tax and began to persecute the Hindus. He destroyed many temples and built mosques over them. This large scale oppression against the majority Hindu community led to a major backlash. A series of revolts and rebellions broke out in the Hindu community that ultimately destroyed the Mughal Empire and decisively ended its tyranny. Such a huge population could not be ruled for long without its consent. Three major centres of military resistance arose in India. These were:-

• The Sikhs of the Punjab under Guru Gobind Singh
• The Marathas of the West Coastal region under Chhatrapati Shivaji Maharaj and
• The Ahoms under their famous General Lachit Burpukhan in Assam.

The Mohyals played a very significant role in the rise of the Sikhs. They rallied to the cause of the Sikh gurus. Aurangzeb was persecuting the Kashmiri pundits. They appealed to Guru Tegh Bahadur to help them. The Guru asked Aurangzeb to first convert him before he would convert the Pandits. The Guru, along with his close followers, was arrested. Amongst his closest followers were- three brothers – Bhai Matidas, Satidas and Ratidas. They were tortured to death. Matidas was sawed in half and yet defiantly refused to convert till the end. His brothers were burnt to death. Their supreme courage in the face of such gruesome torture electrified the people of India. Tyranny had reached an unspeakable level of cruelty. Instead of overwhelming the indigenous people it led to outrage and a rebellion that steadily gained strength – till in less than a century – the Mughal Empire was uprooted and overthrown. It was attacked incessantly by the Sikhs, the Marathas and the Ahoms and overthrown decisively.

The first to lead a significant military revolt was a Mohyal General (a Chhibber) called Banda Bairagi. On the orders of Guru Gobind Singh, he assembled a huge army and created havoc in the Punjab. He avenged the deaths of Guru Gobind Singh's martyred sons, (who had been entombed alive by cementing them into walls). Banda had the Mughal Governor Painda Khan who had committed this atrocity- trampled under the feet of elephants. The Mughals were terrified. Ultimately they assembled a large Army and surrounded him. There was a fierce battle. Banda Bahadur was finally captured and killed by horrible torture. This cruelty and depravity sounded the death knell of the Mughal Empire. Within next 70 years it was comprehensively destroyed.

Maharaja Ranjit Singh

The Sikhs now arose as a major military force in North India. They drove the Mughals and Pathans out of the Punjab and then they attacked and captured Afghanistan all the way to and beyond Jalalabad. The entire region, now called North Western Frontier Province (NWFP) and Federally Administered Tribal Areas (FATA) beyond the Indus were captured and subdued by the Sikhs. The rollback of the invaders had begun. Much before the British conquered India, a resurgent Hindu

India had militarized itself in the form of the Sikhs and Marathas and destroyed the Mughal Empire of the Uzbek rulers. Many of the generals of the Sikh armies were the fighting Brahmins of Mohyal clans whose names have entered folklore and history. The Maratha armies in turn were led by Peshwa generals who also belonged to the fighting Brahmin stock that had emerged with the battle axe-wielding sage – Parshuram and the great teacher of war – Dronacharya.

British Rule

The British took advantage of the disunity and internecine conflicts in India and conquered the country using the British Presidency Army, 60% of which was composed of the Bhumihar fighting Brahmins. British attempts at proselytization and their racial arrogance led to the revolt of 1857 – once again spearheaded by warrior Brahmins like Mangal Pandey. The revolt was disjointed and hence was finally crushed. India became a Crown colony. The British now used caste and jati faultlines to divide and rule the people of India. Then they exploited the faultlines of religion, creed and ethnicity to the fullest extent to destroy the very idea of India.

The British however realized and fully tapped the fighting potential of the Indian people. The Mohyal Brahmins played a major role. They were recognized as a martial caste by the British and were recruited in the British Indian cavalry regiments in a major way. In the First World War the Indian Army was expanded to a huge size of 1.3 million men. It played a stellar role in French, Middle Eastern and East African theatres of war. In the Second World War it was expanded to massive body of 2.5 million men. It was the largest all volunteer armies in the history of the world. Once again, Indian soldiers fought with distinction in Europe, Middle East, North Africa and Burma with Mohyal soldiers making a laudable contribution.

Freedom Struggle and Partition. Many Mohyals played a significant role in India's Freedom Struggle. They were active in the Ghadar Movement and later joined the Indian National Army (INA) of Netaji Subhas Chandra Bose. The INA ultimately shook the loyalty of the Indian soldiers of the British Indian Army. That was the real centre of gravity of the Raj and Bose wanted to specifically target this.

In February 1946, there were revolts in the Royal Indian Navy, Royal Indian Air Force and finally the Army units themselves. These terrified the British. Exhausted by 5 years of the Second World War, they saw the writing on the wall and left in just two years in August 1947, but not before partitioning India and creating a tragedy of monumental proportions. The Mohyal Saraswat Brahmins had to flee enmasse from their traditional homelands along the Indus – Saraswati river alignments. Their community was now scattered all over India in a tragic diaspora.

Renaissance in Independent India. Yet they survived this second holocaust. They managed to preserve their unique identity, tradition and mores. The General Mohyal Sabah now came to the fore to help them preserve their culture in the face of such upheaval and change. They renewed and reinvented themselves. Today Independent India has seen three Mohyals rise to the post of Governor (Mr SK Chibber, Bhai Mahaveer and Lt Gen BKN Chibber); 6 Mohyals reached the High Rank of Army Commander and equivalent in the Army and Air Force. 10 rose to the coveted post of Lt. Generals (three star) in the Indian Army and Navy, with 15 becoming Maj Generals and Five Air Vice Marshals in the Air Force. One Mohyal Officer, Lt Puneet Datt got the Ashok Chakra – the highest award for gallantry in the land. Four Mohyals were awarded the Maha Vir Chakra (MVC) and another four the Vir Chakra. Many others won a host of other gallantry and distinguished service awards. Mohyals have done well in all fields in the post-independence era– especially in the film industry, educational sector and corporate world. The Mohyals excelled in Bollywood with names like Sunil and Nargis Datt , Om Prakash and Annand Bakshi etc. Mohyals also did well in the academic and medical fields and as industrialists and entrepreneurs. In fact Mr B D Bali of Mohan Breweries has rendered yeomen service to the community as President of the General Mohyal Sabah for over four decades.

The Saraswat fighting Brahmins of India therefore have been the Guardians of her Gates. For centuries they fought against each and every invader. Whenever tyranny and oppression reached a crescendo of cruelty, they led the revolts against such tyrants. This began with Parshuram in the pre- epic era and continued in the face of Aurangzeb's unspeakable tyranny and later against the British empire. Subjected to unspeakable tortures they did not submit or break in spirit. They inspired their countrymen to overthrow the tyrants who had turned twisted and evil in their attempts to subjugate the Indian people and silence all voices of dissent and outrage.

The Mohyal Brahmins today are not just warriors with a glorious past, they are an intelligent and talented people with an equally glorious future. In this prologue I have given a brief overview of their amazing history – a tale of bravery and grim sacrifice in the face of untold oppression and unspeakable savagery. They did not wilt in the face of brutal torture that tested the extremities of the endurance of the human spirit. They inspired their countrymen to rise above their fears and resist the invaders and overthrow the tyrants. Today, they form a significant component of the leadership of our Armed Forces and are equally excelling in other fields. This then is the amazing saga of an intrepid people who still continue to be the Guardians of our Gates.

2

Genealogy

Reflections on Caste: Saraswat Brahmins and the Mohyal Clans

The word 'caste' comes from the Portugese word 'casta' – a term the Portugese used for the subdivisions they saw in Indian society. Indian languages do not have a word for caste. They used instead the Sanskrit terms of *jati* or *varna (color)* to describe caste. Also the term *'Biradari'* (a conglomerate of several Jatis), *Kula* and *Vansha* are used. Caste is largely a post colonial term which has gained an uncalled for lease of life due to our caste-based politics. Caste is not so unique to the Indian society as is generally thought. All ancient agricultural societies had segmented their population along the lines of functional or occupational groupings.

Thus most agricultural societies comprised three distinct groups- of the priests, the warriors and the tillers of land or farmers. Other societies had four functional groups like in India – priests, warriors, traders and tillers of the soil. In India this formed the four-fold caste divisions or 'Varna', which included Brahmins (priests), Kshatriyas (warriors and rulers), Traders (vaishyas) and Shudras (tillers of land or peasants). Many ancient agricultural societies including Greece and Rome, had huge slave populations – which were given the menial tasks. In Indian societies, defeated tribal populations were possibly integrated with an agricultural society at the lower levels of Chandals or outcastes and consigned to menial tasks. Caste therefore is not as unique to the Indian civilization as is often made out. Functional or occupational groups clearly existed in all agricultural societies. What was unique about Indian castes were the aspects of endogamy – rituals that prescribed marriages within one's own caste/group and the fact that one was born into a caste.

The Mohyals were Brahmins. Brahmins in India are classified into two broad categories:-

- Gaur Brahmins who lived North of the river Narmada and
- Dravid Brahmins who lived to the south of river Narmada.

The Mohyals belong to the Gaur Brahmin category. The Gaur Brahmins were further classified into five sub-categories:-

- *The Saraswats*: These were the Brahmins who lived on the banks of the mighty Saraswati river. The Mohyals were part of the Saraswat Brahmin clans. That is why they later became the Guardians of India as they lay in the path of each and every invader.
- *Kanyakubja Brahmins* (Kannauj Region)
- *Maithili Brahmins* (Bihar Region)
- *Utkal Brahmins* (Odisha Region)
- *Adi Gauda Brahmins* (Bengal Region)

Caste-divisions of Indian society have been reported by Megasthenes – the Greek Ambassador to the Mauryan court. Megasthenes listed seven castes and counted "Charas" or spies as a separate caste – so numerous were the spies of Kautilya, who reported on every aspect of the empire. The Chinese traveller Huen Tsang (602-664 A.D.) was more accurate. He observed the four-fold division of Hindu society along the lines of Varna. He spoke of the first order of Brahmins (purely living) – who strictly observed ceremonial purity; the second order of Kshatriyas – the race of kings; the third order of Vaishyas or class of traders and the fourth order of Shudras or tillers of the land). The members of a caste married within the caste.

The same Varna division was observed by Ibn Kordadbeh (820-912 A.D.) who came to India in the 9th century. However he counted seven castes and included the Chandals and wandering tribes as separate castes. Abu Rehan (973-1048 A.D.), commonly called Al Biruni, came to India in the times of Mehmood Ghaznavi and left behind his observations in a book entitled 'Kitab Tarikh al Hind'. He observed, "that the Hindus call their castes – Varnas or colors and from the genealogical point of view they call them Jatah (Jati). These are four.

The highest are the Brahmins, next came the Kshatriyas followed by the Vaishyas and then the Shudras.

Gotra and Pravara

R.T. Mohan in his most scholarly essay "Origin of Caste System and Mohyal Brahmins" published in the *Itihas Darpan* journal in 2014 tells us that in Vedic times a person was identified by his Pravara, Gotra, Veda and Veda Shakha (Stotra) suffixed to his name. Pravara Rsi (Rishi) was the original progenitor from whom the family was descended. Gotra rishi was the pravara himself or a prominent descendant who started a new sub-branch in his own name. With the passage of time, there could be several gotras (all consanguineous) under the pravar patriarch. Further, since the Vedas were learned only by rote, each Brahmin family had been assigned a specific "Shakha" (branch) of a particular Veda for study. These four attributes were associated with the name of each individual of that family, just as caste is suffixed in the present times. At every Vedic ceremony, the Yajmana or sacrificer had to recite his gotra and pravara at the beginning of the ceremony and in this way the memory of the Vedic ancestors from whom the reciter had descended was kept alive.

Marriage

In the marriage ceremony of the Hindus, which is still performed according to Vedic rites (*Vivah paddhati*) there is a section called *gotrachara* – stating the gotra of the groom. Here the groom is required to identify himself by name, then mention his pravara gotra and then recount three generations of his ancestors (great grandson of so and so, grandson of and son of so and so) etc. Likewise the bride is supposed to identify herself by her gotra and ancestry for three generations.

In India, the law of matrimony centres around the principle of exogamy. Marriage within one's own patriarchal clan (gotra or sagotra) is strictly forbidden. Marital relations therefore have to be outside one's gotra (Exogamy) but within one's varna only (Endogamy). Thus caste in India was not just based on functional hierarchies of the kind of vocation practiced (priest, warrior, trader or peasant/farmer) but equally extended to strict rules of endogamy and exogamy. The entire set of rules regarding marriage almost looked like a genetic engineering exercise that would perhaps lead to functional excellence in the chosen fields of activity in an agricultural society. Preservation of the 'Y' chromosome line of the male parent was sought to be assured.

The emphasis was on preserving the line of descent provided by the 'Y' chromosome of the male parent. It laid the basis of a patriarchal order. Strict rules of exogamy forbade marriage within a gotra. Overtime however – equally strict rules of endogamy came into vogue later, which laid down the group of Jatis or classes into which alone one was supposed to marry. It was these endogamy and exogamy aspects of caste in India that distinguished it from caste like functional groupings of society in most agricultural civilizations of the world. Little mobility was seemingly permitted from the vocation of one varna to another. This mobility however was clearly visible in the early epic period – where as a result of tyranny and oppression by the rulers of that era, the priests took to arms to defend themselves and became Brahma- Kshatras.

As time progressed however, *varnasankara* or cross-varna marriages were strictly discouraged. R.T. Mohan writes, "Where such alliances did take place, they resulted in creation of new caste subsets, where the male progenies of such union or mixed marriages were nominated as a new caste, with specifically assigned menial duties. Thus the son of a Brahmin from a Vaishya mother was designated as Ambastha and had to devote himself to the art of healing. The son of a Brahmin from a Shudra mother was designated as Nishad – who operated boats and caught fish. The son of a Kshatriya from a Brahmin mother was called a Suta and had to attend to the management of chariots and horses.

One is not sure of how strictly these taboos were enforced. Thus Rishi Parashar consorted with a fisher-woman on a boat ride and this union led to the birth of Sage Vyasa – one of the greatest sages in Indian history and the man who compiled the Vedas in written form and wrote the 'Mahabharat'. He also sired the race of the Kauravas and Pandavas. One does not observe any lowering of status in this obvious case of a mixed marriage. The offspring of such a mixed marriage became the greatest sage of Indian history. It was perhaps the vital 'Y' chromosome that was deemed critical to preserve.

There is also the case against the concept of caste as genetic engineering. Genes are no longer considered destiny. Genes are important but nurture and environment of upbringing are considered even more critical to development outcomes today. Possibly the Indian caste system that segmented society as per functional/occupational divisions - aimed at both providing the genetic inputs and learning environments that would ensure excellence in the given vocation.

Nurture became more important than just genetic wiring. Both put together however create a powerful moulding environment that served as a basis for achieving functional excellence. On the flipside, it also made tradition and a particular way of doing things so deeply entrenched and hard wired that it became a major obstacle to change and innovation. Thus the armies of India clung to the war elephant for over a thousand years, when the advent of the explosive paradigm of war fighting had made this nervous beast a major liability on the battlefield. Flaming naphtha arrows and later muskets and canons caused this war beast to run amok. It should have been discarded as a shock arm and command and control platform when muskets and canons appeared on the battlefield. The Indians however persisted with its use and paid a terrible price. The man-war-beast interface was much better in the context of the cavalry – than between man and the war elephants who went out of control with alarming frequency and disastrous results.

The Caste Implosion
R.T. Mohan however writes about a second phenomenon which merits far greater attention. The great shock of the Muslim invasions, military defeat and the political destruction of the Hindu states led to the dire need of a self-preservation exercise. This took the form of an implosion of the varnas into the numerous castes that we know today. Castes of the same varna now bunched together to form inter-marriage endogamous fraternities (*biradaris*). This was a survival mechanism. The destruction of the Hindu political states forced the society to cohere into smaller caste constellations and tightly knit biradaris, which became valuable local support systems in times of chaos, destruction and change. They also controlled behaviour and

social conduct and enforced compliance with tradition by holding out the dire threat of ex-communicating all those who dared to transgress the rules or to buckle and convert under foreign pressure.

The disunited Indian states proved to be weak and brittle. Indian society however turned out to be very strong and resilient. It devised means to resist the Muslim threat and penetration of their society, whereas the indigenous civilizations of Egypt and Iran were completely overwhelmed by Islam as an ideology. The other factor was the sheer size of India. It could never be conquered at one go by any invaders and several parts of it kept resisting the invaders tenaciously for centuries. Despite its military conquests, Islam failed to convert the Hindu population in its entirety. Almost 80 percent of the Indian population under Muslim rule remained steadfastly Hindu -even in the face of severe persecution and forced proselytization by the sword. It was an amazing feat. When the state and governance structures of Hindu India perished, the society deepened the bonds of biradaris and Jati to resist outside penetration. It struggled heroically and successfully to preserve its identity and ethos in the face of cataclysmic change and social upheaval. The more fierce the oppression, the stronger became these local bonds of biradaris. The lieu motif of India was weak state – strong society – a society that ensured the allegiance of its flocks by the threat of ex-communication of those who weakened or strayed. The threat was serious – the refusal to eat together and end all social and marital relationships with those who proved weak and changed their faith under pressure. They were simply ex-communicated. Thus, when the Hindu state perished, the Hindu society sought to preserve itself by deepening the social bonds of endogamous biradaris. Where Buddhism and Jainism also perished, Hinduism survived miraculously even after a 1,000 years of alien rule.

The defence mechanism was precisely this implosion of varnas into innumerable castes and closely knit local biradaris, based upon endogamous groups. Dr. Ambedkar said that in India endogamy was superimposed on exogamy. He however did not pinpoint when this superimposition occurred.

R.T. Mohan identifies that this superimposition of endogamous biradaris as exogamous groups occurred soon after the Muslim conquest of India. When the Hindu states collapsed militarily, society had to strengthen itself to save itself from penetration and being overwhelmed – even as the entire Iran, Egypt, Central Asia and later Afghanistan's populations had been overwhelmed by Muslim invasions and the spread of Islam by the sword. R.T. Mohan posits in his brilliant essay that this was the precise period when the present constellation of seven exogamous biradaris arose in the Mohyal Brahmin clans of the Saraswati-Indus river tracts. The original varnas now imploded into the bewildering cauldron of castes and endogamous biradaris that held on to their flocks by the dire threat of ex-communication. Castes therefore now became a desperate, last ditch line of defence of the Hindu civilization.

R.T. Mohan posits in his brilliant essay that this was the precise period when the present constellation of seven exogamous biradaris arose in the Mohyal Brahmin clans of the Saraswati-Indus river tracts. The original varnas now imploded with the bewildering cauldron of castes and endogamous biradaris that held on to their flocks by the dire threat of ex-communication. Castes therefore were a desperate, last ditch line of defence of the Hindu civilization. The tradition of suffixing castes to names as a marker of one's identity ostensibly began in this period of dire flux and change of the Islamic invasions. This was the time when the seven Mohyal clans emerged as endogamous groups or biradaris.

The Seven Mohyal Clans

Let us therefore take a deeper look at the seven Mohyal clans that emerged in the wake of the Muslim conquest of India. As highlighted earlier – the Mohyals are a branch of the Saraswat Bahmins who had peopled the mighty Saraswati river valley in the Vedic era. They took to arms in the early epic period to oppose the tyranny of Krityavir Arjun. The mighty warrior sage Parshuram (whose lieu motif was his feared battle axe) now became their military leader. The historians now termed them as Brahm- Kshatras. Parshuram routed Krityavir Arjun and captured his entire domains. He distributed the land amongst his Brahmin followers.

Brahmins thus became the owners of land and hereditary warriors. This was a significant shift of roles and the functional- occupational divisions of the agricultural civilization in India. The meek priests had metamorphosed into valiant warriors and kings. Currently, the Mohyals are an inter-marriage fraternity (briadari) of seven castes namely - Bali, Bhimwal, Chhibber, Datt, Lau, Mohan and Vaid. R.T. Mohan writes, "they claim 'direct descent' from their Seven Pravar Rishis – Parashar, Agastya, Bhrigu, Bhardwaj, Vashistha, Kashyap and Dhanwantari."

Veda

R.T. Mohan says, "they belonged to the Yajurveda and its Madhyandina Shakha".

Datta in his elaborate *History of the Mohyals* traces out a mythological account of the origins of the Mohyals. He goes into a hoary past that stretches back to the creation of the cosmos per se. The Shastras say that Brahma had four mind-born sons (*Manasputra*). These were Bhrigu, Angira, Marichi and Atri. From these were born the Seven Sages – Parashar, Agastya, Bhrigu, Bhardwaj, Vashistha, Kashyap and Dhanwantari. These are said to be the Gotrakara Rishis of the Seven Mohyal Clans. These seven clans are:-

- *Balis:-* Their gotrakara rishi is said to be the renowned sage Parashar. He belonged to the family of Brahmarshi Vashistha. He was the father of the world famous sage Veda Vyasa who first set down the four Vedas in the written form. The Vedas had till then been transmitted from generation to generation in the oral form ie entirely by memorization of the oral tradition. He also composed the Mahabharata's original recensions (called Jaya).
- *Bhimwals:-* Their gotrakara rishi is Agastya Mahamuni. He was a famous rishi of southern India.
- *Chhibbers:-* Their primal rishi is Bhrigu. In this lineage were born the famous rishis like Richika, Jamadagni and his warrior son Parshuram. Parshuram became the great Battle Axe-wielding Brahmin warrior of the epic period who overthrew the tyrant called Krityavir Arjun and became the master of most of North India. He is deemed the Sixth Incarnation of Lord Vishnu and the first to assume human form. He also colonized the western Ghats and led major campaigns in South India.

the seven sages

bhrigu chhiber

bali parashar

agastya bhimwal

vaid dhanvantri

mohan kashyap

vasishta lau

bharadwaja datta

- *Dattas*:- Maharshi Bhardwaj is regarded as their gotrakara rishi. His famous son was Guru Dronacharya. He had learnt the art of war from sage Parshuram and later became the famous teacher of the Kauravas and Pandavas and played a significant role in the Mahabharata.
- *Lau*:- They trace their origins to the great sage Vashistha. Vashistha had been married to the daughter of the sage Kashyap.
- *Mohan*:- The progenitor of the Mohans was the great sage Kashyap. Legend has it that Rishi Kashyap had drained the Satisara Lake to create the vale of Kashmir.
- *Vaids*:- Their gotrakara rishi is the famed sage Dhanvantari, who is said to be the founder of 'Ayurveda' – the great Indian system of medicine.

Thoughts on Caste in the Modern Era

Caste therefore arose as an implosion of the four fold Varna organization of Hindu society in the face of Muslim invasions and persecution. With the shock of the Muslim invasions, the Hindu states collapsed militarily and politically (due to their persistent failure to present a unified front to the Turko- Mongol and Uzbek and other foreign invaders). When the Hindu state collapsed – the Hindu society was forced to step in to strengthen bonds and save itself from penetration and being overwhelmed by the faith and ideology of the invaders. India thus was characterized by the weakness of its state institutions but the strength of its social structures. When the macro state failed to protect itself, the people bonded themselves into close-knit local castes (biradaris) that held their flocks together by the threat of ex-communication and social boycott of those who strayed.

Overtime however, the same deeply entrenched caste faultlines have become barriers to national integration, when a new nation state has emerged in India. They have served to prevent the emergence of a strong state in India. The British saw the bewildering array of castes, jatis and biradaris. They were shaken by the armed revolts of 1857. They resolved to exploit these caste faultlines to the fullest to divide and rule their Indian colony. The most significant faultline they exploited was the caste faultlines. They made people register their castes in the District Collectorates. In 1872 Sir John Risley held the first caste-based census in India. Risley wrote, "as long as there is caste, there will be no India."

When the Indian state failed, Indian society had to fall back on jati, biradari and caste to protect itself. Now that we are once again a nation state, these self-serving castes and jatis are an anachronism and an obstacle to national unification. It is my strong personal belief that we need now to downplay castes and biradaris and strengthen the state in India. Industrialization, as it is, leads to urbanization where the sharp divisions of agricultural era occupations are no longer relevant. The population gets mixed in a homogeneous fashion. Caste and creed become largely irrelevant. Unfortunately in India, the kind of politics we practiced has given an uncalled for fillip to the caste and creed identities at the cost of the larger national identity. This is fast becoming a dangerous failing as a nation state.

3

The First Rebellion

The Battle Axe of Parshuram and the Rise of the Fighting Brahmins

Tracing our Roots

My father used to often recite to me the legend of the great Battle Axe-wielding sage Parshuram – the progenitor of the Mohyals. He was the torch bearer of the Mohyals in general and our Chhibber clan in particular. It was by a strange quirk of fate that I stumbled upon the exact site where Parshuram had been born and spent his early years.

When I was a Major in the Army, I was posted to Jalandhar in Punjab. I was once tasked to conduct a map reading examination of our soldiers. To conduct such an exam you need to be atop a hill feature so that map to ground and ground to map targets can be designated to test the skills of the men. My problem was, where precisely in the Punjab plains, would I get such an elevated platform? I took out the Quarter inch map sheets of the region and began to search for any hill feature in the vicinity of Jalandhar city. To my intense surprise I noted an isolated hill feature on way to Phagwara that arose abruptly in the middle of the vast expanse of the flood plains. I looked closely and was surprised to learn that it was called Parshuram Tila – the Hill of Parshuram.

I studied the adjoining area closely and found a prominent river that meanders in huge loops in the vicinity of the isolated hill feature. It is called the Renuka River. A shock transfixed my being. The Ashram of Rishi Jamdagni (Parshuram's father) was said to be situated on the banks of the Renuka River. The very next day I took a jeep and went to reconnoiter the site not just for the map-reading exercise, but now for my personal quest for locating my own roots.

We reached the place in the evening. We crossed the bridge. The locals still called that river 'Renuka Nadi'. There before us, was a hill that arose so abruptly from the flatness of the plains. Our queries to the locals revealed that yes indeed the hill was called' Parshuram Tila (Parshuram's Hill). The locals told us that this hill had arisen due to the piled up ash of the Yagyas (Yajnas) that sage Parshuram used to perform here each day. A road snaked up the flanks of that hill. We drove up to the summit. There we found a temple with an impressive idol of Lord Parshuram – the Sixth Incarnation of Lord Vishnu. Reverently I bowed low before the statue. I had indeed retraced my roots by a happy coincidence.

That temple is amongst one of the few temples dedicated to Lord Parshuram in the entire country. There is one said to be located near a lake in Arunachal Pradesh (Parshuram Kund) and perhaps some in the Western Ghats – from where he is said to have hurled his Battle Axe into the sea after his numerous wars and victories. Parshuram is not just a myth or fable. The map and oral tradition of that place testified to the authenticity of that very ancient account of a warrior sage with a celebrated temper, who was the true progenitor of the fighting Brahmins, who would, for centuries on end, be the Guardians of the Gateways of invasions into our civilization.

The incarnations of Lord Vishnu – the preserver of the Hindu pantheon (and a part of the trinity of Brahma, Vishnu and Mahesh) have a curious evolutionary progression which the famous evolutionist JBS Haldane had noted in the last century:-

- *Matsya Avatara* The first Avatara of Vishnu was in the form of a fish *Matsya Avatara* – the Great White Whale who saved the Noah's Ark during the Great Flood. Life emerged in the marine environment and grew to a huge size in the whale.
- *Kurma Avatara.* The second was the Kurma Avatara or the Amphibian form of life that was moving inwards from the high seas to the land. The Kurma Avatara appeared in the form of a gigantic tortoise.
- *Varaha Avtara.* The Third Avatara was Varaha Avatara – Vishnu in the form of a gigantic boar or a quadruped mammal who fought and killed the demon who had hijacked the earth.

- *Vamana Avatara.* The Fourth incarnation was as a pygmy-sized Brahmana called Vamana. He was the representative of the dimunitive Ramapithicarus or the pre-human stages of man's evolution when the primates evolved into a dwarf humanoid form that walked erect.

- *Narashima Avatara.* The Fifth incarnation was the Narsimha Avatara – the half man – half lion, who probably signifies the wild -maned cave man of the Stone Age.

- *Parshuram Avatara.* It is only with the Sixth incarnation of Lord Parshuram, the Battle Axe-wielding warrior- sage that we reach full human form – in the form of a warrior Brahmin with a Battle axe – to not just cut down foes but also reclaim forest lands for cultivation and human habitation.

- *Rama Avatara.* The Seventh Avatara is Rama – the ideal, principled human, the ethical exemplar and role-model of the Indian civilization – the ideal King and ruler, the ideal son and brother – the exemplar on how to conduct human relationships and obligations – a great warrior and noble ruler who led major military expeditions into South India and the island of Sri Lanka.

- *Krishna Avatara.* Krishna Avatara is the divine hero, a great soldier, statesman, philosopher and exemplar who ushered in democracy (in the form of clan republics that elected their leaders – in the ancient era of hereditary monarchies). The monarchies of that era all banded together to destroy this nascent democratic form of government. Krishna saved his people by his long march or strategic retreat to Dwarka (in Gujarat).This was much like Mao's strategic retreat or long march in 20th century China. He subsequently played a pivotal role in the geo-politics of South Asia. Indeed it is said that Krishna engineered the Mahabharata War so that the leading monarchial powers of that era would mutually destroy one another and the Republican Yadavas would emerge as the leading power by default. As a grand strategy of conflict – avoidance and inducing clashes amongst one's principal rivals, it was a masterstroke. Krishna gave us the Gita – a remarkable text on the doctrine of desireless action and how to manage fear and guilt on the battlefield.

- *Gautam Buddha.* In the Gautam Buddha the Avatara series reaches a recognizable historical name. The Buddha is recognized as the Ninth incarnation of Vishnu. His saffron-clad army of monks spread the soft power of Buddhism to all corners of Asia. It was a remarkable exercise in the projection of soft power of a civilization that remains unparalleled to this day.
- *Kalki Avatara.* The Puranas mention a 10th incarnation of Vishnu who is yet to come. He will be a great warrior on a white charger who will destroy the current industrial era based on fossil fuels (Kali Yuga) and usher in a brand new civilization that is sustainable and benign to the environment.

JBS Haldane had noted this curious evolutionary progression of the series of Avataras of Vishnu. They proceed from fish to amphibian, to mammal ,to a humanoid of short stature, to the Stone Age man with a wild mane and finally to full human form with the Sage Parshuram, who is a great warrior.

The Legend of Parshuram

With this overview of the entire series of the 10 incarnations of Vishnu – let us now examine the legend of the warrior sage Parshuram in greater detail. In more ways than one, Parshuram is regarded as the true progenitor of the race of fighting Brahmins or *Brahm-Kshatras*. A study of this legend seems to indicate that the Varnas in the Vedic period were based largely on occupational groups or guild corporations of professions. They had not become deeply entrenched, endogamous groups as yet. Thus Lord Parshuram was the great grandson of Bhrigu Rishi – the founder of the *Bhriguvansha*. Bhrigu's son Richika was married to the daughter of King Gadhi named Satyavati. As such this was a marriage between a Brahmin sage and a Kshatriya princess. Satyavati's mother, a Brahmin lady, in turn was married to King Gadhi – himself a Kshatriya. Mixed marriages thus were apparently quite a common occurrence in the Vedic and early epic periods, where rules of endogamy did not seem to have been enforced very rigidly. By the time of Mahabharata however, these caste hierarchies had become endogamous and deeply entrenched. Legend has it that one day Satyavati asked Sage Bhrigu that both she and her mother be blessed with a son each to continue their lineages. The great Sage Bhrigu prescribed for them a ritual of worshipping a particular tree. It is said that he asked them to drink a glass of medicated milk each as part of this ritual . Due to an error, the glasses of milk got interchanged and the rituals got mixed up. When told of this, Bhrigu predicted that Satyavati's son would be a great warrior and her mother's son would be a great sage.

Satyavati was quite shaken. She pleaded with Bhrigu Rishi that this should happen not with her son but her grandson. The Great Sage agreed. Thus Rishi Jamadagni was born to Sage Richika and Satyavati. He was the father of Parshuram. Years later Sage Jamadagni married Renuka, the daughter of King Prasanjt. They had five sons of whom Parshuram was the youngest. Inspite of being born in a Brahmin family, Parshuram very early on began to display traits of being a great warrior. He was very fond of playing with weapons, showed great courage and developed an excellent physique. He had great strength and was quick to fly into a rage.

Reactions to Tyranny

In those days, the Emperor who ruled over much of North India was a mighty king called Krityavir Arjun. It was reputed that he had a thousand arms and was a great warrior. Hence he was called Sahastra Arjun. He belonged to the Haihayas, a very war-like tribe of North India. Legend has it that his capital was in Mahishmati (present day Maheshwar in central India or Madhya Pradesh. Other accounts however locate him in present day Gujarat). The tragedy is that Krityavir Arjun was a great tyrant. He had spread a reign of terror in North India. His cruel warriors roamed the land and took what they wanted. They tortured and killed anyone who dared to oppose them. It is said that the Haihayas of the lunar dynasty had sacked the holy city of Kashi and killed the kings Haryaswa and Sudeva of the Solar Clan (*Suryavansha*). They had also dethroned the king of Ayodhya, who also belonged to the Solar Clan. Krityavir Arjun had defeated the Nagas. The Five hordes (Panch Ganas) of the warlike Shakas, Yavanas, Kambojas, Phalvas and Paradas had aligned themselves with Krityavir to wreak havoc in North India. They had occupied Ayodhya. Within the kingdom the soldiers had let loose a reign of terror and anarchy. Might was right and the powerful Haihaya warriors did what they wanted. The people were groaning under the terrible persecution but were terrified into meek submission.

One day, the Haihaya King Krityavir Arjun along with an army of camp followers came to the Ashram of Rishi Jamadagni on the banks of the Renuka River. The Rishi's son was then away in the forest cutting wood for his Yagyas. The sage and his followers welcomed the King and his men. With the help of Kamdhenu (wish-fulfilling cow, also called Surabhi) they offered a feast to the King and his entire army. Krityavir Arjun was astonished. How had the sage managed this? Proudly they showed him Kamdhenu and her calf. The king now demanded that the sage hand over the cow to him. The sage refused saying he needed her for performing the rituals. Krityavir Arjun flew into a rage. His soldiers mercilessly beat up the sage and his followers. They devastated the Ashram and marched off with Kamdhenu.

Parshuram heard all the commotion and rushed back. By the time the looters had left and the Ashram was in ruins. Thus began the mortal enmity between the Haihayas and the Bhargavas, which the Mahabharata epic cites repeatedly. Apparently, Parshuram assembled an army of Brahmins and raised the banner of revolt against the tyrannical Krityavir Arjun and his dreaded Haihayas. Legend however has it that Parshuram had done great penance and pleased Lord Shiva. From him he had received the miraculous weapons of war – the Battle Axe called Parshu (from which he drew his name) and the dreaded Brahmastra – the ultimate weapon of mass destruction.

Like the mighty Hercules (Herakeles) he now charged up to the palace of King Krityavir Arjun and demanded the return of Kamdhenu and her calf. Krityavir Arjun sent his armies to kill him. Parshuram reputedly slaughtered them with his Battle Axe and shower of arrows. Krityavir Arjun then came out himself on his mighty war chariot. There was a fierce battle. As per the myth – Parshuram cut off the thousand arms of Krityavir Arjun one by one and then slew him with his Battle Axe. He returned triumphantly with Kamdhenu and restored her to his father's ashram.

The sons and clansmen of Krityavir Arjun were enraged. They attacked the ashram of Sage Jamadagni at a time when Parshuram was away. They brutally killed his father. When Parshuram returned, he saw his hysterical mother grieving over his father's corpse. He saw her striking her breast twenty-one times in her grief. Parshuram was truly enraged. He vowed to exterminate the Haihayas and slaughtered the sons and all kinsmen of Krityavir Arjun. He launched 21 campaigns to exterminate their very race from the face of this earth. In the bargain he conquered vast tracts of land. He thus conducted the Ashwamedha sacrifice and challenged all kings to either submit or face annihilation. Those who chose to fight were destroyed. Parshuram was now the master of a great empire. He gave away all the land to Rishi Kashyap and the Brahmins. Thus it is that the priestly Brahmins became the masters of the land or 'Mahipals'. This later morphed into the clan of the fighting Brahmins or the Mohyals as also the Bhumihars and Tyagis etc. They gave up alms , their priestly vocations and instead – became proud owners of vast lands. They became the Shalin Brahmins instead of the Yayavars who made their living by the priestly vocation. Many went on to found their own kingdoms and became the Guardians of the Gateways to the Indian civilization. From Afghanistan to Sindh, many Mohyal dynasties arose and barred the path of all invaders.

Guru Dronacharya: When Lord Parshuram had given away his vast wealth and distributed all the lands – he was approached by the poor Brahmin Guru Dronacharya. Parshuram said, "I have given away all my wealth and lands. I have nothing more to give." "Lord then please teach me the Art of War and grant me the secret of the celestial weapons," said Dronacharya. So Parshuram taught Dronacharya the Art of War and Guru Dronacharya became the greatest teacher of war in all of India. He taught the Kaurava and Pandava princes the Art of War. He was based in the village of Gurugram (erstwhile Gurgaon in Haryana).

He took the royal princes across the Shivaliks to Dehradun and established a camp on the banks of the River Tons. The word Dehradun incidentally comes from the words *"Dera-Drona"* or the

Camp of Drona. Its quite curious that the present-day Indian Military Academy (IMA), from where officers of the Indian Army receive their training and become commissioned officers, is located virtually at that very spot. The main parade ground of the Academy has a huge Gate that is called "Drona Dwar- the gate of Drona". It is an interesting synchronism of our history that purely by chance – the present day Academy for teaching the art of war to Indian Military officers was unintentionally located where Guru Drona had set up his school to teach the Royal Princes of the Mahabharatan era the Art of War.

A few kilometers ahead of the IMA, we have the Drona Gufa or the cave where Dronacharya had sat and meditated. Dronacharya had just one son called Ashwathama. The Guru had taught his son all the Arts of War and made him a mighty warrior. His son was the Guru's blind spot. He doted on him. His other blind spot was the great Pandava prince Arjun. He was his favourite disciple and he ensured that he became the greatest Archer and warrior of all times.

Eklavya: Though he had risen from humble origins – Dronacharya had become somewhat arrogant. He refused to teach the art of war to a tribal boy called Eklavya. He also refused to accept Karna because he was ostensibly low born and the son of a Soot (*Sootputra* – son of a charioteer). The crestfallen Eklavya created a statue of Guru Dronacharya and became a self taught archer of amazing skill. It is said that many years later Dronacharya and his band of disciples reached Eklavyas forest. He was then practising archery. A dog began to bark at him. Annoyed, Eklavya shot off a bunch of arrows into the dog's mouth with such skill that he did not wound him. This action forced to dog to be silent. The royal princes were left amazed by his skill. Even Arjun admitted that he could not shoot with such skill. Dronacharya then asked Eklavya who his teacher was. When told that it was Dronacharya himself – the Guru asked Eklavya for his thumb as *Guru-Dakshina*. He wanted to ensure that Arjun remained the greatest archer in the world. Such was his love and blind spot for his favourite disciple. It is said that the great tribal warrior Eklavya unhesitatingly cut off his own right thumb and gave it to his Guru. It is said that in the honour of the great Eklavya, the tribals of Central India still do not use their thumb while shooting arrows.

Karna: The other disciple that Dronacharya refused to teach was Karna – the son of the Sun God. Unfortunately, because his unwed mother Kunti had cast him away at birth, he had been brought up by a humble charioteer. The Guru who taught the princes, felt it beneath his dignity to teach a mere *Sootputra*. Sadly rebuffed and hurt, Karna sought out Guru Parshuram. He told him he was a Brahmin and requested him to teach him the art of war. Parshuram was deeply touched by Karna and his devotion. He taught him the art of war, Towards the end of his training there was a sad episode. The Guru was resting at noon with his head in the lap of his beloved disciple. A scorpion crawled up Karna's thigh and stung him. So as not to disturb the sleep of his revered Guru, Karna stoically bore that intense pain. Blood from the bite fell on Guru's face and he awoke. He was amazed but then outraged, "Only a Kshatriya could bear such an intense pain. You are not a Brahmin, you've lied to me", he thundered. Karna ruefully admitted the truth. The Guru cursed him, "You have wrongfully learnt the art of war. You will lose this knowledge when you will need it the most."

Thus it was that Karna's head was in a daze at the most critical time of the Mahabharata War. His chariot wheel got stuck in the mud. When he jumped down to extricate his chariot, he was attacked and killed by his hated rival Arjun.

Bheeshma. The third great disciple of Guru Parshuram was the mighty Bheeshma – the grandsire of the Kauravas and Pandavas historically. It is said that he had become as powerful as his Guru and in trials of skill they proved to be equal. The other great disciple of Parshuram is said to be Balram – the brother of Krishna. All the four great disciples of Parshuram played pivotal roles in the Mahabharata War and the politics of that era.

Southern Expeditions

Legend has it that Parshuram is immortal – that he is around even in the present day and age – perhaps hidden in some cave in the Himalayas, engaged in deep meditation. It is said that the 10th Avatara of Vishnu – Kalki – will also be a great warrior and Parshuram will emerge to teach him the art of war.

Parshuram in West and South India

It is said that after his conquest of North India Parshuram distributed all his wealth and lands to the Brahmins – who thereafter become owners of land and later even rulers in their own right. Parshuram then wandered all over India performing heroic deeds. Apparently he saved the Konkan region from being submerged in the sea and founded the clan of Chitpavan Brahmins. He also waged war in Kerala and Karnataka. In the South he destroyed the Nagas and gave the land to the Nambudhri Brahmins. The art of Kaliyari Pattu, the martial art of Kerala – from which Karate is said to have been developed, is credited to Parshuram. Parshuram is a *Deerghajeevi* – he had acquired the secret of Soma – the divine elixir that rejuvenates and reverses the ageing process. It is secreted in the brain as enkephalins and endorphins in deep meditation. Possibly it is the secretion of these neuro-chemicals that enhances the lifespan. A verse in the Rig Veda says, "The cows that were old became young again." Rishi Aurobindo, a modern day sage, spent his lifetime in this quest for the secret of longevity.

Whatever the facts may be – legend has it that Lord Parshuram was around not just in the times of Ramayana but also during the period of the Mahabharata. He is said to have been present during the Sita Swayamavara – where Rama, the seventh incarnation of Vishnu broke Lord Shiva's bow. The bow was presented by Lord Parshuram to King Janak. He was present during the age of Sri Krishna – the 8th incarnation of Vishnu. The very same Sri Krishna, who engineered the Mahabharata War and possibly brought about the mutual destruction of the Jedi knights of that era who had mastered the cult of secret and esoteric weapons. Parshuram is counted as one of the *Deerghajeevis* (long-lived ancients) of the Indian civilization and an incarnation of Vishnu the preserver. Today Wikipedia lists some 28 temples dedicated to Lord Parshuram. Most are in the Western Ghats and southern states. There is one in Arunachal Pradesh and the one near Jalandhar in Punjab.

The Cult of the Samurai and the Band of Fighting Brahmins

The Samurai of Japan are said to be the poet- warriors – equally skilled in the gentler arts of poetry, painting and ceremonial tea drinking as they are in the martial arts of war. With the warrior sage Parshuram begins the tradition of fighting Brahmins. In this present age they are called scholar-warriors. Parshuram, ostensibly had led a revolt against a highly tyrannical and unjust ruler whose Haihaya warriors were terrorizing the region of North India. The fight against oppression and state terror is a just war and the Brahmins of that ancient era – led the uprising against such unjust and cruel rulers. Thus the Brahmins, who in the Vedic era had confined themselves to priestly duties, piety and renunciation now transformed themselves into warriors who took up arms against tyrannical rule. We see them now becoming owners of land (Mahipals) and even rulers of kingdoms. Their fighting tradition continues and they become the *Brahm-Kshatras* – the Fighting Brahmins of India. These warrior Brahmins now became the Guardians of the Gateways into the Indian civilization – from the Khyber to the Bolan Pass. From Sindh to Baluchistan, these fighting Brahmins of the former Saraswati River tract had stood squarely in the path of every invader, whether Greek, Hun, Scythian, Saka, Arab, Mongol, Turkomen or Pathan. The story has so many similarities with the cult of the Samurai in Japan who became feudal lords and the protectors of Japan.

Their history becomes a series of ballads of bravery that is preserved by the court poets or family bards. Some two millennium after the epic age of Ramayana, at the time when Mughal Emperor Aurangzeb unleashed another reign of terror against the indigenous people of this country – it is the warrior Brahmins of the Punjab who rose in revolt. Soldier saints like Baba Paraga and Banda Bairagi arose (who were both Mohyals of the Chhibber clan), who lead a military revolt. There are also martyrs like Bhai Mati Das and his brothers. In a gruesome act of torture – Bhai Matidas was sawed to death by the Mughals. His brothers were boiled and burnt to death – in a bid to terrorize the Indian population into meek submission. Instead of meekness, the response was of intense outrage. Inspired by the courage and extreme stoicism of their martyrs, the Sikhs of Punjab arose in red hot revolt under their Gurus – their soldier-saints who were so well served by the Mohyal Fighting Brahmins. In less than a century, the tyrannical Uzbek Empire was overthrown and destroyed.

The cult of the soldier saint now turned into the military brotherhood of the Sikhs who led an Indian military revival. In the South, Shivaji and later the Peshwa Brahmins led the revolt of the Marathas. Between the Sikhs and the Marathas, the Uzbek Empire (turned ruthlessly tyrannical) was comprehensively destroyed. In India we have the unique tradition of the soldier saint – the "Sant Sipahi" – the Brahmin priest who becomes a fierce warrior and fights ethically and bravely for what is right. When tyrants terrify the people and try to crush their spirits – it is these self same Fighting Brahmins who lead the rebellions that overthrow the oppressors and destroy the tyrants. Their courage and stoicism in the face of extreme torture – designed to terrify a population into meek submission – had the exact opposite effect. A fire storm erupted that swept the tyrants into oblivion. Not only did the Sikhs destroy the Mughal Empire, they also attacked Afghanistan and conquered all Pathan territories west of the Indus (present day FATA and NWFP). They became the torch bearers of an Indian Military Renaissance.

When it comes to standing steadfastly against foreign invasions – it is the self same warrior Brahmins who were in the forefront. They barred the path of every invader. They became the bulldogs of the border and the Guardians of our Gates. This is the uniquely Indian tradition of the scholar warriors. Modern day Armed Forces are highly complex organizations that use cutting edge technology. To master these, present day war leaders must therefore be 'scholar–warriors'. This scholar-warrior or Fighting Brahmin tradition emerged in India with the advent of the warrior sage Parshuram. In fact, it merits mention that Parshuram was not the only Brahmin warrior in the epic period. The other was Ravana – the King of Lanka and his brothers and sons. Ravana had similarly propitiated Lord Shiva and won many boons. He had learnt the art of war and won for himself celestial weapons and a fabulous kingdom. However, he had strayed far from the path of righteousness and had abducted Sita. Ram had led a massive military campaign against him across the sea and this entailed the construction of the Adams Bridge (Ram Setu) that links India to Sri Lanka. In a tale that bears a remarkable similarity to Homer's Illiad (and the Story of Helen of Troy) – a massive campaign was launched to rescue Sita –

the princess of Ayodhya. Like Troy, the capital of Ravan's Lanka was besieged and finally destroyed by Prince Ram along with an Army of Monkeys. That is the other tale of fighting Brahmins who went astray in the epic period.

Courtesy : Karanvir Vimanika

4

Guardians of the Gate

Facing the Greeks of Alexander

In the early and later epic period we see the Brahmin Sages taking up weapons and becoming warriors. The primal push towards this dramatic change of Varna based roles from priests and savants to warriors came from Parshuram. He led the revolt against the tyranny and loot perpetrated by the Haihaya warriors of Krityavir Arjun. Parshuram killed the tyrant and freed people from his tyrannical rule. In the bargain he became the master of a vast empire. He distributed all his land and wealth amongst the Brahmins. The priests of the Vedic period now became the Masters of the Land – Mahipals or Bhupatis (later Mohyals). They refused to take alms or live on charity anymore. Instead they took up arms and in time, many of them became rulers of kingdoms and even empires. From the Yayavars or priests , they became the Shalin Brahmins.

The main Brahmin warriors of the early epic period were Parshuram and Ravana and of the later epic period of Mahabharata – it was Guru Dronacharya and his son Ashwathama. There is then a long gap in which India fragmented into a large number of squabbling kingdoms and clan republics. In historic terms – 16 major states or Mahajanapadas had formed in India by this time. Besides these major states there were a large number of smaller Janapadas or principalities – especially along the Northern border.

Kedar Sharma: In 585 B.C. we next hear of a Brahmin ruler called Kedar Sharma from Khoistan (Afghanistan) from the areas between Herat and Ghazni. He extended his kingdom down till the Shivaliks. He came down to the plains and established a massive fort at Kalinjar in Bundelkhand. Ruins of this massive fort are still visible today and cover an area of some 7 sq. kms.

Assumption of Power by the Shudras and the Vaishyas

Changes were now taking place in the Art of War itself. In the period of the Mahabharata the chariots were the primary arm of the army. The chariots were manned by the Maharathis – the great car warriors, who were all Kshatriyas. Gradually – after the Mahabharata War, emphasis began to shift towards greater use of elephants. War elephants were manned by the people of the Shudra caste. Thus gradually, we see the Shudras gaining political power. The Nanda dynasty and the Mauryan dynasty were both formed by Shudra kings.

The Vaishya or Merchant class became very prosperous. They needed peace for the pursuit of commerce and trade. Hence they were more inclined towards pacific faiths like Buddhism and Jainism. The rulers needed their wealth and so we find an increasing trend towards state patronage of Buddhism. The Brahminical order was opposed to this and we see a great deal of latent tension based upon the clash between state patronage for Buddhism or Brahminism. This saw the consolidation of the Mauryan empire and later its overthrow by Brahmin military rulers. This is the social milieu in which Mahapadma Nanda, a Shudra ruler, came to power in Patliputra. He then had the biggest army in India. Armies since the epic period had acquired a four arms or a *"chaturang-bala"* character. The four arms are – the Chariots, the Elephants, the Cavalry and the Foot Soldiers.

In the North West there was a mosaic of clan republics and small kingdoms mainly ruled by Mohyal Brahmin rulers, who were considered the Guardians of the frontier tracts and the defenders of the gateways to the Indian civilization. Some historians called these brave fiefdoms the Bulldogs of the Borders. One such kingdom was that of King Porus or Pourava – the ruler of the trans-Jhelum tract. He was a Mohyal Brahmin and a powerful warrior himself. Some legends say he was seven feet tall. His neighbor was Ambhi Raja of Taxila – a petty and jealous ruler. It is said that these two states went to war and Ambhi Raja was soundly defeated. He never forgave Porus for this humiliation and at the first opportunity sought revenge. The opportunity was not long in coming.

The Invasion of Alexander: In 319 B.C. Alexander, the Greek Emperor had set out on a mission of conquering the known world with a combat hardened army of just 32,000 Infantry phalanxes and some 4000 soldiers in his cavalry. This Greek army had emerged from years of internecine wars between the Greek city states in which they had perfected their organizations and tactics for close combat. Alexander thus set out for world conquest with the help of a Greek army which his father – King Philip had raised and used extensively in various inter- Greek wars. To the intense surprise of all - he defeated the vast army of the Iranian King Daraius by leading a direct charge at the command and control node of this army led by the Iranian emperor himself. He then defeated the Central Asian states on the banks of the Syr and Amu Darya (present day Uzbekistan, Kyrgystan, Tajikistan etc.) He then overran Afghanistan. India was now his primary target. By 327 B.C., he was set to invade India.

The Greek Army had been combat hardened by decades of internecine struggles between the Greek city states. They had perfected the art of fighting with a combination of very well drilled Infantry that fought in company and battalion-size phalanxes, supported by Heavy and Light Cavalry for manoeuvre and shock action. Alexander's way of war was to surprise his enemies by rapid and unexpected speeds of advance to gain contact, and in battle his strategy was to dentify and target the enemy's centre of gravity – his command and control centre from where the opposing ruler exercised the control of his vast forces. In most cases, Alexander would personally lead a cavalry charge onto this node and unhinge the enemy. He had done this with great success against the Iranian King Darius, who had a vast army of 600,000 but was overwhelmed by the much smaller Greek Force that identified his command position and attacked it in a sudden charge.

The Greek Military Organization: Alexander's father Prince Philips had created a standing professional Greek Army and evolved the hoplite phlanx organization for fighting. This was not a conscripted levy but a standing professional army. Greek pages did an apprenticeship of five years to join either the heavy or the Light Cavalry. It was thus a standing professional army and not one that was hastily mobilized in times of war. It would be pertinent to take a closer look at the Greek Military Organization of that era.

The Cavalry: The Greek Cavalry was organized into three distinct classes:-

- The Heavy Cavalry of the Companions Unit
- The Heavy Cavalry of the Thessalian Cavalry Units and
- The Light Cavalry

Let us examine these in detail.

Companion's Unit: Heavy Cavalry – These were heavily armored cavalry units like the Knights of the Middle Ages. They wore horse-hair plumed bronze helmets, fish scale bronze cuirass or armament plates that covered them from neck to waist. They had long greaves wrapped around from knees to toes. They were equipped with light hide covered wooden shields, long spears and Celtic swords. Their horses were covered with a head piece and breast plates of armour and were superbly trained.

The Companions were the elite forces of the Greek Army and comprised of the Barons. Each Baron was accompanied by a maximum of three pages (who were apprentices and learnt the craft of being companions from the young age of seven years). All Army commanders, generals and civilian administrators were selected from the Companion Units. The Companions had a total strength of some 2,000 horsemen in Macedonia. They were grouped into eight squadrons of some 250 men each. They used shock tactics and their charges generally decided most of the battles that Alexander fought. They generally executed the deep outflanking manoeuvres to attack from the flanks or rear – and executed the Single or the Double Canne manoeuvre or otherwise led the charge on the main command and control node of the enemy's army.

Thessilian Cavalry Units – This was similar in composition to the Companion Unit and was manned by Greek noblemen from Thessaly. They traced their origin to the Greek God Heakles (Hercules) and were part of the Heavy Cavalry.

Light Cavalry – The Light Cavalry consisted of horsemen armed only with a shield and sword. Being lightly armed they could move swiftly. These were manned by mercenaries or soldiers from allied nations. They were used for reconnaissance or lightening charges across enemy lines to disorient and act as a reserve to exploit the success and shock action of the heavy cavalry. Units of archers and lancers on horseback would often accompany the light cavalry for attacking the enemy flanks.

Greek Infantry – The Greek Infantry was superbly trained and could march upto 40 kms a day with heavy loads. They normally carried a month's rations and supplies with them. King Philip had made them more agile and mobile by replacing the heavier bronze helmets and shields with toughened leather hide helmets and shields as also the breastplate armour was replaced by lighter, toughened leather. The Greek Infantry would march in Brigade columns but fight in company and battalion-size phalanxes.

The Heavy Infantry Phalanx

King Philip had made some revolutionary changes to make the Greek Phalanx a formidable fighting organization. As stated, the bronze helmet and breastplates had been replaced by toughened leather helmets and plates to reduce the weight on the soldier. The older 3-foot-sized shield was reduced to a circular shield of just 2 feet, This was hung around the neck and could be shifted around by shifting the body weight. This freed both hands to hold the long Greek spears (Hoplites). These were increased in length from 8 ft. to 14 ft. The sword was replaced by a small stabbing dagger.

A Greek Phalanx was generally a rectangular column of some 128 soldiers wide and 8 to 16 ranks deep. The first 5 ranks held their spears pointing forward and the balance pointing upwards. Now at least the spears of the first five ranks could strike the enemy at the first collision. The Greek Infantry did not fight individually but as a cohesive unit. The Greek Phalanx was formidable. It resembled a pack of centipedes moving sideways. They could also adopt oblique, concave or convex formations. Rear reserves could move up from both flanks and squeeze from three sides. Experienced soldiers held the side and back rows. The long spears outranged all swordsmen and short spear armed opponents of that era. The phalanx therefore had a major tactical advantage. It enabled these units to fight as a well-integrated formation that did not lose its cohesion at the first shock of contact with the enemy. The Greek Army also had Light Infantry units armed with just shields and spears that followed through behind a heavy cavalry charge and exploited its success seamlessly.

Logistics: Alexander was a great logistician. His Army had specialists like botanists, zoologists, meteorologists, surveyors and cartographers. One of the Alexander's top generals (Parminion) held the logistics department. An advance team was sent to capture supplies and establish advance bases. Only then did the main forces move in.

Size of Alexander's Army: After defeating the Iranians some 30,000 Persians had joined the Greek Force of some 40,000 Infantry and Cavalry. After defeating the Central Asian kingdoms. Alexander was joined by another 40,000 Central Asian horsemen and foot soldiers. Thus Alexander's Army that came down the Hindu Kush had a massive force of about 1,20,000 strong at the very least. These had 80,000 troops and 40,000 followers. To make matters worse, Ambhi Raja, the King of Taxila had also joined Alexander and contributed over 20,000 soldiers and guides to the Greek invading force. It was a hopeless contest. Facing this mammoth force were petty border chieftains. Porus was perhaps the most significant of these. He had an Army of

- 30,000 Infantry
- 5,000 Cavalry
- 300 Chariots
- 200 War Elephants

The mightiest power in India at that time however was the Nanda Army of Patliputra. It had at that time

- 200,000 Infantry
- 20,000 Cavalry
- 2,000 Chariots
- 3,000 War elephants

Correctly speaking, only the Nanda Army was well equipped and of sufficient size to not only take on Alexander, but defeat him comprehensively. Accordingly, Kautilya had gone to the court of Mahapadma Nanda to exhort the king to march to the west and confront Alexander. He asked him to rise above the petty politics of that era and think in civilizational terms. The Indian civilization was under attack from the Greek civilization. India was then divided into 16 Mahajanapadas and many smaller Janapadas. These were constantly at war with one another. It was India's period of the warring kingdoms. The need now was for a unified defense to confront the foreign invader.

Mahapadma Nanda however could not think beyond the petty geo-politics of South Asia and failed to think in civilizational terms as Kautilya had asked him to. Kautilya had reached his court by noon time and by then the Nanda ruler was usually drunk. He was struck by the Brahmin's impudence. His passionate appeals failed to move him.

In a fit of exasperation, Kautilya saw his drunken state and said, "You are not fit to rule." Mahapadma Nandawas enraged. He had him caught by the tuft of hair on his head and had him thrown out of the court.

Kautilya swore not to tie his tuft of hair again till it was bathed in Nanda's blood.

A dejected Kautilya then returned to North India. Ambhi Raja had by then already aligned himself with the invader. The situation was tense and hopeless. Alexander's forces had moved in two columns. The main column had come via the Khyber Pass and was led by Hephaestion. Alexander meanwhile had moved north with a smaller column to secure his northern flank formed by the ancient Mt Aernos. He entered the Valley of Kashmir along the Poonch River. Here at Bafliaz he fought a major battle where his black horse Bucephulus was killed. This place was just below the Pir Panjal Pass and is still called Bafliaz after Alexander's famous horse. When I was commanding a Division in the area of Rajouri-Poonch for Counter-Terrorist Operations (CT Ops), I had personally been to Bafliaz to see the spot where Alexander's famed horse had reportedly fallen. Having secured what he thought was the highest mountain to his North and thereby having secured his flanks, Alexander turned and rejoined the main Greek column. The stage was now set for the battle of the Hydaspes (present-day Jhelum River) with Porus.

The Battle on the Jhelum

The two armies were now camped on the opposite banks of the Jhelum River in the Karri Plains. Alexander made many repeated feints to the south. Each time Porus sent his force and shadowed the Greeks in these futile up and down movements. Alexander then sent a smaller force south as a feint while he moved north with the main force and effected a surprise crossing of the Jhelum with his army. Possibly Ambhi's men who had aligned with him showed him a ford for effecting this crossing. When he heard of it Porus now sent his son forward to contest this crossing. His son moved up with a force of war chariots. The chariots soon got bogged down in the marshy river banks and the command element was separated from the accompanying Infantry, and was decimated. The Indian archers with long bows used to hold the lower end of the bows with their toes. In the slippery soil they could not discharge their long, lethal arrows, which could penetrate the armour of the Greeks. Porus now moved up with his main force. He adopted the T-shaped '*Sakata Vyuha*' formation (shaped like the axel of a cart). This was a mistake. Given Alexander's almost 3:1 superiority – he should have adopted a Chakra Vyuha or circular formation to cater for attack from any direction.

Even as a frontal engagement commenced – the Greeks first came in contact with the 200 war elephants of Porus. The huge beasts terrified them. Alexander soon recovered from his shock and rallied his men. The Greeks clattered their shields to make a din to try and frighten the elephants. They showered arrows on their feet to make them turn and run. The elephants however took a heavy toll of the Greeks. Porus was riding on the biggest elephant and showering javelins and spears to kill the Greek soldiers.

Repeating his tactic of attacking the command and control node of the enemy forces, Alexander personally led a charge on the huge war elephant of Porous. The huge elephant reared up menacingly and Alexander was thrown off his horse. He now sent the Central Asian horses on a wide outflanking manoeuvre to attack from the flanks. Even as Porus' Army turned to face them, another contingent attacked them from the rear. The battle was the fiercest the Greeks had ever fought anywhere in the world. The huge war elephants had truly

alexanders invesion

shaken them to the core. Unfortunately, as the sun went down, the vast size of Alexander's army (also accompanied perhaps by the Taxila forces of the turncoat Ambhi Raja) slowly wore the army of Porus down.

The men fought fiercely and very bravely, but the odds were heavily against them. By evening Porus was almost alone fighting on his elephant. Porus was now extremely tired and exhausted. The battle had raged on for the whole day. Finally he had exhausted his spears and javelins. Alexander was struck by the bravery and composure of this man in the face of certain death. Finally a weary Porus got down from the elephant and asked for water. He was taken prisoner and brought before Alexander.

"Porus – you are my prisoner now. Tell me how should I treat you?" Queried Alexander.

"Just as one king treats another", Porus replied with great calm and dignity.

Alexander was deeply moved by the gravitas, bravery and composure of Porus. He made Porus his ally and returned his kingdom to him. The Greeks had at long last won this battle. It was their toughest encounter and the first time, they had faced the war elephants. The huge beasts terrified them and even as they sat around their campfires, they talked in hushed tones about the fury of these wild beasts.

Psychological Warfare

Kautilya had meanwhile returned from his failed mission to exhort Mahapadma Nanda to move up and stop Alexander. He sent his spies forward and got the full details of the battle between Porus and Alexander. He pondered deeply over the reports. A new weapon system – the war elephants had apparently terrified the Greeks and made a huge impression on them. The chariots however had failed dismally. They were not capable of cross country movement. These had been bogged down on the marshy river banks and separated the command element from the rest of the army. The elephants could move in all terrains and had a massive shock impact in the battlefield. He pondered over how to stop the Greeks of Alexander.

Slowly an idea formed in his mind. He was now aware of the truly shaken state of the Greek army. The men were homesick and worried about entering a strange new land. What had terrified them most were the war elephants. Kautilya pondered deeply. Then he sent his array of spies dressed as snake charmers, acrobats, performers, gypsies and nautch girls. They hobnobbed with the Greeks. They told them lurid tales of how Nanda's Army had 9,000 war elephants. "Their elephants", they said, "were much bigger in size; and trained to pick up enemies in their trunk and toss them to the ground to break their armour. Then they would gore them with their tusks. They were trained to crush skulls with their huge feet and practiced by crushing coconuts! Such lurid tales filled the Greek Army with dread and foreboding. The fear of the unknown magnified their dread. Soon there was -visible unrest in the Greek Camp.

Alexander had now reached the Beas. He was camped at a place called Tibor (modern day Tibri in Punjab?). The Greek army mutinied. It refused to go any further. Alexander was a great orator. He gathered his men and harangued them for hours. He exhorted them to complete their mission of global conquest. He reminded them of the great battles they had fought and won, the impossible odds they had overcome. The Greek army however had enough. They had left home in 319 B.C., some 8 years ago. They had fought innumerable battles and won huge piles of plunder and booty. They wanted to return home with this loot. The war elephants had shaken them and the rumors of what lay ahead terrified them. Such is the impact of a new and unfamiliar weapon system upon the minds of soldiers. Despite all Alexander's oratory, they simply refused to go forward. They were egged on by their generals who were also keen now to get back home. One General, Coenus, was most vociferous in his protests and incited the men to refuse to go any further. Subsequently Alexander had Coenus killed.

Ultimately, Alexander knew it was of no use. He went to his tent and sulked for three days. Then he had seven fire altars built to mark the farthest point of his advance and agreed to his men's demand to return homewards. His army now marched along the banks of the Indus to get to the sea and commence the journey homeward. The

Greek soldiers now fought with renewed vigor and hope. They were eager to get back home with the booty and fought fiercely on their way homewards. They carried out mass slaughters, wherever they were opposed, to terrify the locals. These massacres were ruthless and brutal and designed to open the path home. These virtually amounted to genocide. The system of war that had evolved till then in India was highly chivalrous. Armies of India left the civilian populations alone. Now they encountered a foreign army that slaughtered civilians so ruthlessly and without any remorse.

The Mohyals of Multan

As the Greeks retreated along the course of the Indus river, they came upon the Mohyal kingdom of Multan. The Greeks called them the Malloi. There, the Bali Mohyal-led clans gave the Greeks the toughest and bloodiest fight of their whole world- conquering expedition. There was a fierce clash near Multan along the course of the dried out Saraswati river. A fierce defence was put up by a confederacy of Republican clans of Mohyals (Malwas) and the Kshudrakas.

Taking a leaf from the Greek war- book, the Mohyal warrior Brahmins now made a special effort to locate the Greek generals and commanders. They ambushed them and shot them down with their meter long arrows that could penetrate the leather hide armour of the Greeks. The Greeks were stung by these skirmishing tactics. They laid siege to the fort city of Multan. A major battle took place outside the city gates. Once again the Indian longbow archers picked out Alexander on his horse. They took careful aim and shot the meter long arrow. It pierced Alexander's body armour and he fell off his horse and fainted with the pain.

The Greeks were enraged when they saw their famous, world conquering general fall. They thought he had been killed. In a wild rage they now fell upon the city of the Bali Mohyal kings. They began a frightful slaughter of all its men, women and children. It was an unspeakable massacre. Suddenly Alexander regained consciousness. He had been shot in the liver and this wound would subsequently lead to his death in Alexandria.

"What are you doing?" He asked his comrades.

"We thought they had killed you – we are slaughtering the whole population to avenge your death", his comrades said.

"Don't", he expostulated, "These are the best fighters I have seen in the whole world. Take them with you."

The world conqueror on his globalizing mission was ever on the lookout for gaining brave allies in his bid for world domination!

So the Greeks took with them the remaining Mohyal population of Multan. Men, women and children – were now forced to march down with Alexander's retreating Army. In effect, Alexander's much touted invasion of India never amounted to anything more than an extended border raid. It failed to break out to the Indo-Gangetic plains of India or deal with the main Indian power of that era – the Nandas of Magadh. It merely dealt with the border kingdoms of the fighting Brahmins, who put up such a tenacious resistance that Alexander was forced to retreat home. It is true that his men fought fiercely on their way home, but they also carried out genocide and large scale massacres enroute. This was something that South Asia had not seen so far.

The Greek Armies along with their caravans of loot and captured slaves reached the mouth of Indus. Around the Port of Karachi, they began to build a huge armada of ships on which they would sail back with the loot and plunder of their conquests. Once the ships were built, Alexander divided his army in two. One would sail in the ships along with the plunder and loot, while the other would march in parallel along the Makran coast into the dreary sands of Baluchistan as a flank guard of sorts and to pacify these areas of his empire. The land column suffered terrible thirst and privation in this long march, but Alexander led them from the front. As always, he personally led the most dangerous and difficult part of his mission.

Many months later – the two columns converged and finally sailed to Alexandria in Egypt. Alexander and his armies had laid the foundation of some 80 new cities through his vast and far-flung empire from Asia Minor to Iran, Central Asia, Afghanistan, North India and the upper portions of North Africa. Alexander died of his wounds in the city of Alexandria – the wounds inflicted by the fighting Brahmin warriors. A large contingent of them had been taken to Alexandria by the Greeks. Alexander named no successor before his death. The

Greek Empire split up into a large number of satrapies (provinces) ruled by the local Greek satraps. The Greek satrapies in Baluchistan and Afghanistan came under the rule of Selukos Niketor – the local satrap.

In the melee and confusion following Alexander's death, it is said that the band of Mohyal warriors taken from Multan somehow crossed over into Saudi Arabia and Iraq and settled down there. They lived there for centuries. Somewhere in the 7th Century A.D. – the descendants of the Mohyals of Multan – a clan led by one Rahab Datt Sultan would play a historic role in the epochal battle of Karbala (680 A.D.) between the Shias and Sunnis. They would fight on the side of the grandsons of Prophet Mohammad – Hasan and Hussain. Sadly it was a war that they lost. The grandsons of the Prophet were slain, but the Datt warrior Brahmins would gain the everlasting gratitude of the Shias for their bravery and valor. But that story is recorded in detail later in this book.

It was the strangest fallout of Alexander's invasion and it caused a class of Indian Fighting Brahmins to settle down in Iraq and much later perhaps, play a pivotal role in one of its most epic battles of the Muslim world – the Karbala War.

5

The Bhumihars of the Imperial Mauryan Army and the Sunga Dynasty

Meanwhile North India lay ravaged and shaken in the aftermath of Alexander's most brutal invasion. Wars had been fought for centuries in India but the civilian population had hardly ever been touched. A chivalrous form of war had crystallized, in which armies fought one another in straight combat governed by the tradition of *shaurya* and chivalry. Raj Dharma enjoined that the unarmed civilian population should not be touched. For the first time, the Greeks carried out systematic and large scale slaughters designed to terrify the civil population. This did not really work.

Despite the genocide of the civilian population – the Greeks were astonished by the ferocity of the resistance they encountered in India. The sole and greatest tragedy was that instead of uniting to fight the Greeks – the various small Janapadas, kingdoms and clan republics failed to unite and present a joint and unified front to the invaders. They all fought singly and in succession, and were thus overwhelmed by the vast and combat hardened Greek invading force. This force had received huge infusions of Iranian and Central Asian soldiers and horsemen.

The hostile Greek lack of sense of self now served to crystallize the Indian sense of self and identity. The Greek invasion inflicted a major shock on the Indian sense of self. Till then, India had great unity and uniformity as a cultural entity. However, politically India was badly splintered into a series of Mahajanapadas and even smaller Janapadas. These squabbling kingdoms and clan republics could not present a united front to any foreign invader – Alexander's Greek Armies had fully exploited this disarray and lack of unity to cut through North India and leave behind a wake of terrible destruction and genocidal killings. The slaughters were horrific and the whole of North India was reeling in shock and disarray. The lands had been ravaged and plundered – the populations slaughtered. The bravery of the Mohyals of Porus and Multan had been of little avail. The need of the hour was unity.

Kautilya had closely followed the progression of the Greek Armies down the Indus river course. He was deeply pained by how easily the foreigners had defeated our squabbling armies and ravaged our people, one by one. India was a great civilizational entity but it totally lacked political unity and military cohesion. The Indians were simply too busy fighting themselves to deal unitedly with any invader. It had led to a monumental tragedy of truly Greek proportions. What Kautilya saw was a ravaged land – burnt and looted cities, raped women, slaughtered populations and vultures feasting on the dead.

This was unacceptable. Individually, our soldiers had fought heroically. Their bravery and tenacity had shaken the Greeks. Alexander finally died of wounds inflicted by the fighting Brahmins of the frontier tracts of India. But overall, we lost because we failed to present a unified front to the foreign invaders. In the bargain North India had been ravaged and its people slaughtered.

Kautilya pondered deeply on the lessons of the Greek invasion that had hit North India like a hurricane. The idea of India is millenniums old. Every Hindu ritual commences with a recital of where it is being held – on *Jambudweep* (the world's island of Jambu – the Asian continent(?) – *Bharat Khande* – the land of Bharat or India). Yet our British historians told us that there was no concept of India down the ages. Nationhood was a gift of the British. What is amazing is the number of Indians that still subscribe to this colonial thesis. The colonial masters used the concept of Imperial Justice to justify their rule. India, they said, was no nation. It was just a mass of feuding castes, creeds, religions and ethnicities, forever at war with one another. They needed an external power to rule them, so that it could provide even handed Imperial Justice to a squabbling population – forever at war within itself.

The simple fact is that the Atharva Veda poetically talks of the concept of *"Rashtra"* or nation. There are so many verses expressing the patriotic sentiment – *"May my motherland grant me the lustre of Gold."* There are verses worshipping the brown and ruddy earth of India. There is the concept of the *Chakravartin Samrat* (all conquering ruler- emperor of all directions) who unified all under heaven. All other kings accepted his suzerainty. Kautilya pondered deeply on how to convert India's great civilizational unity into political unity. The need for political unity was paramount and Alexander's brutal invasion had just served to underline this dire need.

The question was – HOW?

The strongest kingdom in India then was that of the Mahapadma Nanda's Magadh. It had a vast army but it had let Alexander go unchallenged. Nanda's had not moved forward to contest his advance. Nor had he tried to create a coalition of Indian states to oppose the invader. That was left to a Brahmin teacher of the University of Taxila – where Indian princes and court officials were taught the art and science of war and statecraft.

Kautilya had tried to rouse the Nandas to do their civilizational duty but had failed dismally. He now saw the carnage that resulted from this lack of unity. The first need was to unify India politically under a strong and centralized rule. India was a strong society. It needed an equally strong state to safeguard its people. Without such a strong state, it would never be able to safeguard its wealth and values.

The Rise of the Imperial Mauryan Army

The first need was to raise a strong and mighty army that would unify India. Kautilya and Chandragupta now traveled down the ravaged Indus river tract. The people of this river tract were brave and tenacious fighters. They had experienced first-hand, what an external invasion meant. They had suffered terribly. Acharya Chanakya (Kautilya) and Chandragupta Maurya spoke to them of the need to unify India to prevent such terrible invasions. The Greek invasion had caused a tsunami of death and destruction. The Mohyal Brahmins of the Indus and Saraswati tracts needed little convincing. They flocked to the Mauryan banner in thousands. It was in the wake of the brutal Greek invasion that Kautilya went about recruiting and raising the Imperial Mauryan Army with the help of which he would later conquer and unify the whole of India. To secure power in Magadh – the most powerful kingdom in Northern India, the Nandas of Maghada had to be defeated and overthrown.

Why Magadha?

The eastern parts of Bihar, Jharkhand and Odisha had dense jungles from where the war elephants came. They also had huge reserves of iron, which would revolutionize weapons metallurgy. From bronze weapons, the Mauryan army had shifted to the much sturdier and stronger weapons made up of iron. Magadha dominated all trade routes. Its alluvial soil was rich and the Ganga sustained agriculture, which could produce a huge surplus to fill economic coffers. Chandragupta and Chanakya now set about recruiting a huge Imperial Mauryan Army from amongst the ravaged ranks of the Mohyals of the Indus-Saraswati river tracts, who had suffered terribly at the hands of Alexander. Quite obviously, they needed little persuasion after this bitter experience of results of a complete lack of unity. So it was with an Army of these sentinels of the border (*Seemant Pradeshon ke Rakshak*) that the Imperial Mauryan army was raised and formed.

These Mohyal fighting Brahmins of the newly raised Mauryan army, then attacked and conquered Magadha. They overthrew Mahapadma Nanda. Chanakya installed Chandragupta Maurya on the throne of Patliputra, which was then the primary centre of political power in East India. The fighting Brahmins from the North West now formed the core of the Imperial Mauryan army. They settled down in the Eastern UP, and Bihar and in time came to be called the *Bhumihar Brahmins* – the landowning Brahmin aristocracy of Eastern India. Their accounts indicate that the Bhumihars migrated from the Kanyakubja Brahmin society of Kannauj. They are today a confederation of 18 castes including Dwevdi, Dixit, Malaviya, Pandey, Pathak, Rai, Shahi, Tripathi, Vajpayee, etc. Other scholars trace them to Madarpur in Kanpur. Almost all of these trace their ancestry to Sage Parshuram and later Pushyamitra Sunga- the General of the Mauryan Army who overthrew the last Mauryan ruler. They were thus the core of Imperial Mauryan Army that went on to unify the whole of India in the wake of Alexander's brutal invasion. Two of the most famous Bhumiars however are not soldiers but great poets, Goswami Tulsidas who wrote the *Ram Charitmanas*- the rendition of the Ramayana into the folk language of Avadhi, and Surdas – the blind poet, famous for his devotional songs in praise of the god- child Krishna. The rulers of the holy city- state of Varanasi were also Bhumira Brahmins of distinction.

Reorganizing the Army

The Mahabharatan military paradigm was premised upon an Army of four fighting arms – the Chariots, the Cavalry, the War Elephants and the Infantry. Pride of Place was given to the war chariots. Kautilya observed that these war chariots lacked cross country mobility. They were all right for set-piece battles on huge flood plains, where the two armies would converge for a tournament of sorts with laid down rules of chivalry and conduct. But the Greek invaders did not observe these rules. They slaughtered our civilian population. The Greek armies were premised on mobility. Their infantry could march 40 kms a day with heavy loads. Their cavalry could outflank and disorient with shock charges. They fought not on set piece battlefields like Kurukshetra or Panipat, but anywhere and everywhere. The battle with Porus had taken place on the banks of the Jhelum and the Indian chariots were completely bogged down in the mud and slush. The command element thus got separated from the soldiery. Elaborate rules of war and chivalry observed by South Asian kingdoms were not followed by the invaders. This Indian sense of self only crystallized in the wake of such a brutal invasion by a hostile non-self. The people who suffered most were best placed to appreciate the ideas and ideal of national unity. These were the fighting Brahmins of the Saraswati- Indus river tracts.

Kautilya analyzed the recent wars with the Greeks and drew some pertinent lessons. The chariots were now useless in a mobile war. Hence they were consigned to purely ceremonial purposes. The War Elephants had performed superbly. They were capable of rapid cross country movement in any and every terrain including plains, mountains , jungles and even deserts. They carried 8 soldiers armed with bows and arrows and spears and lances – opposed to just one car warrior in the chariots. In terms of firepower therefore, the elephants completely outclassed the chariot. The same was even more evident in terms of relative mobility. The elephant was a much more elevated command and control platform. Alexander's cavalry charge against the elephants of Porus had failed dismally. Used in the mass – the war elephants could generate shock and awe.

So, Kautilya made the war elephants the primary combat arm of the Imperial Mauryan Army. He now took a leaf from Alexander's much more mobile form of war that entailed rapid marches and quick outflanking manoeuvres. He first attacked the Nandas in Magadha and overthrew them to establish the Mauryan Empire centred on Patliputra. There he raised the size of the Elephant Corps from 3,000 to 9,000 war elephants. Elephants are hugely expensive to maintain and the Mauryan state needed massive economic resources. Kautilya monetized the Mauryan economy on the silver standard. He issued silver and gold coins. He brought new land under cultivation and created mines, eating/gambling houses and liquor vends – all under state-control to raise revenue. Of the *Kosha* (treasury) and *Danda* (Army) he felt that the former was far more important. A mighty military power could only emerge on the basis of seizing economic power. The Mauryan state therefore was elaborate and tightly centralized. Officials were centrally appointed and paid in gold/silver coinage. Kautilya now raised a vast Army of some 600,000 Infantry; 8,000 chariots; 9,000 war elephants and some 30,000 cavalry. Megasthenes has left behind elaborate accounts of this vast standing army and its shock arm of war elephants. Elephants now became the key to victory. *"Where there are Elephants there is Victory"*, said a Sanskrit proverb. Elephants used in the mass could generate shock and awe. For the next 10 centuries, the elephant became the core of all Indian armies. It did extremely well initially as a platform for mobility, command and control and inducing shock action.

The era of the elephant ended however the day the explosive paradigm of war began. The Chinese, Turks, Mongols and Arabs soon made explosives, Naphtha flaming arrows, huge siege canons and then muskets and field artillery. Their very noise frightened and panicked our elephants, who became unruly. India's fatal flaw was to hang on to the elephant long after it had become a liability on the battlefield. In the Mauryan Era the shock arm of 9,000 War Elephants however, helped the Mauryans unite the whole of India in just 25 years after Alexander's brutal invasion.

Driving out the Greek Power

Having consolidated his empire in India, Kautilya now asked Chandragupta Maurya to train his guns northwards to fortify India against any more foreign invasions. Kautilya did not want to wait to be attacked. Instead the Imperial Mauryan state mounted a massive pre-emptive attack on the Greek Satrap, Selukos Niketor – whom Alexander had left behind to hold the outposts of his empire in Central Asia, Afghanistan and Baluchistan. Future danger could come from here and Kautilya was in no mood to let it crystallize and happen again. He embarked on a forward defence of the new Indian Union.

Thus, in 305 B.C., merely 22 years after the Greek invasion, the Imperial Mauryan Army mounted a major offensive on the Greek Empire. Selukos Niketor and his Greeks were routed. Selukos had to give his daughter in marriage to Chandragupta; and cede the satrapies in Aria (Herat), Archosia (Kandahar), Parepanasadoi (Kabul) of Afghanistan and Baluchistan. So much for Greek conquest! Kautilya had sealed the traditional invasion routes of the Khyber and Bolan Passes and gone far ahead and occupied the Hindu Kush ranges. He had thereby acquired for India a very scientific and easily defensible frontier- something that the British tried for in vain many centuries later but could never do. India was now secured from any further foreign invasion. How scientific this civilizational boundary was established in the 7th century AD when the Hindu kings of Kabul and Kandahar stopped the world conquering Arab armies on the ramparts of the Hindu kush and forced them to turn back- utterly humiliated. It was the zenith of Indian military power. That was how the chapter of Greek conquest ended in India. The Indian response was to unify the whole country under the banner of the mighty Mauryan Empire that unified India from Afghanistan to Kamrup and from Kashmir to Karnataka. Then it attacked Greek power on the borders and pushed them beyond Baluchistan and Afghanistan to give depth to the defences of the Indian civilization in the North West and acquire a scientific frontier along the formidable Hindu Kush range.

It was a remarkable feat of turning defeat into victory. For the first time India had provided strategic depth to its northern frontiers and had acquired scientific borders along the Hindu-kush mountains that were so easily defensible with a minimum of troops. Kautilya, the great teacher from the faculty of the Taxila University of war and statecraft, now abdicated his role as the National Security Advisor (NSA) of the Mauryan Empire. He appointed Mudrarakshasa – his former greatest adversary and NSA of the Mahapadma Nanda to that post. He had consolidated the Mauryan Empire and secured the northern invasion routes. He had driven the Greek power not just from India, but also from neighboring Afghanistan and Baluchistan. He had managed to unify India into a strong centralized empire. A few years later Chandragupta Maurya converted to Jainism and abdicated the throne. His successor Bindusara (298-237 B.C.) extended the Mauryan Empire down south till Karnataka.

Ashoka: The Great (273-232 B.C.)
Ashoka began his career as Chanda Ashoka – the terrible and ruthless. He killed his brothers and all contenders to the Mauryan throne. The kingdom of Kalinga was the only power holding out against the mighty Mauryan empire. Ashoka attacked it in 261 B.C. and there was a terrible battle leading to a large scale bloodbath and casualties on both sides. Reportedly, a 100,000 men were killed and some 50,000 held prisoners. Ashoka was sickened by the bloodletting. He turned for peace to Buddhism and was transformed. He now stopped the pursuit of hard power and military conquest and turned instead to Dharma-Vijay or the conquest of hearts and minds. He sent out an army of saffron-clad Buddhist monks to spread the doctrine of the Buddha to lands as far afield as Tibet, Myanmar, South East Asia (Laos, Cambodia, Thailand and Vietnam), Sri Lanka, Korea, China, Japan and parts of Central Asia and Mongolia. It was a remarkable ideological or soft power offensive which converted great parts of Asia to the Indian creed of Buddhism. It was a remarkable projection of soft power of a vast state. Ashoka's rock edicts are today found all over India.

This soft power projection was perhaps at the expense of the hard-military power of the state. It atrophied. After Ashoka's passing away, the Mauryan Empire went into decline. It lasted merely a century and a half thereafter, but it had for the first time politically unified the whole of India. The Lion of Ashoka is the emblem of our Republic today. They are part of the rank badges of the Armed Forces and even the Police, Para- military and Central Police Organizations today. The present Indian Republic traces its origins to the imperial Mauryan empire that first unified the sub- continent as a political rather than a civilizational area and cultural entity.

The Revolt of Pushyamitra Sunga

The weakening of Mauryan military power undid the political unification and consolidation of India. As Mauryan military power declined – the various regions began to assert their influence and make inroads into India. The last of the Mauryan rulers was Brihadrath. He was a very weak and indecisive ruler. Under him the Greeks began to make deep inroads into the Mauryan Empire and the entire security consolidation of India was undone. Brihadrath now wanted to sign a treaty with the Greeks, which was seen as a virtual sell out. The Commander in Chief of the last Mauryan Emperor was Pushyamitra Sunga. He was a warrior Brahmin of the Kashyap Gotra. He was enraged by Brihadrath's plans to sell out to the Greeks. He was also livid about the rise of the power of the Buddhist clergy and its corroding influence on India's military power. Sunga staged a coup in a military parade and overthrew the last Mauryan King who was killed in 184 B.C. The Commander-in-Chief now took charge of the faltering Mauryan Empire. Its pacific policies, he believed had been its undoing. Demetrius – the Indo-Bactrian Greek king now attacked India. He captured Taxila, Rawalpindi, Sialkot and Mathura and then stormed into Magadh and was knocking on the gates of Patliputra itself. Pushyamitra Sunga now launched a counter attack. He defeated the Greeks and steadily pushed them back to the border. In the final assault, the Greek king Demetrius was killed in 175 B.C. and Greek forces pushed beyond India's borders once again.

Pushyamitra Sunga now performed the *Ashwamedha Yagya*. His sway extended from Patliputra to Kabul and Swat Valley in the North; in the West it touched the Arabian Sea and in South, it reached Kalinga and flanked the Satvahana Empire. The great Sage Patanjali flourished in his time. There was a great revival of brahmanism. The Manusmriti was written in this period as part of this massive drive to re-Hinduise Indian society and bring about an eclipse of the pacific religions of Buddhism and Jainism in India. Pushyamitra Sunga founded the Brahmin Sunga dynasty that reunified the Mauryan Empire and ruled for the next 150 years. Pushyamitra Sunga was celebrated by Kalidas in his immortal play *'Malavika Agninetram'*, Panini, the grammarian was his contemporary.

According to the Puranas, some 10 Kings of the Sunga dynasty ruled for a period of 112 years (184 to 73 B.C.). The last monarch in the line was Devabhuti. The Buddhists were decidedly unhappy with the overthrow of the Mauryan dynasty, which had given them state patronage. They even sided with the Indo-Bactrian kings and then the Greek armies. This enraged Pushyamitra Sunga, who took reprisals by razing Buddhist monasteries and killing a large number of Buddhists for siding with the Greeks. He was largely responsible for hastening the decline of Budhhism in India. He pushed back resurgent Greek power in India and consolidated his hold upon the whole of Northern India from Afghanistan to Bengal and beyond. The Bhumiar Brahmins trace their descent to Pushyamitra Sunga.

The Satvahana Empire (236 B.C. to 230 A.D.)

Towards the end of the Sunga dynasty a new Brahmin empire had emerged in the South. These were the Satvahanas (also called Andhras in the Puranas). This dynasty was founded by Ling Simuka who destroyed the Kanva rulers who had succeeded the Sungas. The Satvahanas ruled for over 300 years with their capital at Pratisthan, in the upper Godavari (modern day Paithan). The Satvahanas revived the Vedic religion.

The Vakatakas

In the 4th Century A.D., another Brahmin dynasty called the Vakatakas flourished in the region South of the Narmada. It was founded by Vindhya-Shakti and his son Pravarsena-I. Their's was a powerful kingdom and even Chandragupta Vikramaditya (376-

415 A.D.) had to establish marital alliances with this dynasty. He gave his daughter Prabhavati in marriage to Rudrasena-II of this dynasty. The famous Ajanta frescoes were painted in the reign of the Vakatakas. Kalidas had composed his famous work *'Meghadootam'* at the Vakataka court.

The Rashtrakutas

The Rashtrakutas ruled over Maharashtra (753 - 932 A.D.) with a line of 14 kings. The Ellora cave temples were built in this reign. The world famous Ellora temples, which was built top down and entailed a removal of 4,00,000 tons of rock, were built in the reign of Rashtrakutas. The famous Elephanta rock cut caves are also ascribed to this dynasty. The Ellora temples are so magnificent and the fact that they were carved top- down from sheer rock faces has led some people to make fantastic claims that these cave temples were the work of extra- terrestrials who had apparently done a form of 3D computer printing on to the sheer rock face!

The Chalukyas

This was another Brahmin dynasty founded by Pulakesiri-I and ruled in the Deccan for 230 years from the middle of the 6th to the 8th Century A.D. To check the further expansion of this power, Harsha had attacked Pulakesiri-II but suffered a defeat at his hands. His capital was at Aihole – where Parshuram had washed his blood stained Battle Axe. They built hundreds of famous temples in Aihole, Pattadakal and their capital Badami. The Chinese pilgrim Huen Tsang had visited the Chalukyan Empire and was wonderstruck by the grandeur and glory of this Brahminical Empire.

The Gupta Dynasty

The Brahmins occupied high positions at the courts of the Gupta kingdom (320-540 A.D.). The army commanders of both Samudragupta and Chandragupta Vikramaditya (376-415 A.D.) were both Brahmins namely, Harisena and Virsena. Virsena had reportedly defeated the Sakas in one of the most epic battles of Indian history.

Harshvardhan

Harshvardhan had ascended the throne in 606 A.D. at the young age of 16 years and ruled for 41 years. He had a massive Army consisting of 500,000 Infantry, 100,000 Cavalry, 6000 Elephants(?)

A great proponent of military mobility, he was also a great patron of learning and had founded the Universities of Tarala, Ujjain, Nalanda and Vallabhi. He was a great devotee of Shiva and Surya (Aditya). His poet laureate Bana Bhatt had written the *Harsha Charita* (620 A.D.) and *Kadambari*.

6

The Arab Interlude: The Heroic Role of the Brahmins in the Karbala War

Husseini Brahmins in the Kabala War

Let us turn the clock back a little to the 7th Century A.D. to recount in some detail a very curious episode of the history of the Mohyals – their foray into the heart of Arabia and participation in the primal Shia-Sunni conflict – the Karbala War that took place on 9 October in 680 A.D. Legend and folklore tell us that one Rahab Datt Sultan and his Mohyal clansmen had rushed to the defence of the grandsons of the Prophet and had taken heavy casualties to protect the last scion of that revered family. This strange tale was made famous by Russel Tracey's history of the Mohyals- first published in 1911. He had reconstructed this episode from the bardic accounts of Mohyal history left behind by the Kavits or court poets of the Datt clans. The bardic accounts repeatedly mentioned *"Arab kiyo asthan"*, – "they settled in Arabia". This account was later popularized by the famous Hindi writer Munshi Prem Chand. Prem Chand was a great votary of Hindu- Muslim unity and wrote a play called *Karbala* in 1924. Herein he based his play on the account left by Stracey. This story was later picked up by a Muslim Shia writer-Shah Nazir Hashmi Ghazipuri who wrote a lengthy article in the *Alnataq* Urdu news paper of Lucknow(1926)- entitled *"Shahidan Karbala ke Fidai Hindu."*The learned Mohyal historian R T Mohan however feels that this account requires confirmation. He feels that the battle under reference was not the Battle of Karbala but that of Kufa which took place six years later. Both bardic accounts however refer to Datt Mohyal participation in the Shia – Sunni conflict in Iraq in the 7th century AD.

But how did the Datt clans reach Arabia and Iraq? There are many speculations of about how this happened. As stated in Chapter Four – Alexander had encountered the toughest fight of his career against the Malloi of the Multan district. In fact, he later died of the wounds he had received in the fierce battle. Legend has it that he was so impressed by the bravery of the Mohyals that he took a whole contingent of them along with him in his retreat – first to the mouth of the Indus and then by the sea and coastal route down to Alexandria in Egypt. There he died without naming a successor and his empire split into many parts governed by the local Greek satraps. In this confused situation, the Mohyal column made its way out to Saudi Arabia and Iraq, and settled down there in Basrah. It is said that around Sixth century A.D. 1400 Husseini Brahmins lived in Baghdad alone. This was then the centre of learning of the Islamic civilization and the Brahmins made a significant contribution to maths and astronomy of the Arabs. They had brought with them the Brahminical knowledge of mathematics, algebra, the zero, the decimals and astronomy. This they taught to the Arabs and gained renown as men of honour and learning.

Another set of legends traces the history of these Mohyal clans in Arabia to the warrior son of Guru Dronacharya – Ashwathama. He had been exiled after the massacre he carried out on the Pandava children after the Mahabharata War. It is said he had wandered as far as Ayodhya with some of his clansmen. And later it was he and his clansmen who reached Iraq and settled there.

Another story has it that Porus after his formal alliance with Alexander had sent a column with him and it was this column which had travelled all the way to Iraq.. In recent times a third version has also been put forth. The grandson of the Prophet had some kinship ties with Samudragupta and he had sent a column of Mohyal cavalry to give him aid in the battle of Karbala. R T Mohan has talked at length about the extensive trade and commercial contacts that existed between India and the Middle East. He writes- "There was maritime intercourse from early period between India and the Western World, including Arabia and Persia. By the third decade of sixth century inter-oceanic trade had developed reaching from China through Indonesia and the east coast of India up to Ceylon, and extending thence along the west Indian coast to Persia, Arabia and Ethiopia. There were corresponding land trade routes. Kabul was a great trade mart for goods exported from India by land route. From Kabul, the trade caravans moved north via Balkh to join the 'silk route' from China to Europe. Others turned west towards Ghazni for destinations in West Asia. Likewise, there were close cultural links with West Asia. Starting with Mecca, Islam has been systematically decimating its pre-Islamic Pagan heritage in the area, but considerable evidence has survived this religious vandalism". He also cites rare historical manuscripts that were discovered in the Makhtab –e –Sultania library in Turkey (called Siyar- ul -Okul) which talk of scholars sent by a benign King Vikram and also mention the four Vedas – thus pointing to extensive contacts between the pagans of Arabia (Mecca) with India.

Personally, I'm inclined to go along with the thesis that these Mohyal clans were those that accompanied Alexander's Army in their retreat from India – whether as allied columns sent by Porus or as the Malloi or Mohyal clans that were taken after the fierce battle in Multan. There are detailed mentions of these clans in the Mohyal oral history traditions and graphic accounts of the Karbala War in the Shia tradition. The Kavits specifically talk of *Arab kiyo asthan* (they settled in Arabia).Movement to South Asia has therefore not been a one-way street of successive invasions from the West towards the East. Oral history traditions recount several instances of movements from East to West, from India into Central Asia and the Middle East. Whichever way they reached Iraq – the fact that they were there simply cannot be denied or overlooked and this episode merits further research. It is said then an ancestor of Rahab Datt named, Sidh Viyud Datt had been conferred the title of Sultan and made Iraq his home. He was a tenacious warrior and a worshipper of Brahman. He was also called Mir Sidham. He in turn was the descendant of Sidh Jidha (Vaj), a saint who lived in Arabia around 600 A.D.

The Karbala War

After the death of Prophet Muhammad, there were three Caliphs – Caliph Abu-Bakr (632-634 A.D.), Omar Caliph (634-644 A.D.), Osman Caliph (644-656 A.D.).

All three were related to the Prophet by marriage alliances. Osman, who was somewhat unpopular, was unfortunately assassinated. After his death, Hazrat Ali – the son-in-law of Prophet Muhammad (also his first cousin), who was married to the Prophet's third daughter (the only surviving issue) became the 4th Caliph. Amir Moaira, a protégé of Osman, strongly opposed the caliphate of Hazrat Ali. There was bitter fighting for five years. Finally Moaira had Hazrat Ali murdered in the mosque of Kufa (and his mausoleum still stands in the town of Najaf in Iraq).

After the killing of Hazrat Ali, Moaira now usurped the caliphate and turned it into a kingdom in Iraq. After Moaira's death, his notorious son Yazid (679-683 A.D.), the Omayyad tyrant, became the next caliph. His claim was however contested by Hasan and Hussein – the grandsons of Hazrat Ali. In the internecine struggle – Hasan abdicated his claim to the crown. Later he died of poisoning. It was suspected that his own wife Jedah had administered the poison. His younger brother Imam Hussein was incensed by this assassination. He had been living a secluded life in Madina.

Imam Hussein now came out and challenged the usurper Yazid. A bitter conflict followed, which saw its denouement in the Battle of Karbala fought on 9 October 680 A.D. The participation of Rahab Datt Sultan is borne out by the Shia accounts of this war, which have been so graphically preserved in the Shia oral traditions. The Datts were part of an entourage of 200 men and women including 72 members of Hasan's family (40 on foot and 32 on horseback). He had left Madina and made an arduous trek to Karbala, where he had a large following. After an 18 days march, he was near Karbala – on the banks of the Euphratus River. It was then that Yazid sent a 35,000 strong army from Mecca and other places. They surrounded Hussein's small column. 6,000 soldiers cut them off from the river Euphratus and ensured that not a drop of water reached this pitiful band. By the third day, most of this column had died of thirst. This included Hasan's brother Abbas (32 yrs), his son Ali Akbar (22 yrs), daughter Sakina (4 yrs) and 6 months old infant Ali Asghar. Asghar, the infant was killed by an arrow while in the lap of Hasan.

Then these blood thirsty hordes moved in for the kill. Hasan himself was brutally killed and the horsemen trampled over his dead body till it was mangled beyond recognition. The assassins then rode off with the severed head of Imam. At the time of Karbala War, Rahab Datt, the leader of the Datt clan in Iraq, was a highly esteemed figure due to his close relations with the family of Prophet Muhammad. In this war, he was the only chieftain who dared to come forth for the defence of the grandsons of the Prophet. He fought alongside with him and was reportedly, with Imam Hussein in the Battle of Karbala. They were overwhelmed. When the soldiers of Yazid were riding away with the severed head of Hasan, Rahab Datt and his men gave them chase till the castle of Kufa and after a bitter fight recovered the head of Imam. They washed the holy man's head reverentially and carried it to Damascus.

Enroute their camp was surrounded at night by Yazid's men. They demanded the head of the Imam. Legend has it that Rahab Datt cut off the heads of one of his own sons and offered it to them. When they refused, one by one, Rahab Datt beheaded all his sons and offered their heads to protect the sacred relic in the form of the severed head of the Holy Imam. Miraculously they managed to save it. A year later, it was buried at Karbala along with the rest of Imam's body.

The Datts now rallied around Aamir Mukhtar, the follower of the Imam who led the resistance against Yazid's forces. The Datts fought with extraordinary heroism and valour and captured and razed the Fort of Kufa. This was the seat of Yazid's Governor Obeidullah, the butcher. Having scored a resounding victory on the battlefield, they sounded the drums and announced that they had avenged the innocent blood of Imam Hussein.

This battle of Karbala is recounted in harrowing and grisly detail by the Shias every year in their mosques. The men weep copiously. In every Muharram procession, they flail themselves to atone for the sin of not being there to defend the Imam. *"Hai Hasan – Hum na the"* (Alas Hasan – we were not there) – they still cry piteously.

History records that after the Datt attack on Kufa – the Sunnis unleashed a reign of terror on the Shias and Datts. Around 200 A.D. the Datts decided to return to their homeland. They came via Syria and Afghanistan and finally settled at Dananagar in the district of Sialkot. Some drifted as far as Pushkar in Rajasthan. Their long retreat back to home is a saga by itself. It is said that they fought their way through Syria and Asia Minor and into Afghanistan. Enroute they captured Ghazi, Balkh and Bukhara. They then annexed Kandahar and converged on Sindh. They crossed Sindh and at Attock, they entered Punjab, their original homeland.

Hazrat Bal

Another unsubstantiated story states that as the descendants of Rahab Datt migrated to India, they carried with them the sacred hair of Imam Hussein (Moo-e-Mubarik) and deposited these at the Hazrat Bal shrine in Kashmir. This relic had come into their possession when they had retrieved the severed head of Imam Hussein from the assassins of Yazid. This incident however remains to be corroborated for its historical authenticity.

By any account, this is a strange and astounding tale of bravery and adventure that spans the civilizations. It is a rare story of Hindu warriors fighting for the Imam and grandson of the Holy Prophet. The Shias, the followers of Hasan and Hussein, honoured the Datts with the title of "Husseini Brahmins" and treated them with great reverence, in grateful recognition of their supreme sacrifices in the war of Karbala. As per the *Jung Nama* written by Ahmed Punjabi (p.175-76), the Shias were instructed to recite the name of Rahab Datt in their daily prayers. Even till recently, it is said that when Muslims in the Punjab suffered from boils – they asked the Husseini Brahmins to spit on these for cure.

Even today, *Anjuman-e-Husseini* – an organization of Shia Muslims is striving to involve the Husseini Brahmins of the region – the Mohyals – in their Muharram processions. They wish to express their profound gratitude to our ancestors who sacrificed their lives to protect Imam Hussein in the Battle of Karbala.

Karbala led to a bitter faultline war between the Shias and Sunnis in Islam, which has unfortunately carried on to this day. Even as we write this piece, the lands of Syria and Iraq are wracked by a brutal civil war between the Shias and Sunnis. Iranian troops have gone to help their Shia brethren in this bitter conflict – which has become a war of identity that is being fought to the finish. It is fascinating and amazing therefore, to learn of the stellar role played by a band of Mohyal Brahmins from India. Their bizarre adventures read like the fantastic tales of Sindbad – The Sailor.

The exploits of the Mohyal Datt clans are recorded in the oral histories of Shias as also the *Kavits* and bards of the Mohyal clans. One line of tribute from a Muslim savant stands out for its sincerity and genuine gratitude – *'Wah Datt Sultan – Hindu ka Dharm – Musalman ka Imam'*--- praise be to the Sultan Datt; he has the faith of the Hindu and integrity (iman) of the Muslim. The Mohyal clans of Rahab Datt Sultan indeed spanned the bridge between two distant and virtually antithetical civilizations. It forms an amazing interlude of history that testifies to the adage – *"Truth is indeed stranger than fiction"*.

It is an astonishing tale of adventure that spans not just countries and continents but also the centuries. It is a saga of courage, sacrifice and devotion that deepens the ties between diverse faiths. It deserves to be widely disseminated. This is a tale that must be told – again and again for its one scintillating message – *the oneness of mankind and the commonality between faiths*. It is an amazing tale of Hindu-Muslim unity forged to protect a world famous family of mystics descended from the holy Prophet himself. As a saga of inter-faith dialogue, it is unparalleled and breathtaking in its sweep.

7

The Shahi Mohyal Brahmin Dynasty of Afghanistan
Halting the Arab Invaders

Thus Islam had arisen as a small sect in Saudi Arabia. Within the space of just one century however, it had unified the diverse Arabic tribes into a formidable fighting force and became a major political power that swept across large parts of Western and Central Asia, North Africa and even reached the continent of Europe.

It soon became a powerful political force with the Caliphs. However, the fourth Caliph was rather tyrannical. Disputes arose between various claimants to the post of Caliph. These led to bloody wars and assassinations. From the early egalitarian bias of Islam, the emphasis shifted to the oral tradition about the sayings and doings of the Holy Prophet. These became the *Hadiths*. Soon a priesthood of sorts arose – the community of *Ulemas* – the scholars who knew not just the Holy Koran but also the tradition of the *Hadiths*. Gone was the early emphasis on *Ijma* and *Ijtihad*- the doctrine of independent reasoning- whereby every Muslim was free to read the Koran and come to his own independent conclusions ; as also the emphasis on the consensus of the community was forgotten as the cult of the dictatorial Emir emerged out of the fierce battles for succession.

The Arab tribes were living in the sparse and barren desert. The desert hardly produced anything more than a subsistence diet of dates and camel meat and milk. So in the political economy of Arabia, major, emphasis was placed traditionally on the *Ghazu*. The tribes occasionally resorted to the *Ghazu* – the raid to seek wealth, plunder and slaves from the fertile and settled lands on the fringes of the deserts. Arab armies were now unified. The Arab cavalry boasted of excellent horses and camels. This Arab cavalry now stormed out of the Middle East not just for raids for loot and plunder but on wars of conquest designed to subdue distant lands and convert people to Islam by the sword. These thundering Arab armies virtually destroyed the ancient civilizations of Syria, Egypt, Iraq and Iran. They were all entirely converted to Islam by the sword. The Arabs then conquered Central Asia and huge parts of North Africa from modern day Libya, Algeria, Morocco and Sudan. They pushed out towards Europe and conquered Spain. The Arab armies of Islam seemed invincible and unstoppable.

The amazing but little known fact is that the world conquering Arab armies were checked for the very first time on the slopes of the Hindu- Kush mountains on the borders of Afghanistan, by the Afghan Hindu armies of the Rutbil of Kandahar and the Shahis of Kabul. This Hindu Mohyal dynasty was then ruling in Afghanistan.- and held off the Arab invasions for at least three centuries They drew the Arabs inside Afghanistan in guerilla fashion and then closed the passes behind them. The Arab armies were virtually starved into surrender in the harsh and barren Afghan landscape that has been the ruin of so many invading armies. The Arabs were forced to buy their way back to safety. This was the very first military disaster that had overtaken the Arab armies and it sent shockwaves all across the vast Caliphate. They were shaken by the very first news of a comprehensive defeat. The cruel Hajjaj- the Governor of Iraq- pushed the Arab armies to attack Afghanistan once again- the very next year. Though they obeyed their orders, they were understandably nervous and soon retreated after a series of extended raids in which they went back with large amounts of booty and slaves. The Hajjaj was clearly unimpressed. The armies were humiliated by the Iraqi governor Hajjaj and ordered to go back and slaughter the infidels. This was the first time that the Arab armies had been stopped and defeated in their all conquering march and the Arab Caliph was not prepared to stomach this humiliation. The tired and angry Arab armies now mutinied and a four year long civil war erupted. This ended the string of Arab conquests. The only place that they had been decisively checked so far, had been India. Thus the Rutbil and Shahi Hindu kingdoms of Afghanistan held off the Arabs for three hundred years. It is a proud feat in the military history of the world. Checked in Afghanistan, the Arabs now tried to get at India from the South.

The Arabs were great sea farers. By the start of the 7th Century, they were knocking on the gates of Sindh, in western India. Sindh was then also ruled by a Mohyal Brahmin King called Chach, who had extended his kingdom till Kashmir. His successor, Dahir fought the Arabs bravely and beat back many attacks. However, he finally succumbed to the Arab invasions by sea due to treachery and infighting by the Buddhists. The primary account of this sea-borne invasion is from Arab sources and is therefore rather unflattering to their enemies – the Mohyal Brahmins. Unfortunately, it is the only account that we really have (apart from the Ballads of the Kavits who tried to preserve Mohyal history in the oral form of poetry).The tale of Sindh will be taken up subsequently in detail.

In this chapter we will chronicle the history of the Hindu Shahi kings of Afghanistan and the magnificent defense they put up against the Arab armies. In fact the only force that had been able to stop the Arabs till then were these Hindu kingdoms of Afghanistan. The Hindu Shahi dynasty had held off the world conquering Arabs for almost three centuries and that was no mean feat. It deserves to be studied in detail. These Mohyal fighting Brahmins were the true Guardians of our Gates for three centuries. They were the true *"bulldogs of the border"* that held off the Arab invasion for 300 years. Unfortunately thereafter, the Mohyals, the Pratiharas, Satvahanas and Rashtrakutas were all competing for power in North India. Thus they failed to present a unified front to the looters who came to plunder India's wealth and then stayed on to rule. It is noteworthy that where the Arabs had failed dismally to conquer Afghanistan and Punjab- the Turkic people that had been converted by the Arabs, were later able to break through into India. This was simply because they were locals and knew the terrain very well and were acclamatised to the harsh environment of Afghanistan that had taken such a heavy toll of the Arab armies. However, it is time that someone recounts the saga of the tenacious defence that did not crumble in a few days or months but held off the Arab invaders for three centuries at a stretch. The saga of how the world conquering Arabs were checkmated in Afghanistan deserves to be told in detail. It is surprising that today so little is known about a glorious period of our history.

I'm again deeply indebted to RT Mohan for his pioneering research in the field of the Hindu Shahi kingdoms of Afghanistan and Punjab. The tales of valour of these Mohyal Fighting Brahmins – the true Bulldogs of our borders, deserve to be recounted in detail. It is something to be proud of. It needs to be recorded for posterity to inspire our present generations. RT Mohan has left behind an excellent record of this period in his illuminating monograph – *'Afghanistan Revisited : The Brahmin Shahi Dynasties of Afghanistan & Punjab'*. RT Mohan also records the Arab invasions in his seminal essay – *'Three Glorious Centuries of Hindu History : Early Indo-Islamic History (CE 640-1000) of Afghanistan and North West India'*. He states that the Koh Hindu Kush range (now in present Afghanistan) was then the true political and physical frontier of India. The Kingdom of Gandhar (present day Kandahar) was always regarded as an integral part of the Indian system of states. It may be recalled that Gandhari – the Queen of the Kauravas and her brother Shakuni had played a key role in the Mahabharata. There are specific references in the Rigveda and Mahabharata to rivers, tribes and rulers, which testify to the close linkages between the Indo-Aryans in Punjab to the people of present day Afghanistan.

After routing the Greeks, the Mauryan empire had extended its sway over Afghanistan and made the Koh-Hindu Kush the scientific and easily defendable frontier of the Indian civilization per se. Fa Hiyan, the Chinese pilgrim had visited India around CE 400. He reported that in the country around Udayan (present day Kabul) – the language then spoken was the same as in Central India. Dress, food habits and drinks of the people were all similar. Buddhism then flourished in the land.

However, by the time Huen Tsang came to India in the 7th Century A.D., Buddhism was on the decline and Brahminism was again on the ascendant – just as it was in the rest of India. Pushyamitra Sunga had been angered by the Buddhists' closeness to the Greeks and had taken revenge upon their Sangha and monasteries. Most notably, Huen Tsang did not notice any Islamic influence in Afghanistan or the rest of India in CE 644.

The Rise of Islam: As recounted, Islam arose in the 7th Century and rapidly became a political force. The ideology of Islam was initially spread by the sword. Very rapidly and with surprising ease it conquered Syria (635 AD), Iraq and Egypt (639 AD), Persia (640 AD), Tripolitania upto North West Africa (670 AD), Khorasan and parts of Central Asia (west and north of the Koh Hindu Kush range) all came under the Arab Caliphate. The entire population of this vast region was converted to Islam and there was not a single holdout or resistance to penetration of any sort. Islamic conquest was complete, thorough and comprehensive. As the great Persian Empire of Iran fell – the Caliphate now acquired a common border with "Al Hind".

Situation in Afghanistan - 7th Century A.D.: Huen Tsang's records make mention of a an able Kshatriya king at Kapisha (60 miles northwest of Kabul) who ruled over an extensive kingdom. In fact, as the Arabs began probing the western borders of India, the Hindu kings were ruling over Southern Afghanistan.

Rutbil (variously called Ratbil, Reital, Zunbil, Santhal etc. by Muslim chroniclers) was the *hereditary* designation of the Kshatriya kings of Zabulistan or South Western Afghanistan. He had his capital at Bast (now in ruins) and his territory extended westward upto the borders of Persia (Iran). As stated, Rutbil was not the name of this king but the hereditary title of all kings of this line. As such we encounter the same name some two centuries down the line, when the Turkic invasions began.

A Buddhist dynasty (named Turk Hindu Shahis by Al Baruni) ruled over South Eastern Afghanistan with its capital at Kabul. They were closely associated and the Muslim chronicles often refer to the whole region south of Koh-Hindu Kush as the Kingdom of Kabul.

The First Arab Military Disaster: The simple fact is that the Rutbil Kingdom and the Shahi dynasty of Kabul (called 'Turk Shahi') put up a spirited defence that kept the Arabs at bay for well over 200 years (CE 643 to 870). Thus, Zabulistan and Kabulistan were then the frontline states of India that barred the path of Arab armies to the Khyber Pass. Kabulistan comprised of the northern territories of Sirat, Laghman, Kabul, Nangrabal (modern Jalalabad) and Gandhar valley touching Wai Hind or Udabhandapura of Rajat Tarangani. Zabulistan was the area southwest of Kabulistan and held sway upto the borders of Eastern Iran. Rutbil's kingdom thus also held sway over the Sistan province of Iran. Sistan fell after heroic resistance and the Arabs now mounted a series of raids into Zabulistan. Surprisingly however, the all conquering Arab armies were checkmated on the high ramparts of the Hindu Kush mountains.

Abdul Malik had taken over the reins of the Caliphate (684-705 A.D.). He appointed Hajjaj bin Yusuf as the Govrnor of Iraq (CE 694-714). He let loose a wave of tyranny in the conquered lands. Later, the entire Eastern Caliphate came under the sway of the cruel Hajjaj. Hajjaj equipped and despatched three armies with different targets assigned to each:-

- **The First Army:** under Qutaiba went North, crossed the Oxus (Amu Darya) and conquered Bukhara, Samarkand and the Ferghana valley of Uzbekistan – north of the Hindu Kush.
  It even penetrated upto Kashgar in Sinkiang (Xinjiang province, China)
- **The Second Army:** under Mohammed Bin Quasim was despatched via Sistan and Makran to subjugate Sindh, the Kingdom of Dahar.
- **The Third Army:** This was sent by Al Hajjaj under his experienced General Obaidullah bin Ali Bakr in 698 CE with the orders to lay waste the Zutbil's lands, destroy his forts and kill and enslave his people. This campaign was described by Al-Bibduri as the 'Army of Destructors' (Jaish al Fana).

Thus in 698 CE, Hajjaj ordered Obaidullah to invade the kingdom of Rutbil and not come back till he had conquered and destroyed this kingdom that had held out for so long. Obaidullah launched a massive attack across the Hindu Kush range. Rutbil cleverly retreated and drew the Arab armies deep inside till the Gates of Kandahar.

Once they were fully extended – Rutbil sent his forces behind them to block the passes and defiles on the Hindu Kush and trap the Arab armies. He completely cut off their lines of retreat and supplies. Checkmated at Kandahar and with their retreat blocked, the Arab armies soon were facing starvation and thirst in that stark, barren landscape. Obaidullah was caught in a hopeless situation. His armies suffered badly. Finally he had to pay a huge ransom of 700,000 Dirhams to go back intact. He had to deposit this princely sum with the agents of Rutbil and promise never to raid Rutbil's territory again. A large number of Arab forces had died of thirst and hunger. He had no option but to accept these humiliating terms and seek safe passage across the defiles of the Hindu Kush. Obaidullah died of grief at his inglorious defeat and the humiliation and the sad plight of his army. The First Arab invasion of India had ended in a total disaster. The harsh mountain terrain had unhinged the logistics of the Arab Army and there was nothing in that barren landscape to live off. It was a total and unmitigated disaster.

The Second Invasion: The despotic Hajjaj was enraged. To retrieve Arab honour, he now despatched Abdur Rehman, son of Mohammed Ibn Astah at the head of a massive army of 40,000 Arab warriors. These were then the best equipped force in all the Arab armies and were despatched to batter down the Indian defences on the ramparts of the Hindu Kush. Around CE 700 the Arab armies launched their second attack. They gained some initial success and made many penetrations into Zabulistan. However, they encountered very stiff resistance. His soldiers now went into an orgy of loot and plunder. He captured a large amounts of booty. He now tactfully decided to return to Sistan and avoided any further battle by bashing his head against the deep defences of Kandahar. He came back to Sistan and sent glowing reports of the success of his raids. The Hajjaj was livid. He accused him of cowardice and turning away from the Jihad against the infidels. In no uncertain terms he threatened to sack him unless he went right back and captured Zabulistan before the end of that very year.

The Arab armies not surprisingly had enough. They had taken heavy casualties battering through the Hindu Kush defiles. They were well aware of what had happened to the previous Arab expedition and the ignominious end it had met. Abdul's forces were in no mood to be trapped by the snow and the Kabulis in that treacherous terrain. Abdur Rehman got into a huddle with his senior commanders. They refused to obey the orders of the Hajjaj and there was open rebellion (Fitna) against the Caliphate. This was unprecedented and sent a shockwave across the entire Islamic empire.

To secure his position in the event of retaliation by the Caliph, Abdur Rehman now entered into a treaty with Rutbil - that in case Rehman was defeated by the forces of the Caliph, he would grant him asylum. In case Abdur Rehman won, Rutbil would be absolved of the need to pay any kind of tributes to the Caliph. The Ummayad throne and the tyrannical rule of the Hajjaj was badly shaken. Abdul Rehman declared war against Hajjaj. Rehman gained some initial success. He now took to the field with a 100,000 men and now turned on the Caliph himself. The caliph tried to buy him off with promises of Governorship and liberal pay and pensions for his men. His forces were buoyed up by their initial victory and refused to yield. The Caliph now turned to Al Hajjaj. A major battle took place in CE 702. Fierce fighting broke out.Unfortunately, Abdur Rehman and his forces were defeated in Sistan.

Abdur Rehman now retreated to Zaranj (where Indian engineers have recently completed a road connecting Dilaram in Iran to Zaranj in Afghanistan – where it joins the circular Ring Road linking the main cities of Afghanistan). The Governor of Zaranj was his own appointee. But Rehman had lost the battle against the Caliph and the city of Zaranj closed its gates and denied him entrance. Abdur Rehman now retreated to Bust – where the governor was also his appointee. Initially, he was warmly received but soon treachery reared its ugly head. Abdur Rehman was put in chains and was to be delivered to the tender mercy of the Hajjaj for exacting a terrible revenge.

At this juncture, The Hindu Raja Rutbil heard of this treachery. Without wasting time, he marched out at the head of his army and rode hard to Bust. He secured the release of the Arab General who had allied with his. Abdur Rehman thereafter stayed as the honoured guest of his benefactor Rutbil. This battle had aroused the interest of the entire Caliphate. Rutbil now became a celebrated hero of this holy war. "Rutbil", writes RT Mohan, had became a formidable foe, who had made Sistan an ill-omened frontier for the Arabs."

He had put a grinding halt to the triumphant march of Islam which had gained such swift and surprising victories against many ancient civilizations in Iraq, Syria, Iran, Egypt and Tripolitania. The Arabs had also conquered Spain. For the first time, they were checkmated on the frontier of India. Their world conquering armies revolted and refused to go any further. Afghanistan has been the graveyard of many military reputations. Arab expansion was now checkmated completely for the next over 200 years. This revolt of the Arab armies sent to attack India has many curious parallels with what had happened earlier to the Greek armies of Alexander who had similarly tried to conquer India in the 3rd century BC.

Checkmate in Europe
Thus, the Hindu kingdoms of Kabul and Zabul (Kandahar) held out triumphantly against the world conquering Arab armies and drove them back. They fought skilful and mobile battles that drew the enemy deep inside this territory and then trapped them decisively. The treacherous and barren terrain and the bitter cold did the rest. The Arab armies now had to pay a huge ransom to extricate themselves from this trap. It was a masterstroke and stopped the Arab steamroller at the very gates of India.

The second invasion was an even greater disaster and culminated in a revolt in the Arab armies, which next morphed into an insurrection in the entire Arab Caliphate. This led to a four year long civil war. This drained the Arab empire of its energy for any further conquest. Exactly the same had happened earlier to the Greek dreams of conquest in India. The ferocity of the Indian use of war elephants had spread panic in the Greek ranks. The Greek armies had mutinied and that was the end of Alexander's spree of conquest. Exactly the same process was replicated with the Arab invasion of India. The heroic guardians of the gateway to India stopped the marauding Arabs dead in their tracks. The world conquering Arab armies tasted their first humiliating defeat at the gates of the Hindu Kush mountains range. In Arab history and folklore this decisive defeat rankles deeply. That is why Koranic legends still talk of the Ghazwa- e – Hind, the final war for the conquest of India that will take place in the end of times (near our present era). Gazwa- e- Hind represents the vistages of the Arab dream to conquer India that had failed so miserably. This defeat has left deep scars on the Arab psyche and to this day the Arabs wistfully talk of the Gazhwa-e - Hind, the final battle for the conquest of India. This is where the Arab steam roller advance had been decisively checked. The ISIS has in recent times, revived this talk of the Ghazwa- e Hind, of now attempting the final conquest of India in which they had failed so dismally the first time. We all know of Porus' heroic stand against Alexander, but very few know the history of the even more successful and heroic resistance of the Hindu kingdoms of Afghanistan against the all conquering Arab armies from the Middle – East. Curiously both these invading armies which had defeated foes all over the world, were decisively checked in India. When pressed to resume advance, both armies had mutinied and refused to go any further.

The weakened and demoralised Arab empire suffered its next major setback in France. In 732 A.D., the Arab armies that had captured Spain now tried to make a foray into France across the Pyrenees and Alps. The French forces decimated them and saved Europe from the marauding Arab hordes. Between India and France – the Arab armies had been checkmated from any further conquest. A combination of terrain and tenacious and dogged defenders had beaten the world conquering Arab armies. In hindsight it appears that the Arabs were poor mountain fighters and their advance was decisively held and turned back by the Hindu kings of Zabul and Kabul. India was the very first nation to resist and stop the advance of the till then invincible armies pouring out of Arabia like a scourge - pillaging, looting and destroying ancient civilizations.

The Arabs were then at the zenith of their military glory – when they received this decisive checkmate at the hands of the border states of the Indian civilization. The Arab empire went into deep decline thereafter and it was only after a gap of 300 years that the Turkic Ghaznavid empires could resume the Islamic advance. This time they were aided by excellent cavalry, formidable archers and invaluable local knowledge of the terrain. They had flaming naptha arrows whose fire power proved lethal to the war elephants that had become the mainstay of the Indian way of war. Above all they were not Arabs from distant lands but locals of ethnic South Asian stock who had been converted to Islam. Thus they knew the terrain and were used to the local climatic conditions.

The real pity is that this great feat of arms – of checkmating the Arab military storm emanating from the heart of Middle East has been completely obliterated from our historical memory. We have forgotten our tremendous successes and remember only our defeats. In his seminal work *'The Decline and Fall of the Roman Empire'*, Edward Gibbon has summed up the situation in these words:-

"When the Arabs first issued from the desert, they must have been surprised at the ease and rapidity of their own success. But when they advanced (further) in their career of victory to the banks of Indus and the summit of the Pyrenees – when they had (repeatedly) displayed their scimitars and the energy of their faith, they might be equally astonished that any nation could resist their invincible arms; that any boundary should confine the domination of the successors of the Prophet."

In military – technical terms what stopped the Arab advance was a combination of the difficult mountain terrain of the Hindu Kush and Pyrenees, and the bitter cold and snow-laden passes. The Arab horses and even more, the Arab camel caravans possibly could not take this bitter cold. As such their system of logistics support broke down completely. The Arabs could not live off the harsh and barren mountain terrain. They were not prepared for the intense cold and snow.

This cold desert sapped the strength of their armies and cooled their ardour for further conquest. Chanakya, the NSA of the Mauryan empire had done well by selecting a scientific frontier for the Indian civilization. It was easy to hold and defend the Hindu Kush mountain range and the very terrain took its toll of invading armies. It was forward defence based on natural ramparts and it worked brilliantly. It had completely checkmated and stopped the firestorm erupting from the heart of the Arabian desert with its epicentre in Iraq, Syria and Saudi Arabia.

8

The Invasion of Sindh

Chach and Dahir. Resistance by Mohyal Brahmin Rulers

Stung and exasperated by the Arab failure in Southern Afghanistan, Hajjaj turned his attention towards another frontier region of Al Hind. He now targeted Sindh. Al Hind had become a magnificent obsession with the Arabs. Khorasan had become the graveyard of their military reputation. The final battle for the conquest of Hind or what is known as Ghazva-e-Hind had become part of the Arab folklore.

It was as a part of this obsession with the conquest of Hind, that the Hajjaj now dispatched strong armies to break into India from the South. Maulana Nadwi in his '*Indo-Arab Relations*' states that between 638 and 711 the Arabs launched as many 15 attacks against the Indian province of Sindh. As was stated in the last chapter, Hajjaj had sent the second group of Arab armies under Mohammed Bin Quasim via Sistan and Makran to conquer Sindh.

It is extremely unfortunate that the sole historical record of the Battles for Sindh is a highly jaundiced and prejudiced account by Ali Ibn Hamid Kufi (originally of Kufa in Syria) called the *Chachnama*. This was an account written by the invaders. It had a transparent agenda of magnifying the apparent heroism and achievements of the Arab armies and being a hagiography for its invading generals. What however detracts from its objectivity, is its outright attempt to depict their enemies – the Hindu Brahminical kings of Sindh as debauched, depraved and incestual heretics who had to be destroyed. This supposedly historical account has the flavour of the stories of '*Sindbad – the Sailor*', and tries to craft a narrative that shows the defenders' culture as decadent and rotten and therefore ripe for defeat by the all conquering armies of Arabia. It qualifies as clever propaganda and spin doctoring, rather than an objective historical account of the campaigns.

It is sad to see some writers quote the Arab text in its entirety. It cannot but be a rough guide and a rather lop-sided and jaundiced account of that campaign.

Unfortunately, it is the only account that we have.

The Arab account is a classic example of spin- doctoring as it deftly tries to paint a lurid picture of their adversaries- the Chach Mohyal Brahmin dynasty that ruled Sindh. Apparently, these Mohyal Brahmins originally came from the region of Mathura. In the 6th Century A.D. Rai Narsingh Das , a Chhibber patriarch, was the *dewan* of Mathura. He had two sons, namely Rai Chach and Nahar Singh. After the death of their father, the sons became disenchanted with the ruler of Mathura. A dispute with the King forced them to emigrate. Rai Chach – a Mohyal Brahmin of the Chhibber clan was a very erudite scholar of Sanskrit and statecraft. He migrated to Sindh through Bhatinda and Bikaner. In Sindh, he got a job at the court of Raja Sahasi (also called Rai Sinhasana, who was a Brahmin). Rai Sinhasana was the last ruler of his dynasty. He had no issue. He saw great talent in Rai Chach and appointed him his Prime Minister.

Ali Ibn Hamid's account goes into lurid details of how the childless Queen Sobhi, the wife of Raja Sahsi,apparently fell madly in love with the handsome Chach. In actual fact – the king had died childless. The widowed queen had no option but to turn to her trusted Prime Minister to save her life. She kept the news of the king's death a secret as the neighbouring king – Dhamrat, a brother of her husband, coveted their kingdom. To safeguard herself and preserve the kingdom's independence, she now married Rai Chach. Dhamrat challenged Rai Chach to a duel and was killed by him in combat. Rai Chach now became the King of Sindh and was possibly the first to use the apellation of Chhibber (from the Sanskrit *Shiv-var* or righteous person).

Rai Chach proved to be a very energetic and aggressive military leader. He made his brother Nahar Singh the defacto ruler of Sindh, while he went out on a campaign of conquest. In an impressive military campaign he extended his kingdom to the borders of Kashmir. He successively conquered Brahmanabad, Thatta, Sohistan and Multan. It is said that he marched up the Makran coast and had also conquered Baluchistan. His vast kingdom now extended to Kannauj in the East, Kashmir and Kabul in the North and Iran in the West. It was an impressive feat of arms. He built a mighty fort at Alwar. He had two sons – Dahir and Dahersia.

Raja Rai Chach died in 674 A.D. after a glorious rule of 40 years. After him, his brother Nahar Singh (also called Chandar) was crowned king. He however became a Buddhist and devoted most of his time to meditation and study of scriptures. Taking advantage of this the ruler of Sohistan named Mehta, (whose kingdom had been captured by Chach) declared war on Sindh. He was joined by the king of Kannauj. They were beaten back by the forces of Dahir who refused to join them against his uncle.

Raja Nahar Singh died in 681 A.D. after a brief rule of 7 years. Dahir was made king of Alwar and Nahar's son Raj became ruler of Brahmanabad. Raj died after a year and was succeeded by Dahersia – the second son of Rai Chach. Dahersia also died prematurely in 687 A.D. and Dahir now took charge of the whole kingdom. He was now attacked by Raja Rawal of the neighobouring state. He had hardly repelled this attack, when the Arab invasion commenced.

As stated in the last chapter, Hajjaj-bin-Yusuf, the governor of Basra had sent in armies to attack Afghanistan in 698 A.D. This invasion turned into an unmitigated disaster. The next year the Hajjaj sent Abdul Rehman with an even stronger force. Shaken, Rehman's men made some forays for loot and plunder but wisely avoided going deep into Afghanistan (lest they be cut off like Obaidullah's forces the previous year). The enraged Hajjaj now charged Abdul with rank cowardice. He ordered his armies to go back again and not come back till they had destroyed the Rutbil's kingdom. The shaken armies mutinied. A four year long civil war followed. Abdul was defeated and finally taken prisoner. The Hindu Raja of Zabul, Rutbil rescued him and gave him asylum in his kingdom. Exasperated, the Hajjaj was livid with rage. He now thought of attacking Al Hind from other directions.

Between 638 A.D. and 711 A.D., it is said the Arabs had launched as many as 15 raids against Sindh. The Chachnama recounts these raids:-

- **Earliest Raids:** These were launched in the reign of Caliph Umar (634-43 A.D.) to pillage Thane (near Mumbai), Broach (Bharuch, Gujarat) and Debal (Devbal near Karachi). There was bitter fighting and the Arabs were driven back. A second raid was launched by sea soon thereafter. This was also beaten back decisively.
- **Attacks Through Bolan Pass:** Under the reign of Caliph Ali (661-79 A.D.) a total of six attacks were launched through the Bolan Pass and Kaikan (Quetta). These were mostly raids for loot and plunder. India was the fabled land of riches. The Caliph's state received one fifth share of the plunder and loot and the rest was distributed amongst the soldiers. These being purely raids for loot, plunder and slaves, failed to subdue Sindh.

The First Invasion of Sindh

The Arab chronicles have conjured up a provocation for the attack on Sindh, in terms of an Arabian ship of pilgrims that was ostensibly kidnapped by pirates near the coast of Sindh. Hajjaj now held Raja Dahir responsible and sent his legions to invade Sindh. It was a rather flimsy pretext. Consequent to the ship hijacking incident – the Hajjaj now sent Obaidullah bin Nabhan to mount a determined attack against the seaport of Debal near Karachi. This initial attack was repulsed and the assaulting Arabs were slaughtered to a man. The Hajjaj was truly getting exasperated. He wrote to Budail (or Bazil) to proceed to Debal with a large army. The citizen of Debal sent a messenger who rushed to Raja Dahir. He informed him of the arrival of a large Arab Army under Budail, which had landed at Narun (some distance from Debal). Dahir now sent his son Jaisiya (Jai Singh) with an army of 4,000 soldiers on horse and camel. They proceeded with great speed by forced marches and reached Debal. A pitched battle ensued. In the end the Muslim Army was completely routed. Budail himself was killed and many Arab soldiers were taken prisoners.

The Hajjaj was deeply affected by this rout. He vowed to avenge this indignity of an ignominious defeat. He now made intensive preparations and assembled a huge army under his own son-in-law Imdad Mohammed-bin-Quasim. His parting exhortation to Quasim was:-

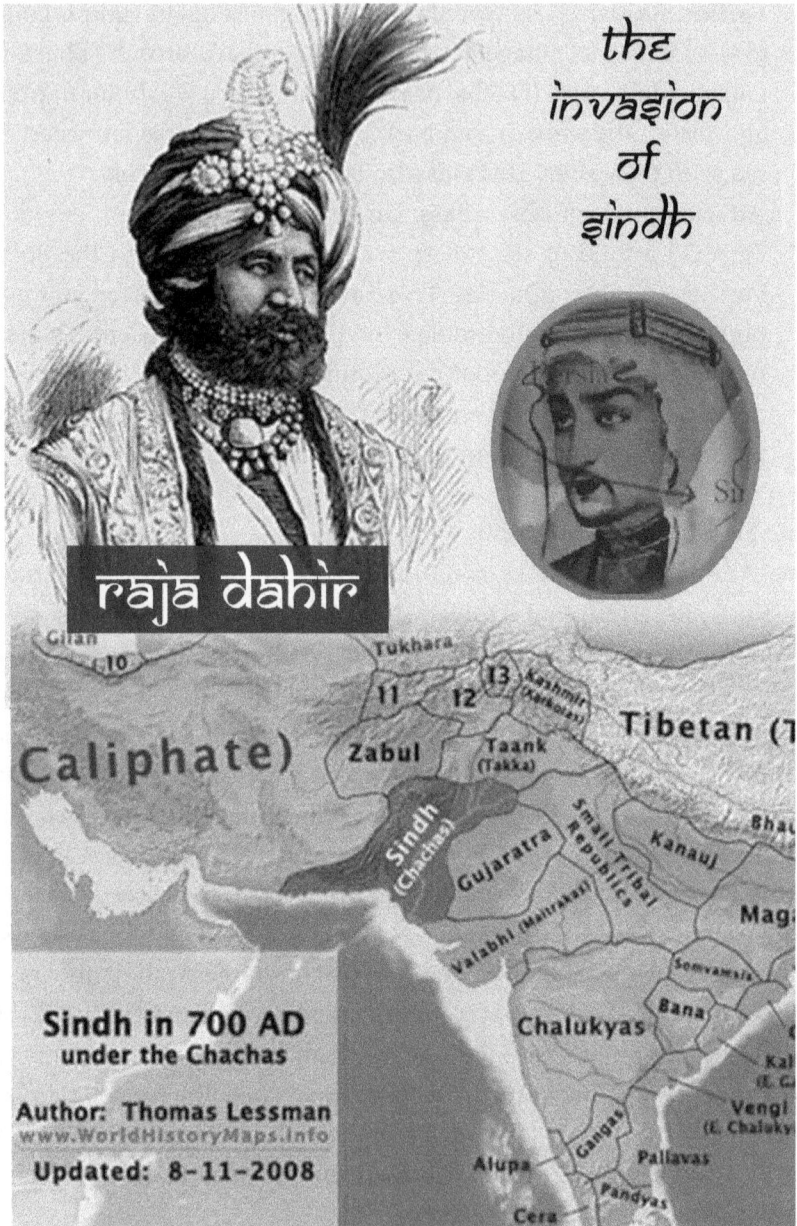

the
invasion
of
sindh

raja dahir

Gilan
10
Tukhara
11 12 13 Kashmir (Apikulas)
Caliphate) Zabul Taank (Takka) Tibetan (T
Sindh (Chachas) Gujaratra Small Tribal Republics Kanauj Bha
Valabhi (Maitrakas) Somvamsis Mag
Bana
Sindh in 700 AD Chalukyas
under the Chachas Kal (E. C
Author: Thomas Lessman Vengi (E. Chaluky
www.WorldHistoryMaps.info Gangas
Updated: 8-11-2008 Alupa Pallavas
Pandyas
Cera

"I swear by God that I am determined to spend the wealth of the whole of Iraq that is my possession on this expedition and the flame of my fire will never go down until I take revenge (of Budail's death)."

The Second Invasion of Sindh

In 712 A.D., Imdad Mohammed-bin-Quasim marched on Sindh with an army of 6,000 horsemen and 3,000 camels. Some accounts speak of an army of 15,000 men. Part of it marched along the Makran coast while most of the heavy equipment (including the stone throwing catapults) were brought in by sea. The Iraqi forces had flaming naphtha arrows to deal with the Indian war elephants. Things were not going well in the luckless Dahir's camp. The Buddhists had risen in revolt. The Buddhist leader Samani (ruler of Neron) and the disgruntled Jats had openly sided with the Arab invaders. Dahir had employed an Arab called Ilafi to head some of his legions. He defected to Mir Quasim with valuable intelligence about the forts and defences of Dahir. His trusted aide, Seosagar also deserted him at this crucial hour. Thus, though as per Arab chronicles, Dahir had an army of 20,000 infantry; 10,000 cavalry and 80 war elephants, his men seemed demoralised and riven by dissensions and disarray. Having won two initial battles, Dahir himself tended to underestimate the enemy and was dismissive about the threat.

Quasim now laid seige to the Devbal Fort. In the centre of the fort was a turret from which a sacred Red Flag fluttered proudly. Some local citizens (mostly Buddhists) deserted the Fort and went over to the enemy. They advised Quasim to topple the tower and bring down the flag. It would severely demoralise the defenders, who would take it as an ill omen. Quasim used his catapults to good effect. They flung huge stones that demolished the tower and brought down the flag. For some strange reason, it severely demoralised the defenders. The defences crumbled under the bombardment of the catapults. The Arabs broke into the walls of Devbal Fort. They began to slaughter its citizens and rape the women. Many women immolated themselves in the burning pyres. The sacred Hindu and Buddhist shrines were destroyed and the town was sacked and razed to the ground.

Having captured the fort city of Devbal (which had beaten back two earlier assaults), Quasim marched his army to the banks of the mighty river Sindh. The valiant Jai Singh was defending this river front. There was a bridge over the Sindh river, which was said to be guarded by two mighty brothers Moka and Rasal. Astonishingly, they were bribed. The gates of the bridge were suddenly flung open and the Arab armies swarmed across. Jai Singh still put up a determined fight. It is said he held the Arabs at bay for over 50 days, before he was finally forced to pull back.

Raja Dahir and his family had sought refuge in the Rawar Fort. The fort was commanded by Sardar Kik, a relative of Dahir. Dahir valiantly charged out of the besieged fort at the head of his army. He was riding his huge white elephant. For a time it looked as if his sudden charge had shaken the Arabs and won the day. The Arabs however brought forward their naphtha arrow equipped archers. An archer shot a flaming arrow at the Howdah of Dahir's elephant. The howdah caught fire and the elephant panicked and went out of control. It charged out of the battlefield and plunged into the river. Separated from his men – Dahir and his mahout were swept away by the river. A skilful Arab bowman aimed an arrow that hit him in his chest. The wounded Dahir splashed out of the river to face the Arabs on foot when he was killed by a group of Arab swordsmen.

With the death of their king – the armies of Sindh lost heart and disintegrated. Dahir's queen had stayed back in the Rawar Fort. She fought on bravely for three days. Jai Singh had taken up defences in the fort of Brahmanabad and could not come to her aid. After three days the fort fell. The invaders again unleashed an orgy of plunder, rape and killing. The brave Queen along with many other women committed Jauhar by immolating herself in the fire.

Sir HM Eliot writes that two very beautiful daughters of Dahir – Surya Devi and Paimal Devi were captured alive in Sindh. They were sent to Iraq to be presented as slaves for the Caliph's harem. The girls however had their revenge. They told the Caliph that they were not fit for his bed as Mir Quasim had already defiled them for three days. The Caliph flew into a terrible rage. He ordered that Mohammed bin Quasim be killed and his body sewed in a hide and be presented to him. This was done. He proudly showed the dead body of Quasim to the brave girls. They were delighted to see the corpse of the man who had laid their fathers kingdom waste. Their revenge complete they now turned and mocked the Caliph and said Quasim had done nothing to their person. But he had destroyed the kingdom and the girls had taken their revenge for their father's killing. The enraged Caliph had the girls killed by being dragged to death behind the horses. But even while dying, the brave girls had taken their revenge.

Mohammed bin Quasim, the invader of Sindh , was dead.

Meanwhile the Arabs had captured Brahmanabad, Niron, Deran, Thatta (Multan) and almost reached Kannauj. At each fort they had to put in long seiges and faced fierce resistance. The neighbouring Rajput kingodms of Rajasthan and Gujarat now combined forces to check any further Arab advance into India and managed to confine the Arab penetration to Sindh. So even as the Northern ramparts held in Afghanistan – the bastion in Sindh had collapsed suddenly- mostly due to internal dissensions and treachery. However , the Arab invaders were not permitted to proceed beyond Sindh.

After the execution of Bin Quasim, Yazid was appointed the new Governor of Sindh by the Caliph. Taking advantage of this disarray, Jai Singh launched a fierce counter attack. He recaptured Brahmanabad and liberated large parts of Sindh. The Caliph now sent a huge force by land and sea to retake the province. In the major battle that ensued, Jai Singh was killed and his brothers migrated to Delhi and Punjab. After the fall of Sindh, the descendants of Raja Dahir – namely, Maharaja Narain, Bhavan, Chham and Jangri moved to the Punjab and settled in various districts. Maharaj founded his state at Bhadravati, on the banks of the Jhelum. Narain became the ruler of Sialkot, Bhavan and Chham became the chiefs of Bhatner (present day Hanumangarh), while Jangir was given a high post in the kingdom of Delhi. This was the sad end of the Mohyal Brahmin dynasty in Sindh that had once ruled over a vast kingdom stretching up to Kashmir and Kannauj.

A Military Technical Analysis

The Arab invasion of Afghanistan had failed miserably. The Arabs had now turned their attention to Sindh. Their invasion was mounted by land and sea. The initial forays were beaten back and in one case the entire force exterminated and its leader killed. This made Raja Dahir complacent. Unfortunately the terrain in Sindh suited the Arab cavalry and camel corps. They used technical innovations like catapults, which could hurl huge rocks to batter down forts. The major innovation was the use of naphtha fire arrows to neutralize and panic the Indian war elephants. This is how Raja Dahir was killed. This demoralized the Sindh army.

The Muslim chronicles have tried to paint the Rai Chach and his successors as decadent, depraved and superstitious. A dispassionate reconstruction of the battles however presents a different picture. Fierce resistance had been offered. Many initial Arab forays were routed. It is only when the defenders grew complacent that Mohammed Bin Quasim got his breakthrough. The defenders in Afghanistan had the advantage of fighting on treacherous mountain terrain, which was not suited for the Arab camel caravans. The Arab logistical support had broken down. The barren landscape ruled out any living off the land and the invading Arab armies were starved. They had to buy their way out.

Their next invasion was an even greater disaster. They were hesitant to go in too deep and get cut off like the last time. Hence they confined themselves to shallow raids and retired quickly behind the Hindu Kush. When pushed to invade again, they simply mutinied.

The defenders of Sindh however did not have the advantage of terrain. Sindh was on the fringes of the desert and hence suitable terrain for the camel based logistics of the Arab army. They brought their heavy catapults and stores by sea. Dahir's defence was riven by desertions and betrayals by the Buddhist population. The naphtha fire arrows, the siege catapults and their excellent cavalry won the day for the Arabs. They however encountered stiff resistance as they proceeded northwards and the Rajputs now combined forces to limit the Arab penetration to Sindh.

The Brahmin Shahi kingdom of Afghanistan held out almost for 300 years. They foiled all Arab attempts to invade and conquer their territory. The India of that era was no pushover for Arab conquest. It offered stiff and tenacious resistance at every step. The Arab armies were finally checkmated in Afghanistan. However, after repeated forays, they did get a local breakthrough in Sindh in 712 A.D. Afghanistan's frontier defences of the Indian civilization however continued to hold out for 300 years – defiantly and resolutely. The Bulldogs of the Border had tenaciously resisted the Arab penetration and for the first time in history, brought the all conquering Arab armies to a grinding halt on the borders of Afghanistan.

9

The Turko-Mongol Invasions
Holocaust from Afghanistan

The Arab armies of Islam had finally been checkmated in Afghanistan. The Arab cavalry had swept across Iraq, Syria and Egypt and had captured Tripolitania (Libya), Algeria, Tunisia and Morocco. They had vanquished the great civilization of Persia (Iran) and the kingdoms of Central Asia. They followed this up swiftly with a series of serious attempts at invading India via Iran but were held and turned back. The Arabs then shifted the centre of gravity and attacked India via Sindh. The Rajputs however confined their conquest to Sindh. The Arabs had captured Spain but failed to fight across the Pyrenees and Alps into France. Mountains posed an impregnable barrier to Arab invasions. They could not fight in the cold mountains and the expansion of their empire was brought to a grinding halt. The mutiny in the Arab armies after the second failed invasion of Hindu Afghanistan and a four year long civil war that followed, drained the Arab empire of its energy and appetite for further conquest.

India therefore was the first nation that brought the victorious march of the invincible Arab armies to a grinding halt on the ramparts of the Hindu Kush. This was when the Arab Empire – the caliphate was at its peak of military glory and power. Two failed attempts at invading Afghanistan had led to a revolt and a civil war in the Arab Caliphate. The Arabs did manage a penetration later in the Sindh – but this was confined to that province alone and Arab advance into the rest of India was effectively checked. The Arab invasion like Alexander's therefore, was a limited penetration at best. Far more significant than the immediate impact of conquest was the long term impact of the thorough proselytization that the Arab armies had carried out in Syria, Iraq, Egypt, Triploitania, Iran and later in Central Asia.

It was these converted Central Asian empires (later called the Gun Powder empires) that were subsequently able to effect a breakthrough some 300 years after the first failed Arab invasions of India. They were able to effect the breakthrough because they had created a superb cavalry and skilled archers. These Turkic khanates had subsequently learnt the use of explosives from the Mongols. They had also exploited the Mongol invention of the stirrup – which enabled their cavalry to fight mounted. Later under Babur they also employed the flint matchlocks, muskets and horse- drawn field artillery. This had thus created a local Revolution in Military Affairs (RMA). This enabled small but highly mobile Turko-Mongol armies to defeat much larger hosts in Afghanistan and later in India.

The Indian tragedy lay in continuing to place heavy reliance on their war elephants. The Indian war elephants with their huge ears were ultra-sensitive to the sound of guns and musket fire and tended to panic completely and go berserk on the battle field. The Arabs had used naphtha fire arrows to neutralise the war elephants. Since the kings and commanders were almost always mounted on these war elephants – the entire command and control broke down as soon as these elephants panicked and in most cases trampled their own men in their uncontrolled flight. It was India's failure to keep pace with revolutionary changes in military technology and techniques that cost them so dearly. The bulldogs of the border who had held the Arabs at bay for 300 years, now unfortunately failed to hold the Turko-Mongol invasions. Not only were the Turko-Mongols using Mongol-style cavalry, but had the advantage of knowing the local terrain and being used to the harsh local climatic conditions which had stumped the Arab armies.

The other major military cause of the defeat of the Hindu Kings in Afganistan was not their meekness but their impetuosity and over-aggressiveness. Time and again instead of expoiting the tremendous defense potential of the mountainous terrain- with its steep and narrow passes , the Hindu kings of Afgahnistan launched aggressive and pre-emptive attacks upon Ghazni. These cost them heavy and needless casualties and weakened their military power to stand up to subsequent invasions. It may have been better for the Hindu kings of

Afghanistan to have let the Gaznavids launch the initial attacks, inflict heavy casualties on them and weaken them sufficiently to deliver the final coup de grace. A failure to adopt this prudent and cost –effective strategy in the mountains, opened the gateways of India to a new sucession of Muslim invasions- now by the converted populations of Central Asia and later Afghanistan itself. The tragedy is that the initial breakthrough against the Rutbils came via simple treachery.

The rise of the Turkic Empires

In theory, the Caliph as the successor of the Prophet was the fountainhead of all political authority. All Muslim kings and tribal chiefs were subordinate to him and his legal sanction was needed to provide legitimacy for their authority. With the waning of the political and military might of the Caliphate however, its governors in Khorasan set up their own strong kingdoms; and actually threatened the Caliph militarily to seek his sanction for their rule of these territories. When it came to fighting with India, the Turkic empires had a great advantage vis-à-vis the Arabs. These were local people accustomed to the mountains and harsh local terrain and well-conversant with the geography of the area. Hence, after conversion, they fared much better than their erstwhile conquerors – the Arabs, in the forays into Afghanistan and then into India. The two major Turkic empires that rose in this region were the Samanids and then the Saffarids.

The Samanids (CE 819-1005): Samn Khuda, a converted Persian Zoroastrian King of Bukhara, was the founder of the Samanid dynasty. It was the first native dynasty to rise in the region and was virtually independent of the Caliphs. The Samanid kingdom held sway over a wide area. Transoxania (present day Uzbekistan) and Khorasan (bordering region of Iran and Afghanistan) really flourished under the rule of the Samanids. There was great development of industry and commerce. The Samanids were great patrons of art and soon Bukhara and Samarkand became flourishing cities and great cultural centres that now rivaled Baghdad. This area became the new great centre of power in the region.

The Samanids now began to employ the Turkish slaves from beyond the frontiers (the Jaxasteres) in their Army and other offices of state. By the latter part of the 10th Century, the Samanid Amirs (rulers) were largely occupied with high culture. They generally gave the command of their armies (including even the governorship of the provinces) to Turk generals. Ultimately, a Turk Hajib (doorkeeper) established an independent principality at Ghazni. In time this kingdom of Ghazni became a major military power that posed a severe threat to every other kingdom between the Oxus and the Ganga. This was the Turkic empire that was later to break through the defences of India. During the reign of the Samanids however, peace had prevailed with the Hindu kingdoms of Afghanistan.

The Saffarids (CE 867-879): RT Mohan writes in his seminal essay, that Yaqub-i-Lais, the Saffar – an upstart from Sistan had established himself as a power in the Ghazni region. Soon he became very powerful and threw off the yoke of the Samanids and even the Caliph. He now began to make forays against the Hindu kingdom of Zabulistan (Kandahar region). The Rutbil, the traditional Kshatriya Hindu ruler of Zabul was alarmed. He decided to launch a pre-emptive attack. In doing so he lost the inherent advantage of being a defender in very difficult and defensible mountain terrain. It was this cold terrain that had helped his ancestors defeat the Arabs from the hot deserts of Iraq and Syria.

The problem was that now his enemies belonged to the same region and were of similar ethnic stock. They were locals and knew the terrain very well. The Rutbil was a strong leader and chose the offensive method. He had almost pulled off a military coup and scattered the gathering forces of Ghazhni. Yaqub-i-Lais was frightened by the huge hordes that descended from the Hindu Kush. He now decided upon treachery. He offered to pay homage to Rutbil and invited him over on this pretext. Rutbil trusted him and made a fatal mistake. Once in Yaqub's camp, he was assassinated by the treacherous Saffarids.

With their leader lost, true to tradition, the Hindu armies of Zabulistan simply lost heart and buckled. Caught off balance in an offensive posture, they were suddenly overwhelmed and the Saffarids swept into the kingdom of Zabul. The heroic resistance to Arab and Muslim invasions that had held the enemies at bay for over two

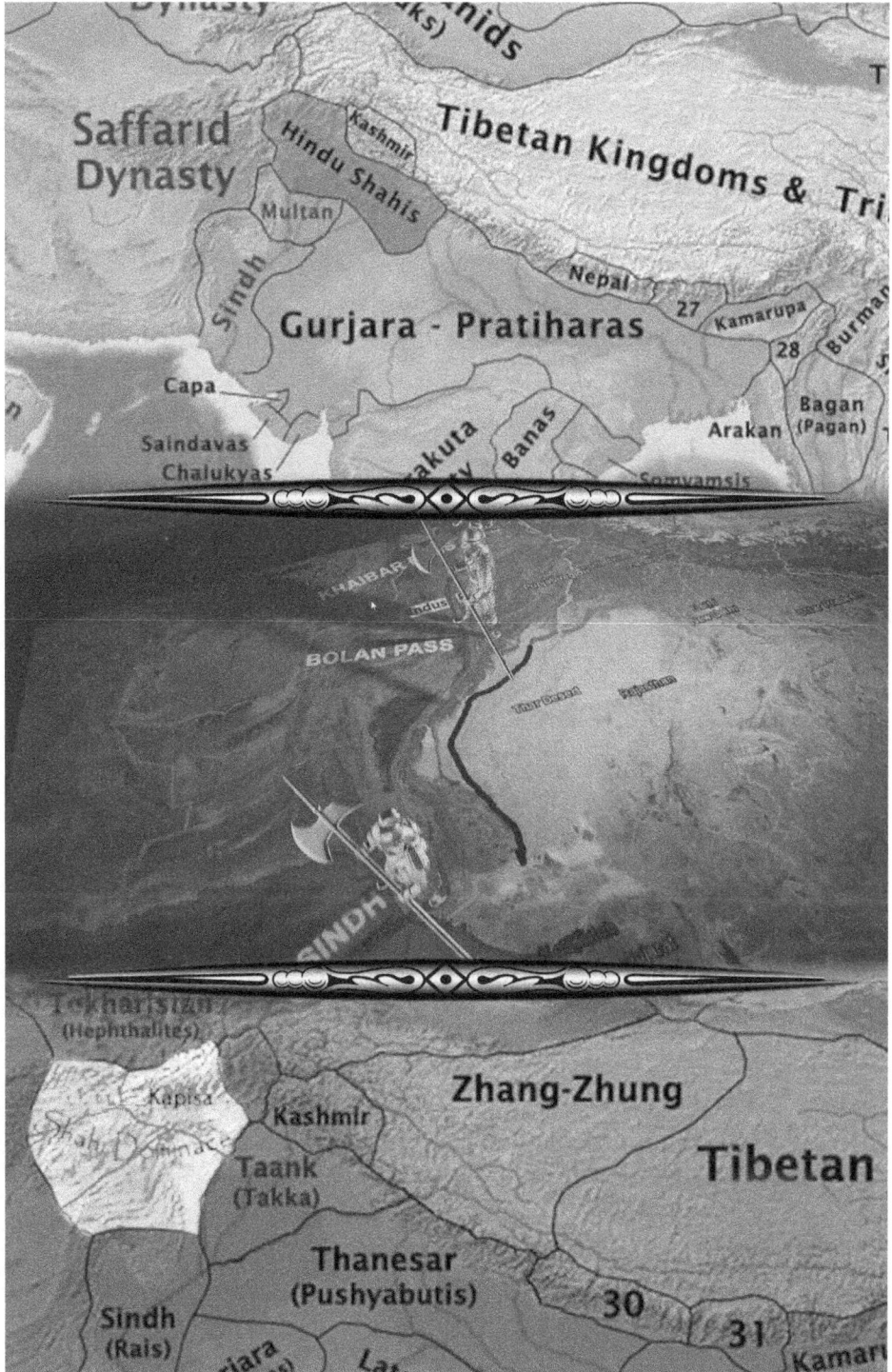

centuries, crumbled all of a sudden due to down right treachery. The Saffarids swept into Zabulistan putting its people to sword; plundering their towns and raping and enslaving their women. Overtime, the entire population was converted to Islam. The first bastion along the Hindu Kush had crumbled suddenly and the gates had been forced open by treachery. Unfortunately, it mattered little that it had been done by treachery. The end result was a sudden crumbling of resistance caused by impetuousity in the mountains. Thus, giving up the advantage of the defender in a highly defensible terrain and being far too trusting with an unscrupulous enemy, was a fatal mistake.

The Brahmin Shahi Kings of Kabul

The Turk Shahi Hindu dynasty had ruled the Kabul kingdom for 60 generations. They were Kshatriyas of Central Asian origin. Kanishka is said to be one of the rulers of the Turk-Shahi dynasty. The last king of this dynasty was Lakutzaman (Kotorman). His Chief Minister was a Mohyal Brahmin, named Kallar (Sanskrit Kalahar). Kotorman had become morally depraved and evil. Kallar staged a palace coup against the degenerate king and put him in prison for correction. The simple fact is that this was a part of the growing ideological struggle in India between traditional Brahmanism and Buddhism. The militarised Brahmins felt strongly and perhaps correctly, that non-violent Buddhism was steadily eroding Indias military power and making it ripe for foreign invasions. Most Brahmanical coups had been staged for this reason – including the coup by Phushyamitra Sunga against the last Mauryan emperor who had turned Buddhist. This coup in Kabul began a new dynasty of Brahman Shahi or Dev Shahi kings of the Mohyal Brahmin dynasty. Abdul Rehman Muhammed Al Baruni, the popular Muslim historian (otherwise known by the title Al Baruni) – has left behind accounts of the Shahi dynasty in his *Tarikh Al-Hind* (History of India). He writes that Kallar was succeeded by the Brahman Samand (Samantadeva), Kamalva (Kamal Varman), Bhimdeva (he died without heir and his kingdom came under Jaipala of Punjab), Jaipala Deva, Andpal (Anandpal), Narayinpal (Trilochanpal) (CE 1001-21) was killed in CE 1021, his son Bhimpala was the last Hindu king of this dynasty.

The first four rulers of the Brahman Shahi dynasty were able to keep at bay all invaders. There were peaceful relations between Kabul and the Samanids (819-1005). As such, there are every few historical records of these kings except those left behind by Al Baruni. A few scattered references to these kings are found in Jami-ul-Hikayat of Mohammed Ufi and the Rajtarangini of Kalhana. Details however ,are very fragmentory. Records have mostly been gathered by the vast hordes of Shahi coins and their scientific numismatic analysis by DW McDowell. These Shahi coins have the name of the person who issued them and inscriptions, have no dates. These have the Bull, Horseman, Lion and Elephant patterns. The coins are in silver or copper.

In recent times, Abdur Rehman and AH Dani, two scholars from Pakistan, have done extrensive research on the Hindu Shahi kingdom of Afghanistan. Rehman has quoted extensively from Persian and Arabic sources. Andre Wink has also written about the early medeival history of India and the expansion of Islam from the 7th – 11th century.

Fresh evidence has emerged in terms of stone inscriptions of the Shahi ruler Veka that were discovered in Mazar-e-Sharief as also the Hund slab inscriptions from the times of Jayapaladeva. The text of these inscriptions was first published in 1979 by the Pakistani scholar Abdur Rehman. It actually praises the valour of Bhima Shahi as well as his successor Jayapaladeva. They talk of them protecting their kingodms from the enemy troops. DW McDowell had published the detailed chronological sequence of Shahi Coins in 1968. All these sources have been combined to piece together a record of the Shahi kingdom of Afghanistan.

Resistance to Islamic Conquest by the Shahis: As stated, the newly converted Persian and Turks established their kingdoms in Sistan and Uzbekistan. They also coveted Indian trade and territory. With the final defeat of the Rutbil of Zabulistan by the Saffarids (who succeeded by treachery), the flanks of the Kabul kingdom were suddenly exposed. The Hindu bastion of Zabul or Gandhara fell. The Saffarids however failed to establish a strong dynasty in Zabul. The powerful Samanid empire of Uzbekistan (Bukhara) also failed to make any headway against the Turk or Brahman Shahis of Kabul who seemed to have fended them off for two centuries. The Brahman Shahis who replaced the Turk Shahis in Kabul tried to prop up friendly Hindu rulers in Ghazni for as long as possible.

When this buffer was eliminated, Jayapala Shahi – the Guardian of the Khyber Pass, twice launched pre- emptive attacks on Ghazni to uproot the nascent Muslim principality under Nasir-ud-Din Sabuktagin. These premature offensives in tough mountain terrain lost them the great advantage that the mountains confer upon defenders. It was better perhaps to have let the Samanids and Saffarids attack first, inflict heavy casualties and attrition and then counterattack and chase them back to their own lands. Perhaps these were strategic errors of judgment born not out of diffidence but impetuosity and aggressiveness but these cost them the advantage of defensive terrain and needlessly weakened them in the face of Turkic offensives that followed.

Four generations of the Pala dynasty continued to stubbornly resist the forays of first Sabuktagin and then his son, Mahmud Ghazni. Superior cavalry and smarter tactics got the better of the Brahman Shahis. A new paradigm of war was making its appearance on the Central Asian battlefields and the Hindus were slow and sluggish in their military reforms. Though they resisted doggedly – in each such encounter they had to cede some territory. The later Brahman Shahis viz. Jayapala, Anandapala, Trilochanpala and Bhimpala (who can be called the Pala Shahis) were engaged in a constant struggle with the Turkish Sultanate that had consolidated itself at Ghazni. These encounters have been recorded by several Muslim chroniclers like Gardizi, Badoni and Ferishta; but more extensively by Utbi – the histriographer at the Ghaznavid court.

When the Hindu state of Zabulistan was lost, as a strategic move the Shahis had transferred their capital from Kabul to Udabhandapura (Wahind Una) situated 14 miles above Attock on the right bank of the River Sindh. From the military point of view it placed the command and control node well behind the frontline in Kabul and was perhaps the initial cause of poor military performance in the subsequent border skirmishes with the Turks.

Historically the real problem however commenced after Bhimadeva. He was a very valiant ruler, who had doggedly held off his enemies for decades. But he died without any male heir. His

Afghan kingdom was thereafter merged with the Mohyal Kingdom of Punjab, ruled by Jayapaladev, who now held sway from Sirhind to Kabul. Jayapala was brave, but he lacked intimate knowledge of the terrain of Afghanistan. Lahore, his capital, was far too laid back to control the battle on the Kabul frontline. This sudden eclipse of the Hindu military leadership in Afghanistan due to the lack of male heirs to the throne, was sadly, the beginning of the end. Let us therefore take a more detailed look at the sucession of Hindu rulers in Afghanistan.

Kallar (Sanskrit 'Kalahar')

He is the Satapatideva of the coins. It is said that he ruled with power and glory – but never assumed the title of king as he had staged a coup and like most military dictators, preferred the military title. He had introduced the Bull and Horseman type of coins. The Bull (Nandi) and the Trident (Trishul) indicated that the new ruler was a devotee of Shiva. This showed a clear break with the earlier state that patronised Buddhism.

We see the familiar motifs of an ideological struggle between Buddhism and Brahminism. This had happened at the end of the Mauryan dynasty – when the Brahmin military commanders – the Sungas had overthrown the king and replaced Buddhism with Brahminism. Pushyamitra Sunga had done much to uproot Buddhism from Indian soil, for he felt they were collaborating with the Greeks (specifically the Indo-Greeks). Was Kallar's revolt based on this religious – ideological tussle for supremacy between Hinduism and Buddhism?

Some coins show the king on horseback with a raised weapon (lance). Possibly this was intended to convey an end of Buddhist pacifism which Kallar may have felt was weakening the Kabul kingdom. These coins were designed to emphasize the rise of hard power as opposed to the soft power approach of Buddhism, based on Ahimsa and non-violence. A stone inscription found recently (CE 2001) at Mazar-e-Sharief makes mention of a king who having occupied the earth, markets and the forts by eight fold forces – had the image of Shiva with Uma installed at Martesya by Pari Mahamatya (Great Minister) i.e. Kallar. During this period the Kabul Shahis had recovered the Northern provinces which had been under the Saffarids since CE 872.

Samantadeva: Kallar was succeeded by Samantadeva. He is generally identified with Lalliya Shahi of the Rajtarangini – which talks of him being placed between the rulers of Darads and Thrushkas, with his throne at the town of Udabhandapura (Wahind Una), situated 14 miles above Attock, on the right side of River Sindh. It merits recounting that when the Hindu state of Zabulistan was lost to the Turks – the Shahis had transferred their capital from Kabul to Udabhandapura. This, to my mind was a strategic error, as it moved the political authority far from the Kabul frontlines and reduced the monarch's influence upon the border skirmishes and battles. Though it made the capital safe perhaps, (as it prevented the outflanking from Kandahar side) it may not have been good for military morale of frontline troops in Kabul and ahead of it.It also diluted local command and control.

Kamalvarman: Samantadeva was succeeded by Kamalvarman – probably around 895 A.D. Amir-i-Lais, the brother of Yaqub-i-Lais had taken over the Saffarid kingdom, which still controlled Zabulistan. The Amir was fighting with the Samanid ruler of Trans-Oxania (Uzbekistan). Possibly these clashes were instigated by the Caliph. This kept the Brahman Shahi rulers of Kabul free from military pressure from this flank. However, the Amir soon sent a governor to Zabul who created serious problems for him.

Fardaghan – the Governor led his army to a large Hindu place of worship called Sakawand. He captured the sacred temple and smashed the idol. This enraged Kalamvarman, who was then the Rai of Hindustan. He collected a huge army and marched on Zabulistan, where the Sakawand shrine was located. According to Mohammad Ufi – Fardaghan spread a rumour that a huge army sent by the Amir was on its way. This stopped the Rai in his tracks. This version however is strongly contested. As per Tarikh-e-Sistan, two Indian kings (Rai of Hindustan) had combined their forces and launched an invasion of Ghazni. Rajat Tarangini meanwhile records a revolt or a palace coup in Udabhandapura, where a rebellious Shahi seized the throne. Forces from Kashmir were sent to restore the rightful ruler and reinstated Kamalvarman.

Bhimadeva: Bhimadeva succeeded Kamalvarman. The Dewai stone inscription describes him in glowing terms as 'Gadahasta, Parambhattaraka, Maharajadhiraj, Parmeshwar Shahi Shri Bhimdeva'. He issued gold coins which had Shahi Shri Bhimdeva on the obverse and Shrimad Gunanidhi Sri Samantadeva on the reverse. This is a touching tribute to an ancestor. Bhimdeva was a powerful military ruler who strengthened the cavalry. He is said to have received an image of Vaikuntha from Kailash in Tibet from the ruler of Tibet via Kira. Mahipal got it from Shahi for a force composed of elephants and horses. Ultimately, the Chandela king set up this image in the Khajuraho temple. Mahipala (CE 914-918), a king of the Gurjar-Pratihara dynasty of Kannauj, is described as a contemporary of Bhimdeva.

Taking advantage of the weakening of the Saffarid Kingdom – Shahi King Bhimdeva stepped up his efforts to regain influence in Kandahar region and soon installed a Hindu king in Ghazni called Laviks. Laviks, the Hindu ruler was wholly dependant upon Bhimdeva for protection and often came to him for safety and succour. Bhimdeva, a powerful military ruler, unfortunately had only one daughter. She was married to King Simharaja, the Lord of Lohar (Poonch-Rajouri area of Jammu). Didda – the daughter of this union in turn was married to Kshanagupta – the king of Kashmir (956-58 A.D.). The illustrious Bhim Shahi, the maternal grandfather of this queen, built a richly endowed temple *'Bhima Keshava'* near Martand in Kashmir.

It is said that in his old age, like many savants and sovereigns, Bhimdeva dedicated himself to Lord Shiva by committing ritual suicide. It was a conscious and pre-meditated decision and since he had no male heir – he decided to merge his kingdom with that of his kinsman's in Punjab – a Mohyal King called Jayapaladeva. Thus the Brahman Shahi kingdom was merged with those of the Mohyal kings of Punjab. India now lost a line of local kings who hailed from Afghanistan itself and were very familiar with its terrain. They had defended it for centuries. Distant kings based in Lahore had little knowledge of the local terrain and border people. Thus, India's hold upon its Hindu Kush frontier was loosened. Command and control centres had successively moved back from Kabul to

Udabhandapura (near Attock) and finally to Lahore in the Punjab plains.

The command and control of the frontier region was greatly weakened and that is how India gradually lost a strong defensive asset in the barren terrain of Afghanistan – which had been made the graveyard of many military invasions and armies. This was the scientific and naturally defensible frontier along the Hindu Kush that had been selected by Kautilya as the natural line of defense for the Indian civilization.

Jayapaladeva: The Hund slab inscription of the time of Jayapaladeva confirms the succession from Bhimdeva to Jayapala. It reads:-

"To the north of Indus there is a city named Udabhandra – therein dwelt the Chief of Kings – Bhima who burnt himself – by Shiva's desire and not through any terrible enemy (action). The King (of that country) is (now) Jayapaladeva."

Al Baruni also confirms this, as does Ferishta – who records that "Jaipal of Brahman tribe reigned at that time over the country extending in length from Sirhind to Lamghan and in breadth from Kashmir to Multan." The Barikot inscription of the reign of Jayapaladeva describes him as "*Parambhattaraka, Maharajadhiraj, Parmeshwara Shri Jayapaladeva*". These were the very same epithets used earlier for Bhimdeva. As recounted earlier by the middle of 10th century, the Turkish slaves had begun to acquire power in the Samanid kingdom and Alaptagin, a Hajib (doorkeeper) was able to establish an independent principality in Ghazni (961 A.D.). This kingdom gradually grew in power. Jayapala then sent his son with a large army to reinstall Lawik at Ghazni but Lawik and his ally were killed in a battle that took place at Chaitla – a place enroute from Kabul to Ghazni. A very severe snowstorm took a heavy toll of the Indians from the plains. The Turks poisoned a spring of water on which the Hindu army depended. Jayapala had now to negotiate permission to retreat from here.

Sabuktagin – the Turk hero of this battle became the Sultan of Ghazni. In the first 12 years of his rule he extended his frontiers to the Oxus on the north and approximately to the present boundary between

Persia and Afghanistan. Concurrently, he began to make forays into the border territories of the kingdom of Udabhandra. The coming conflict with Hind could not be postponed for long. Jayapaladeva - based in Lahore, now adopted an overly aggressive expeditionary approach. Instead of reinforcing the forward defences in Afghanistan, he assembled huge forces and launched two major successive attacks on Sabuktagin. Both failed. The story with the Arabs was fully reversed as the Brahman Shahis failed to exploit the tremendous defence potential of the mountainous terrain and launched attacks into enemy territory that put them at a disadvantage both operationally and logistically. Having beaten the attacking Hindu armies with a combination of weather and terrain, Sabuktagin followed up closely. The Afghan component of the Shahi kingdom that lay beyond the Khyber Pass was now lost to Hindu India forever.

This was the scientific frontier that Kautilya had solicited - as it was excellent mountain terrain to fight a defensive battle. We first lost the local military leadership in this vital frontier region. After Bhimdeva - the political control of this region passed to the Kings of Lahore. From that faraway capital in the Punjab plains - the Afghan border region could not be policed properly. Jayapala and his army later fell back to an expeditionary approach, which wasn't the best way to defend such a mountainous border. Though Jayapala, it is said, left his kingdom in Punjab to his son Anandapala to govern, while he moved up to Afghanistan with expeditionary forces to defend the outposts of his kingdom, he lacked intimate knowledge of the terrain.

Once this natural defence line was breached, there was little to stop the invaders. Through the Shahis, Jayapaladeva and his successors - Anandapala, Trilochanpala and Bhimpala fought tenaciously on the line of the Khyber Pass and later in the Salt Mine ranges above Rawalpindi, the defences had been breached. The needlessly impetuous approach of sending huge expeditionary forces to launch pre-emptive attacks in such a good defensive terrain invited defeat. It was a flawed strategy that completely failed to exploit the excellent defence potential of the terrain as the Rutbil had done earlier against the Arab armies some 300 years earlier.

The loss of the local leadership and thus the steady retreat of the command and control nodes to Udabhandapura (Attock) and then as far back as Lahore in the plains robbed the defence of its dynamism and inherent strength that comes from the leadership locating itself well forward.

Invasion of India

Mahmud Ghazni (son of Sabuktagin) now collected a large force and moved towards the country of Hind in September 1001 CE. Upon reaching Peshawar he pitched camp and then selected an elite force of 15,000 cavalry and best infantry. Jayapala had come up with a force of 12,000 horsemen; 30,000 foot soldiers and 300 elephants. However, he tarried, awaiting further reinforcements, which were on their way. Realizing that further delay would be dangerous and would alter the relative strength decisively, Mahmud launched a sudden all out attack on the hesitant Jayapala. A fierce battle raged till the next noon. Jayapala and 15 members of his family were taken prisoners. Mahmud now followed deep into Shahi territory and captured Hund (Udabhandra) by assault. The people of Udabhandra however continued to resist even after the town was taken. Later the prisoners were released on payment of a large ransom given by Anandapala, son of Jayapala (said to be 250,000 Dinars and 50 elephants). Jayapala like Bhimpala now committed ritual suicide in his old age. His son Anandapala succeeded him in 1002 CE.

Udabhandra had become a famous seat of Saivism and Ugrabhuti - the Sanskrit Grammer teacher, who had taught the same to Anandapala. His book was sent to Kashmir by Anandapala and widely distributed there. Having lost Afghanistan part of their kingdom, the Shahis lost trade tax revenue from caravans and were economically weakened. They also could not recruit soldiers from Afghanistan, most of whom had converted to Islam.

Capture of Bhatia

Before commencing his main assault, Sultan Mahmud of Ghazni sought to secure his flanks by first reducing the major fort city of Bhatia. He apparently marched through Baluchistan to get to that city in the vicinity of Multan (?). It had a huge fort with a ditches outside. The Raja Bijay Ray (Vijaya Raya) came out of his fort with his army of elephants. There was a fierce battle for three days in which the attackers almost gave up and fled. Finally, Mahmud launched a desperate attack and succeeded in capturing some elephants in the centre of Raya's forces. The Raya now withdrew to the fort which held out for some more days. Finally, the city fell and all people were slaughtered or converted to Islam. As Mahmud was returning from this expedition – he had to cross the flooded rivers and lost most of his plunder and booty and a number of his men. Mahmud himself barely managed to save his own life. It had been a tough and bitterly fought campaign.

Multan

Multan itself was then under a Muslim ruler of the Arab invading force of Bin Qasim. He had been quite friendly with the Hindu rulers around. A large temple of Aditya – the Sun – was allowed to remain here due to the fabulous riches and offerings it received from the Hindu devotees. Mahmud next attacked Multan. Anandapala sent an army to aid Multan. There was a battle at Peshawar where this army was defeated. Mahmud now laid seige to Multan. Meanwhile he received news that the king of Kashgar had invaded Ghazni and occupied his capital. He had to rush back to fight Elak Khan. He defeated him using the war elephants taken from India. He had left behind Sukhpala, a scion of the Shahi clan who had converted to Islam to control his Indian territories. Sukhpal abjured Islam and staged a revolt. Ghazni sped back and ambushed Sukhpala who was imprisoned and later killed.

Battle for Punjab

In CE 1008, Mahmud Ghazni once again crossed the Khyber Pass and invaded Punjab. By now, India was getting alarmed over the repeated attacks by the Turks and the slaughters they were causing. The Ghakkars (or Kakkars of Punjab), a warlike tribe also joined Anandapala. He sent his son Trilochanpala ahead with a huge Army. Both forces now camped facing one another for 40 days, each side nervous about commencing operations. The Indian armies were camped around Wahind and Peshawar.

Both sides were apprehensive about commencing the offensive. However, the Hindu armies were receiving a large number of reinforcements by the day. Finally, Mahmud got nervous. He ordered his archers to shower arrows on the Hindu armies to induce them to attack. 30,000 Ghakars now charged his ranks. A very fierce battle ensued in which 5,000 of Mahmud's soldiers perished. The Hindus were within an inch of victory. Just then the elephant on which their prince was seated was targeted by flaming naphtha arrows. The elephant panicked and went berserk. It fled the battlefield. This panicked the Indian armies who lost heart and suddenly gave way to the enemy. It was a familiar litany – born out of the tragic failure to learn military lessons. Retreating Hindu forces were attacked and lost some 20,000 dead. Thirty war elephants were captured. Mahmud Ghazni now raided the temple fort of Bhimanagar (modern day Nagarkot) and plundered immense wealth.

Ghor: Mahmud now turned his attention to the tribe of Ghor that had been raiding and plundering his caravans from their cliff hideouts. He defeated them and converted them to Islam. Later this same tribe would mount a major invasion of India in the wake of Ghazni's raids for loot and plunder.

Anandapala now concluded a treaty with Mahmud of Ghazni to buy time. Anandapala however died between 1010 and 1011 CE in this period of reprieve.

Trilochanpala

The town of Behra on the western banks of the Jhelum has always been a strategic town of the Salt range area (Koh-i-gud). In 326 B.C., Alexander had fought Porus in this area. Nandana temple town situated on the outer Salt range was now the capital of the Shahis. It was midway btween Lahore and Wahind.

In 1013 CE, Mahmud Ghazni attacked Nandana. There was a very heavy snowfall which prevented a crossing of the passes and he had to return. However, he came back again in 1014 CE.

Trilochanpala entrusted the defence of Nandana to his son Nidar Bhima (the fearless Bhima). Bhimpala moved up and occupied the narrow passes with elephants and blocked the enemy advance. Using his favourite tactics, Mahmud Ghazni sent his archers and spearmen forward to provoke the defenders into coming out. When further reinforcements came up, Bhima now came out and attacked (rather than luring the enemy to attack the defiles). A mighty battle now raged fiercely.

A Turkish General leading the vanguard was badly wounded and Mahmud had to send his own personal bodyguards to extricate this commander. The battle sea-sawed for hours. Finally the Turks gained the upper hand. A large number of elephants were captured. Had the defenders stuck to their defence positions and induced Mahmud to attack, they may well have turned the tables and secured the advantage of exploiting the highly defsible terrain.

Mahmud now invaded the Fort of Nandana. It resisted fiercely. Mahmud asked his sappers to dig mines under its walls and make tunnels for seeking entry. His archers rained arrows inside the fort. Finally the fort fell after fierce fighting and Mahmud captured a vast amount of booty.

Meanwhile Triclochanpala simply refused to give up. He now went to Kashmir to seek help from its king Sangramraja who agreed to come to his aid. A fierce battle now developed on the banks of the Tarishi river (modern Tohi). The Kashmir forces were full of confidence. Trilochanpala had learnt his lesson. He advised the Kashmir forces to secure the hill tops and escarpments and induce the Turks to attack. The Kashmiri forces reacted with disdain. They sent out columns that resisted the initial advance guard of the Turks. The Ghazni army had crossed the Jhelum and then advanced through the modern towns of Mangla, Mirpur, Kotli and Poonch. Trilochanpala wanted to establish a proper defence line to slow down the Turkish forces and then engage in battle after imposing serious attrition. The impetuous Tunga of the Kashmiri forces however charged out and suffered disastrous results at the hands of the Turk archers. The Shahi power was broken after this battle. Despite this they refused to surrender. Mahmud Ghazni moved back to Afghanistan laden with booty and plunder. The Shahis returned to the unconquered areas of their realm and reoccupied their territories, once he left. Exasperated Mahmud Ghazni now attacked the seat of their power in Lahore itself.

Seige of Lohkot

In 1015 CE, Sultan Mahmud came back to Kashmir to destroy the last remnants of Shahi power. The hill fort of Lohkot was on the southern slopes of the Pir Panjals. It was a most formidable fort. All Mahmud's attempts to take it failed. The summer season passed. In winter there was heavy snowfall and the position became worse for the Turkish army. Mahmud had to call off operations and return to Ghazni. Enroute to Ghazni, he was deliberately misled by his guides into extensive morasses where most of his armies perished and could not be extricated. This campaign was a monumental failure and showed the great advantage of resorting to defence in the mountains.

The Hindu armies had not failed due to timidity or overcaution, but an impetuousity that led them to charge into battles leaving formidable defensive positions behind. Had they fought like the Rutbil in Afghanistan, some three centuries earlier and cleverly exploited the tremendous densive potential of the mountaineous terrain—history may well have been different. The Afghan tactics were based upon inciting the enemy forces to attack. Then their formidable archers would take a very heavy toll of the charging cavalry and infantry with a deadly shower of arrows. Once heavy casualties had been inflicted and the enemy weakened, Afghan cavalry attacked to deliver the coup de grace to the retiring forces.

In 1018 CE, Mahmud launched another expedition to loot Kannauj and Mathura. This time ,he came with an army of 100,000 horses and 29,000 foot soldiers. The loot and plunder had helped him to recruit even larger number of soldiers to his cause in Afghanistan. Large swathes of North India were subject to widespread slaughter, rape and plunder. It was a terrible carnage.

The Last Shahi Effort to Turn the Tide

The Chandelas of Kalanjar now formed a confederacy of Hindu States. They killed Rajyapala – the king of Kannauj, who had earlier shamefully colluded with Mahmud Ghazni. Trilochanpal Shahi joined this Hindu confederacy for a last ditch stand. In 1019 CE Mahmud again launched an expedition to chastise the Chandelas. He assembled the largest army yet to invade India. Before the confederacy forces could get together, Mahmud moved up in speedy forced marches to surprise them. Trilochanpal Shahi now took position on the river Rahib (either Ramganga or Sije). The Sultan hesitated to cross this turbulent and muddy river. Without his knowledge or permission however, eight of his Muslim officers with their men crossed this river one early morning and took the defenders completely by surprise. The Shahi was defeated in the sudden encounter but managed to escape. Some 270 gigantic elephants were captured.

Trilochanpala tried to join up with the Chandelas but possibly died because of his wounds while still enroute. The Chandela Raja now readied to give battle with a large army of 124,000 infantry; 36,000 cavalry and 640 elephants. Mahmud Ghazni became highly pensive when he saw the huge force encamped. Prostrating before God he prayed for success and victory. To his good fortune – the Chandela king lost his nerve and fled at night – leaving his camp and army at the mercy of the invader.

Historians wonder how this battle might have gone, had the steely Trilochanpala been able to join up with the Chandelas. He had steady nerves and great battle experience of fighting the Turks. Perhaps the history of India would have taken a different turn. It is one of the very sad *"what ifs"* of Indian history.

The Turkish invaders had systematically tried to terrorise the Indians into submission by large scale slaughters – genocide, rape and loot. Large numbers of men and women were sold into slavery and concubinage. Even the enemy however payed a tribute to the noble and valiant Shahis who had fought so stubbornly till the very end and had refused to surrender or give passage to Mahmud Ghazni's Turkish armies. Al Baruni writes – *"The Hindu Shahiya dynasty is now extinct . We must say that in all their grandeur, they never slackened in the ardent desire of doing that which is good and right; that they were men of noble sentiment and noble bearing."*

10

The Mughal Empire

Mahmud Ghazni finally wore down the formidable defences of Fortress India in Afghanistan. He used clever tactics of inducing the enemy to charge and then mowed them down by a shower of arrows from his archers. Once the enemy had suffered heavy losses and the attack was in disarray, he used to launch his counter offensive with his superb cavalry. His archers fired flaming naphtha arrows on Indian elephants setting their howdahs on fire. This panicked the huge beasts and caused them to go berserk. They usually fled the battle, trampling their own soldiers. The Indian commanders who rode those elephants were thus seen in undignified (though involuntary) flight by their own men. This caused severe demoralization and was almost always the turning point of the battles which till then the Indians were winning.

This litany of a complete failure to learn from experience – was the tragedy of Indian Armies in this period. We had used the war elephant as the prize arm of combat from the 3rd Century B.C. to the 13th century – that is for well over a thousand years. The caste system with its genetic engineering and emphasis on carrying forth old traditions and ways of warfare – made us incapable of learning afresh and breaking the habits of the past. This failure to ingest and learn lessons from recent combat experience proved fatal to Indian armies. Learning Suktas by rote is good but rote memorization alone is the enemy of innovative and creative thinking. Set ways of doing things in combat can be fatal. We need to de-emphasize rote learning and encourage innovative thinking and creative solutions in war.

The Shahis had put up a tenacious defence. But instead of exploiting the defence potential of the rugged mountainous terrain in Afghanistan (like the Rutbil had done against the Arabs), they charged out valiantly. Time and again Mahmud Ghazni exploited their impetuosity to induce them to attack and then imposed heavy attrition with his archers and their shower of arrows. In this manner we lost not due to diffidence and meekness, but overconfidence and a tendency to launch brave but foolhardy, Balcalva-style charges on a well-entrenched enemy in the mountains. It was a tragic period. India was attacked repeatedly but its defence was left almost entirely to the Shahis of Kabul and Punjab alone. The Pratiharas, Chandelas, Rashtrakutas and Gujjars just could not come together to present a solid and unified front to the invader till it was too late. The Indian kings largely fought separately and were overwhelmed separately.

Mahmud Ghazni launched 17 expeditions, primarily designed to loot the fabulous wealth of the Indian plains and its rich temples that had became centres of commerce and storehouses of enormous wealth. He launched 17 raids that resulted in widespread slaughter amounting to genocide. Our temples were destroyed and our cities burnt. Thousands of women were raped and carried off as slaves to be sold in the brothels of Bukhara, Ghazni, Kabul, Khorasan, Samarkand and beyond. India was then called the "*Bird of Gold*" (*Sone ki Chidiya*) – the stark tragedy was its inability to protect its gold, its wealth, its women and its honour. A failure to unite against foreign invaders was the primary cause of this tragedy. The fabulous loot and plunder now incited other freebooters to assemble armies to rape and loot. The invaders soon sensed the pathetic inability of Indians to unite and now decided to stay back to rule. Mahmud Ghazni was followed by Mohammed Ghori – the same mountain-based tribe of looters that Ghazni had converted to Islam. They came to establish their rule in a weak and pussillnimous country – weakened by centuries of Buddhist pacifism and the sole concern with generating wealth and riches and wallowing in luxury. India's civilisational failure was its inability to think in military terms and unite against foreign invaders. In our preoccupation with the generation of wealth we overlooked the dire need to defend ourselves against those mauraders who coveted our wealth and our women.

The Shahis had suffered badly as they were perhaps the only kingdom in North India that put up a tenacious and dogged resistance.

They were virtually decimated in their valiant defence – scattered to the fringes of their former kingdoms to survive the repeated onslaughts. Little is heard of the Mohyals in the reign of the Ghoris and the subsequent Muslim rulers in Delhi. These Muslim rulers themselves were hit in their turn by that hurricane from the heart of Asia – the Mongols of Changez Khan, who created a real revolution in military affairs and swept through China,Central Asia, Iran, Afghanistan, swathes of North India and ultimately reached the Middle East and the outskirts of Europe.

This military revolution of the Mongols was based on a simple invention – the stirrup – that enabled the Mongol cavalry to fight mounted with its crossbows and swords. The greatest Mongol revolution in war- fighting however, was the use of gunpowder to usher in the explosive paradigm of war. The Mongols used ponderous seige canons to pound down the walls of the forts in India and elsewhere. They routed the Muslim empires of Central Asia, Iran and thundered into Iraq and Syria. They imprisoned the Caliph himself and devastated all lands with fire and sword. They aimed to spread terror that would collapse the will of their enemies to fight. The Central Asians, Iranians and Afghans who had looted India were now themselves swept aside by this Mongol firestorm from the heartland of Asia.

In the wake of the terrible Mongol invasions – a number of Gunpowder Empires arose in Central Asia. Decades later in 1398, Taimur, the lame burst into India and left another tsunami of loot and devastation in his wake. Babur, the founder of Mughal dynasty was his grandson. He came from Samarkand but counted for little in Uzbekistan. Armed with the revolution in the art of war, fashioned by the Mongols and faithfully copied by the gunpowder empires of Central Asia, Babur now decided to seek his fortune in Afghanistan and India. He established his foothold in Afghanistan and then embarked upon the invasion of India.

Babur swept into India for the first time in 1519 and used muskets extensively in the Battle of Bajaur. He came again in 1526. This time he marched in with a force of just 18,000 cavalry; 2,000 infantry and 5,000 gunners. He had some 1,200 musketeers armed with flintlock muskets. Ibrahim Lodhi met Babur at the First Battle of Panipat with a huge host over 1,20,000 strong and armed with hundreds of war elephants. In purely quantitative terms it was simply no contest. Logically, Babur should have been routed. Instead it was the huge hosts of Ibrahim Lodhi that were slaughtered. The carnage was mind-numbing and the defeat was decisive and comprehensive. It set the stage for the establishment of the Mughal Empire in India – an empire that in its heydays was generating some 40% of the world's GDP. The key question for military historians is – how did such a miniscule force like Babur's, win such a decisive victory over such a mammoth force?

The Revolution in Military Affairs
The answer lay in the military-technical revolution (or the Revolution in Military Affairs (RMA)), which the Mongols had initiated and the Mughals had so greatly improved upon. To understand the impact of this military- technical revolution, we must understand the nature of cumulative technological changes that had dynamically altered the battlefield in the 15th century. These merit some reflection:-

• **The Use of Explosives:** The most sweeping change on the battlefield had come with the introduction of explosives. The Mongols were the first to use seige canons to blast down the walls of forts. As a consequence, all forts in India were moved from the plains to the tops of hills and mountains – so that the heavy seige canons could not be dragged up the steep slopes and the forts per se would be safe.

• **Field Guns:** The Mughal genius lay in developing much lighter field guns that could be pulled by horses – virtually anywhere on the battlefield. Babur's artillery comprised the following class of guns:

  ▪ **Seige Artillery:** These were the old Mongol style heavy mortars. These were huge pieces hauled by 2-3 elephants or 400-500 men. These were mounted on four wheeled carriages and could serve to reduce local forts to rubble. This is what had enforced a major change in the design and location of forts. As stated, these were mostly shifted to remote hill tops where seige artillery could not reach.

  ▪ **Field Artillery:** Babur's primary innovation was the much lighter field artillery that was far more mobile and horse drawn. These field guns were mounted on a two-wheeled carriage with an unwheeled leg projecting behind. Most of the barrel was supported by the under carriage.

Babur had two kinds of field guns:-

- **The Firangs:** These were designs copied either from the Chinese or from the Frankish Culverin of European origin. Apparently Babur had acquired them in 1519, when he had recruited Mustafa Rumi, an Ottoman gunner.
- **Zarb Zan:** This was a gun of Ottoman or Egyptian origin. Possibly these guns were modeled on European designs. In later years, the mobility of these field guns improved as Portugese guns with much shorter barrels and wrought iron were introduced.

Seige guns however continued to be made of brass and bronze in India. This made them inordinately expensive. Only an economically strong power could afford them. Metallurgy for forging these canons and field guns was the most closely guarded secret of the Mughal Empire. In fact, the Mughal emperors kept all these guns under their personal control in a centralised field gun park. They were dished out to the local satraps or governors (Subedars) on an as required basis for specific campaigns. Then they were restored to central control.

- **Muskets:** Babur brought with him some 1,240 Toofanchis armed with Flintlock muskets. These handgunners provided protection to Babur's field artillery. Hand guns had been invented by the Chinese. However, the hand gun that first appeared in Central Asia and South Asia appears to have been transmitted from Europe, through the medium of Ottomans and possibly the Mamluks. Babur had come with just 1,240 muskets. By the time of Sher Shah Suri however, the number of muskets in India had shot upto 25,000. Subsequently, the Portugese iron barrelled muskets spread throughout India and could shoot fairly accurately upto 400 yards with a one ounce shot. Locally produced muskets in India were firing rounds of half the weight over half this distance.

- **The Stirrup:** Lastly, the most elementary Mongol innovation was the stirrup. This enabled the Mongol and Turko-Mongol warriors to fight mounted. They could move with great speed and discharge a volley of arrows accurately from their crossbows. This proved to be a game-changer in combat.

The RMA in Action

The cumulative impact of all these technological innovations put together on the battlefield was phenomenal. It is not that Indian warriors were nay less in physical strength or skill than the invaders. Man for man they were perhaps better. It is just that use of superior warfighting technology left them completely outclassed. To understand this, let us take a closer look at the First Battle of Panipat.

The First Battle of Panipat

In this decisive battle, Babur massed his guns behind small ramparts. To prevent the enemy cavalry from charging them, they had a barricade of leather thongs erected. Hundreds of marksmen were deployed between the guns and behind these leather throngs to create a fire anvil. As stated, Irabhim Lodhi had a massive force of well over 1,20,000 men and hundreds of war elephants. Lodhi looked at the puny force of Babur with thinly disguised contempt. He launched his hordes of elephants to lead a thundering charge designed to trample down the Uzbeks.

The Uzbek guns and muskets opened a terrific barrage. The impact was not just psychological in terms of the noise that could terrify the elephants. The canons and musket fire caused severe physical casualties to the force of war elephants. The elephants went berserk. They turned around in complete and uncontrolled flight. They simply trampled over their own cavalry and infantry that were charging closely behind. There was a fearful bedlam. Some elements of Ibrahim's cavalry charged the guns. They were shot down by the musketeers. At this moment of complete disarray and panic in the enemy ranks, caused by their first exposure to explosive gunfire, two wings of Babur's cavalry charged out from both the flanks. They showered arrows upon the fleeing hosts and inflicted a fearful carnage. The panic multiplied and degenerated into a complete and total rout. Rarely in Indian history had such a small force inflicted such a decisive defeat upon a far larger host.

It was the shock of a new warfighting technology that had given an overwhelming asymmetric advantage to the Mughals. The rest was done by their skilful and superior tactics that synergised the impact of the individual technological innovations in a concerted fashion upon the battlefield. The result was a complete and total rout. Technology was the key enabling factor of this victory and not some moral or physical superiority of the Uzbeks. Technology had generated a complete asymmetry over all Indian adversaries and laid the basis for the foundation of the Mughal Empire.

It would be useful to remember that the Mauryan Empire had also been premised upon an RMA based upon using war elephants in the mass for generating shock and awe and serving as a paltform of mobile firepower – with eight archers (instead of one per chariot), mounted on each elephant.

The pity is the next RMA caused by the use of explosives made the elephant a total liability on the battlefield. India's tragedy lay in its inability to learn and change. Caste and genetic engineering brought about an inability to change and innovate and a rigid clinging to habits of the past that were fatal. The Mughals of Uzbekistan now formed a new empire in India that would last over 250 years.

Akbar – the Empire Builder
Babur introduced the new explosive paradigm of war in South Asia. It was Akbar however, who laid the firm foundation of the Mughal Empire in India with his far more enlightened policies of forming a secular consensus. Akbar was tolerant and broadminded. He established marriage alliances with the Rajput Princes. He utilised Hindu administrative talent to the fullest in organising his empire. The *"Nine"* jewels or wisemen (*Navratnas*) of his court included many Hindus. It was a Hindu economist who helped him monetise the Indian economy on the Silver standard. Fiefs and fiefdom were done away with. Provincial governors and district officials were paid from the central treasury in silver coins.

The agricultural produce and crop yields of different regions were systematically mapped and records maintained over a number of years. Based upon the average produce – taxes and tariffs were imposed in a scientific manner and not left to the caprices and whims of local officials, who tended to be so exploitative that they often sparked off peasant rebellions. This scientific collection of revenue made for a contented peasantry. Agriculture produced a huge surplus which was utilised to build fabulous palaces, forts and mausoleums as also infrastructure such as state highways, wells and sarais (night shelters) for wayfarers. The hated Jazia tax was abolished and Akbar tried to synthesize the best elements of all faiths via his syncretic faith called *'Din-e-Elahi'*.

Management of the Military Labour Market

Akbar had begun his military career at the age of 15. He expanded the Mughal Empire into Rajasthan, Gujarat and then into Bihar, Odisha and Bengal. He stabilised Afghanistan all the way to the Helmand river. He now had a boarder framework for economic and political consolidation of his empire. There were some four million armed men in India during Akbar's reign. These posed a threat to the internal instability. To ensure they did not join his enemies, Akbar's solution was simple – a massive expansion of the Mughal army to absorb the available manpower. Thus Akbar's Mughal army expanded from a mere 40,000 in Babur's time to over 2.5 million men. Thus the word Mughal itself became a byword for sheer size, opulence and grandeur.

Dietmar Rothermund writes that by 1950, there were some 350,000 horses in India and some 4 million Infantrymen in its huge military labour market. The number of horses went upto 500,000 requiring some 30-40,000 replacements annually. As the best horses were procured from Arabia this was a highly expensive proposition. Akbar's central problem was not to disarm but to manage this huge military labour market in India.

Early Muslim rulers had turned to the device of feudalism to support such huge armies. Thus officials were granted jagirs and in return they were supposed to raise a given quantum of horsed cavalry and infantry for the ruler's wars. This gave a great deal of autonomy to the local satraps. They had to recover their own salary and expenses of their troops from their fiefdoms. Thus they had no motivation to inform the central government of the actual yield of the assigned revenue. This also led to heavy exploitation of the peasantry by the *Jagirdars* (feudal lords). This often caused intense local resentment and even sparked rebellions.

Akbar's Economic Reforms: Akbar monetized the Indian agrarian economy on the basis of silver coinage. His most far reaching reform however was fundamental. He cancelled all fiefs and began to pay the officials from a Central Treasury. District officials were now instructed to compile a database of crop yields, prices and revenue collected over a 10 year period. Based upon this database he then fixed an average demand from each region and thus did away with arbitrary annual fixations of revenue which generally alienated the peasantry and was the cause of most disaffection and revolts. Akbar had adopted a hierarchical system of classification (Mansab) of all military and government officials. Each *Mansabdar* was appointed by him personally.

Herman Kulke and Ditemand Rothermund write – "The *Mansabdars* served as sub-contractors who controlled the military labour market for him. It must be recalled that there were some four million troopers of various kinds available in the Indian labour market of that era. It was important to enlist them so that they were not available to adversaries or challengers to the Emperor. The highest ranked Mansab had about 7,000 horses. The lower ranked over a few hundred.The Emperor however retained tight central control of all field artillery, which was given out or allotted to Mansabdars on an as required basis. This tight control of the artillery gun park was the basis of the power of the central authority in India. The key source of power however, came from the treasury."

The Mughal empire flourished in the reigns of Akbar, Jehangir and Shahjahan. All of them were by and large liberal and enlightened rulers whose outlook was largely secular. The Mughals Indianised themselves to a great extent by ingesting local traditions of dance, music, architecture and even paintings. They were great builders and left behind magnificent mausoleums and forts. At that time India was generating some 40% of the World's GDP.

Mohyals in the Mughal Period

This liberalization and expansion of the Mughal empire and its army saw the talented Mohyals being recruited in large numbers into the Mughal army and administration. Many of them rose to high positions based upon their military talents and expertise and administrative acumen. They were intelligent and industrious and soon mastered the Persian language in which all official business was transacted. Their military skills were highly prized by the Mughals, who employed them as officers and administrative officials. Many of them received titles of Sultan, Bakshi, Dewan, Mehta, Raizada and even Khan. They had always been a martial race and their military skills were duly recognised by the Mughal Empire. Many of them rose to very high positions by virtue of their talents and good performance. The Mehtas were generally accountants and paymasters of the Mughal army. Bakshi was a title given to officers of the commissariat and perhaps the Paymaster General. Chaudhuri implied head of the family. Raizada meant son of a king. Dewans were incharge of revenue and finance.

Curiously, patently Muslim suffixes like Beg, Khan and Sultan were also conferred upon Mohyal dignitaries by the Muslim and Mughal rulers. Thus Khandi Beg Chhibber was a Minister in Turkistan while his son was known by the designation of Alawal Khan Datt. In the Reqquat-e-Alamgiri – Fateh Jang Khan Bali has been mentioned as the Commander in Gujarat. Yakke Khan Datt (Tis Hazari) mentioned as a Chief of the Mughal Cavalry(commander of 30,000 horse). His family had prospered in the Mani district of Sargodha for centuries. Such high military ranks would only be given based upon demonstrated good combat performance. Tis Hazari implied a commander of 30,000 men, virtually a corps-sized formation. It is therefore clear that Mohyals also served in combat arms and not just in the commissariat or administrative echelons of the gigantic Mughal Army as paymasters and logisticians.

The Advent of Aurangzeb

Dara Shikoh, the eldest son of Shahjahan and the rightful heir to the Mughal throne was a highly enlightened prince. He had the

Upanishads and other Hindu texts translated to Persian. He would have made a very enlightened, liberal and secular monarch who would have perpetuated the liberal traditions set in place by Akbar for the foundation of the Mughal Empire.

Prince Aurangzeb, however, imprisoned his own father and slaughtered his brothers to seize the throne. He was a religious bigot and the Ulema incited him to end the era of tolerance and liberalism. He reimposed the hated Jazia tax, began to demolish Hindu temples and persecute the non-Muslims. He began a mindless expansion of the Mughal army to pursue his equally mindless wars in the South. This massive expansion of the Mughal army completely derailed the Mughal economy and was the primary factor for the downfall of the Mughal Empire. Aurangzeb's reign of terror and persecution triggered great resentment in the non-Muslim population of India. Overtime three great centres of rebellion arose:-

- **The Sikhs:** in the North were led by Guru Gobind Singh- the last Sikh guru who militarized the Sikhs. The Mohyals made a major contribution to the rise of the Sikh military brotherhood and the revival of Indian Arms.Within a century, the Sikhs had driven the Mughals out of Punjab and northern India and conqured J&K and large parts of Afghanistan.Allied Dogra contingents had captured Ladakh and Baltistan and even invaded Tibet.Their rise will be covered in very great detail in the next chapter.

- **The Marathas:** under Chhatrapati Shivaji Maharaj led the Hindu Revolt in the South. Soon the Marathas became a great military power in India and conquered large swathes of western , central and even southern India and between them and the Sikhs – the Mughal military power in India was comprehensively destroyed.

- **The Assamese:** The Assamese (Ahoms) under their famous Hindu General Lachit Burpukhan – checked the Eastward expansion of the Mughal Empire into the North East. In a major naval battle at Saraighat on the Brahmaputra – Burpukhan destroyed the Mughal naval armada. Thus between the Sikhs, Marathas and the Assamese Mughal rule that had suddenly turned tyrranical was brought to a swift and inglorious end.

11

The Rise of the Sikhs and the Role of Mohyals in the Indian Military Revival

Guru Nanak Dev was the first Guru of the Sikhs who established this syncretic faith. It was an extension of the Bhakti Movement that had brought about a revival of Hinduism in the depths of defeat during Muslim rule. Sikhism began as a gentle and peaceful faith that tried to synthesize the teachings of Hinduism and Islam in a mystic blend.

Baba Paraga: Bhishma of Mohyals

The first Mohyal savant who became a disciple of Guru Nanak was Paraga Sain (probable transliteration *Pragya Sen*). He was the son of Raja Gautam (1507-1638). He had laid the foundation of the township of Karyala – which remained the home of the Chhibber clan of the Mohyals for some 450 years till the partition of India in 1947. Paraga became a disciple of Guru Nanak Dev and came to be known as Baba Paraga. Along with Baba, Mardana and Angad were the closest disciples of Guru Nanak Dev and after his passing away, Baba became the power behind the throne. He was blessed with an unusually long life span and served the next five Sikh Gurus viz. Guru Angad Dev, Guru Amar Das, Guru Ram Das, Guru Arjan Dev, Guru Har Gobind.

Paraga married the daughter of Tara Chand Vaid, the Dewan of Kot Sarang (modern Campbellpur) and had a son named Durga Das. It is said that in his boyhood Paraga had been made captive by the Afghans and was taken to Kabul. He was repatriated to India after the conquest of Kabul by Babur. Baba Paraga helped Guru Arjan Dev in the compilation of the Adi Granth. In the reign of Shahjahan, the Mughal Emperor was incensed by the rise of the power and fame of the Sikh Guru. He deputed Painda Khan, his governor in Lahore to take action against Guru Har Gobind. Baba Paraga was now 131 years of age and was called '*Baba Buddha*' by the locals. In 1628, on the Guru's clarion call, he took up arms and led a force of some 500 warriors (Jatha) against Painda Khan. In the battle, Painda Khan was killed. Unfortunately, Baba Paraga was himself grievously wounded while fighting near Kartarpur and died on his return to Karyala – the Jerusalem of the Mohyals in Punjab. This grand old warrior was truly the Bhishma of the Mohyal community and the Sikhs.

He led the nascent militarization of the peaceful Sikh faith. His mausoleum stands today on the outskirts of Karyala and another monument to him was raised at Charbagh in Kabul. The revival process of indigenous arms in India had begun with this first rebellion against the Mughals. Chowk Paraga Das which lies in the vicinity of the Golden Temple is named after him.

Bhai Mati Das

Bhai Mati Das and Sati Das were the grandsons of Baba Paraga. Their father Bhai Hiranand also came from the Karyala village in Jhelum. He had been initiated into the Sikh faith by Guru Arjan Dev, who had bestowed upon him the title of "Bhai" (brother). The family still bears this name as a title. They saved Guru Harkrishan and later Guru Tegh Bahadur. Their father Durgamal was the Dewan of Guru Tegh Bahadur. As he was growing old, he asked the Guru to appoint his son Mati Das as Dewan and Sati Das as Wazir. The Guru agreed graciously and the brothers assumed charge.

Guru Tegh Bahadur had established the Anandpur Sahib seminary in Himachal Pradesh. He began his march to the East via U.P., Bihar and Bengal. His son Gobind Rai (later the last Guru, Gobind Singh) was born at Patna.

Aurangzeb in the meanwhile, had begun cruel persecution of the Hindus and Sikhs. The repression was most cruel in Kashmir where the Mughal Governor Iftikhar Khan was forcibly trying to convert them to Islam. Guru Tegh Bahadur returned to Anandpur Sahib to raise the spirits of the Hindu and Sikh population. The Kashmiri Pandits approached him for help to save themselves from the wrath of the Emperor and to intercede on their behalf. Apparently the Guru sent a message to Aurangzeb to first convert him before he converted the Pandits. Aurangzeb was enraged.The Guru and his disciples were arrested by a huge force of some 1,200 mounted soldiers. They were taken to Delhi. The Qazi offered them the stark choice – embrace Islam or die. The Guru and his disciples refused to convert and were now subjected to the most terrible and inhuman torture. Before such cruel torture even the crucification of Jesus Christ pales in terms of the sheer intensity of pain inflicted. The Mughal Empire in its determination to rule by sheer terror, had now turned twisted and evil. The Mughal executioners not only beheaded people, they devised abominable means of torturing them publicly. The aim was to terrify the non-Muslim population into meek and abject surrender. The Sikh religious texts recall these gruesome tortures in all their gory detail.

Martyrdom of Mati Das – Sawed to Death

The fate of Bhai Mati Das, a Mohyal was most gruesome and cruel. He was bolted between two planks of wood and then painfully sawed in half by the Mughal executioner. Even as he was being sawed in two Bhai Mati Das kept reciting the Japji Sahib in a heroic gesture of great calm and defiance in the face of the most horrifying and excruciating pain. What was astonishing was that despite this horrible torture Bhai Mati Das refused to forsake his faith. He calmly accepted such pain and suffering but did not bow down to his executioners. Bhai Mati Das's martyrdom is still remembered in the annals of the Sikh faith. The way he was killed is a crime against all humanity.

His brother Sati Das was wrapped in cotton wool soaked in oil and burnt to death in a most horrible fashion. He too refused to relent and forsake his faith.

Bhai Dayal Das was placed in a cauldron of boiling water and scalded to death on 10th November 1675. The Guru and his disciples were made to watch these tortures and executions in turn to make them weaken, tremble and relent. The fact that they refused to beg their executioners for mercy despite such horrible tortures – even today sends a shiver down the spine.

The depravity of it all had reached a crescendo of cruelty and evil. These scream of the tortured and dying sounded the death knell of the Mughal Empire.

On 11 November 1675, after watching all his disciples being tortured so horribly to death, Guru Tegh Bahadur himself was beheaded beneath a Banyan tree opposite the Sunehri Masjid in Chandni Chowk in Delhi. There were public displays of torture and executions designed to terrify the Indian people. The depravity and inhuman cruelty only steeled the faith of the victims. It sent a wave of anger throughout the Punjab. In less than a hundred years, the Mughal Empire was uprooted and destroyed by the anger of those it had sought to persecute in such a savage and depraved manner. Guru Tegh Bahadur's severed head was rescued by his disciple Bhai Jaita, who carried it secretly to Anandpur Sahib in the Punjab, where the nine year old Guru Gobind Singh cremated it with deep reverence. Gurudwara Sis Ganj stands at the spot where Guru Gobind Singh had cremated his father's head. Another disciple stole the headless body under cover of darkness and cremated it by burning his hut.

The last words of the stoic Guru were, "*Sir Diya par Sar na Diya*" (I sacrificed my head but not my Honour). It was a rallying cry that echoed in the hearts of outraged Sikhs and Hindus of Punjab. The harvest of hate and anger it generated, destroyed the mighty Mughal Empire. Subsequently, Gurudwara Sisganj Sahib was rebuilt at Chandni Chowk – the site of the Guru's martyrdom. Gurudwara Rakabganj stands where his headless body was cremated. Like the Jews, the Sikhs had sworn – never to forget. They made the Mughal Empire history.The supreme sacrifice of the Guru and his Mohyal disciples stands as an inspiration for the generations to come of steely courage and fortitude in the face of death by excrutiating torture.

Banda Bahadur: The Military Renaissance Begins

Madho Das was born on 16 October 1670 at Rajouri in Jammu & Kashmir (J&K). He was named Lachhman Dev. Wrestling, horse riding and hunting were his major hobbies. Once while hunting he killed a doe and was shocked to see the mother and her aborted fawn writhing in pain. He had a change of heart. He left his home and became a disciple of a Bairagi Sadhu called Janki Das. The Sadhu gave him the name – Madho Das. With the Sadhu he travelled all over North India. He finally reached Nanded in Maharashtra – where he built a hut on the banks of the Godavari river and began deep meditation. He remained there for many years.

Meanwhile Aurangzeb had died. In the war of succession, his own son Bahadur Shah Zafar sought the help of Guru Gobind Singh. Hoping he would end the tyranny against his people, the Guru helped him. However, after he consolidated his rule, Bahadur Shah Zafar never carried out his promise. The Guru felt betrayed. The Guru held a Durbar where he initiated Madho Das into the Sikh faith and called him Gurbaksh Singh. He handed him five arrows form his quiver as a symbol of temporal authority and appointed him to lead the campaign in Punjab against the Mughals and avenge the murder of the Sikh Gurus and their families and the innocent civilians. More specifically, he asked him to punish Nawab Wazir Khan, who had been most active in committing these atrocities.

He gave Gurbaksh Singh an Advisory Council of five devoted Sikhs (Hazuri Sikhs). They were to announce to the people of the Punjab that Banda Bairagi was the Guru's deputy and nominee, and would lead the expedition against the Muslims of Sirhind to avenge the atrocities against the Sikhs. Twenty-five soldiers accompanied Banda from Nanded to Punjab. The Guru had given him his own sword, green bow, nagara (war drum) and a *nishan Sahib* (religious penant). He ordered him to avenge the atrocities against the Sikhs and eliminate Nawab Wazir Khan, the tyrant of Punjab. 300 Sikh Risaldars accompanied him for some eight kilometers as part of a ceremonial send off from Nanded.

Once in Punjab, Banda Bairagi set to mobilizing an army of Sikh volunteers. He began to train them hard. He now started attacking the Mughal bastions one by one and destroyed them. One by one, the Mughal bastions fell like nine pins. These included Samana, Ghuam, Thaksa, Mustafabad and Sadhura. He now reached the outskirts of Sirhind. This is where the Sahibzadas, the sons of Guru Gobind Singh, had been martyred by entombing them alive in walls.

Banda also saw at first hand, how the Satnami Sect which had risen in revolt against the Mughals had been massacred. He marched upon Hisar and was well received by the local Hindus and Sikhs as a

Leader and Deputy of Guru Gobind Singh. Banda now sent letters to the Sikhs of Malwa to join him in his campaign against Sirhind. He rescued Mata Sahib Kaur and had her evacuated to Delhi under armed escort. There she joined Mata Sundari who was acting as the Head of the Khalsa after the demise of Guru Gobind Singh. In early November 1709, he attacked and looted the Mughal treasury of Sonepat with a band of 500 men. He then raided the treasury of Kaithal.

Samana: Samana town was very strongly fortified. It had a wall all around and every haveli was a fortress. The Mughals had deployed guns for the town's defence. On 26 November 1709, Banda camped at a distance and pretended to lack the will to attack. At night, however, he made a rapid approach march and entered the town beore the gates could be closed. Samna was a special target for the Sikhs. Jalaluddin Jattad – the man who had beheaded Guru Tegh Bahadur lived here. So did Ali Hussain who had betrayed Guru Gobind Singh. Jattad's son had beheaded the two younger sons of Guru Gobind Singh. The entire Sikh peasantry around was outraged by the Mughal atrocities. They joined Banda's army in their thousands and fell upon Samana.

The entire population was massacred in revenge. Banda appointed Fateh Singh as commander of the fort city of Samana and made it his base of operations. He next attacked the Muslim Ranghars and the Damla village of Pathans who had just joined Guru Gobind Singh after being dismissed from the Mughal Army. Later they had betrayed him and switched sides. Banda struck these turncoats in a very concerted manner to bring home to all that the Sikhs would react with vigour against all atrocities and treachery. Damla village was razed to the ground.

A Muslim historian Khafi Khan wrote, "In two to three months' time, Banda had a force of some four to five thousand horsemen and seven to eight thousand foot soldiers. Day by day their numbers increased as abundant money and material by pillage of Moghul treasuries fell into their hands. Many Muslim villages were laid waste and Banda Bahadur appointed his own police officials (Thanedars) and established his sovereignty by setting up collectors of revenue (Tahsildar-e-mal)."

In February 1710, Banda Bahadur established his headquarters at Mukhlisgarh – in the lower Shivalik foothills south of Nahan. He

bhai mati das being sawed to death

repaired and strengthened the Fort here which was at a commanding height atop a hill. Two streams supplied it water. The loot and plunder was stored here to pay for the hiring of soldiers and horsemen. Banda now began to mint coins and issued orders under his seal. Mukhlisgarh's name was changed to Lohgarh and became the seat of his provisional government.

Banda Bahadur's primary target was the fort city of Sirhind. Wazir Khan, its governor was the worst tyrant who had a lot of Sikh blood on his hands. Sikhs were now baying for his blood. Banda began preparations to attack Sirhind. He called for volunteers and reinforcements from Majha and Doaba. Wazir Khan was worried. He sent a strong force under Sher Mohammad Khan of Malerkotla towards Ropar to prevent this force from joining up with Banda Bahadur. There was a fierce battle with vicious hand-to-hand combat. The Sikhs triumphed and the Mughal forces fled. Banda now succeeded in consolidating his entire force for the Battle of Sirhind and began to make final preparations.

Banda's Kingdom: Banda now ruled over the region bounded in the North by the Shivalik hills; in the West by River Tangri; in the East by the River Jamuna and in the South along the line passing through Samana, Thanesar, Kaithal and Karnal. Banda abolished the Zamindari system of the Mughals and declared the actual cultivators as the owners of land. This was a hugely popular move and like an expert guerilla leader – Banda was ensuring popular support for his uprising. Banda spent three months organizing his administration and making preparations for the Battle of Sirhind. His local levies were mostly armed with native matchlocks, spears, swords, bows and arrows. They had few good horses and guns and no elephants. His force now grew to an impressive strength of 30-40,000 men. The Mughals had lost complete control of the present day Punjab and Haryana region.

Wazir's Jihad: Wazir Khan now proclaimed a Jihad – a holy war against the Sikhs. He was joined by the Nawab of Malerkotla and a large number of Muslim Chiefs and Ranghars. Wazir Khan now had a force of six thousand cavalry, eight to nine thousand musketeers (burqundaz) and archers. Besides he had 10 Artillery guns and many elephants. This totaled an impressive force of 30,000.

The Battle of Chappar Chiri

Like Napoleon, Banda climbed a high ground in the battle area and closely observed the opposite army. He kept an elite reserve ready to intervene at a decisive moment. The battle erupted fiercely. Initially Banda lost a lot of men but then he mounted a sudden charge at the enemy's command and control node. So fierce was this assault that it broke the Mughal ranks. They fled and the Sikhs chased them all the way to Sirhind. Wazir Khan fell from his horse and was taken prisoner. Though Banda lost some 5,000 men, he had triumphed. Wazir Khan was now killed and his body hung upside down by his feet from a tree – a standing monument to the fate of all cruel tyrants and opressors.By some accounts Banda had his body trampled under the feet of elephants.

Wazir Khan's severed head was now stuck on a spear by a Sikh soldier. He took his seat on the howdah of Wazir Khan's elephant and the Sikh Army marched to Sirhind. The Mughals fled inside the fort city in sheer panic. The Sikhs besieged the city and rested for the night after the hard fought battle. The next day, refreshed, they fell upon the city with a vengeance. Sirhind was the economic and provincial capital of the Mughals. It had a huge government treasury. From here Banda Singh's men looted Rupees two crore worth of treasure and took it to Lohgarh. In a return gesture, they converted a large number of Mughal warriors to Sikhism. The Sirhind province had 28 Parganas of rich agricultural land. It yielded a levy of Rs. 52 Lakhs annually. He appointed Baj Singh as the Governor of Sirhind with the task of guarding against the Mughal garrisons in Lahore and Jammu. Banda Bahadur returned to Lohgarh, his capital. By 12 May 1710, he was master of a huge kingdom.

Advance to Lahore

In June 1710, Banda advanced from Sirhind to Malerkotla. The town was saved after it paid a ransom of Rupees two lakh. He then marched on to Morinda, whose faujdar had handed over Guru Gobind Singh's mother and his two younger sons to Wazir Khan. He advanced and captured Hoshiarpur and Jalandhar. Banda then crossed the Beas and entered the Majha region. He captured Batala. He reached Amritsar

baba paraga

banda singh bahadur

and made huge offerings. He now advanced on Lahore. Sayyed Islam Khan now mounted canons upon the fort walls and rained shells on the Sikhs. They laid siege to Lahore but were unable to scale the huge walls. They had no artillery to reduce this. However, Banda swept into the rest of the Lahore city and put it to fire and sword. The Mughal Emprie was now truly shaken. Banda's uprising clearly marked the beginning of its end.

Mughal Counter Offensive

The shaken Mughal Emperor Bahadur Shah Zafar now returned from the South to punish the Sikhs. Instructions were issued to the Governors of Delhi and Oudh (Awadh) and all Mughal Mansabdars to march towards Punjab. On 10 December 1710, the Mughal Emperor issued a general order to kill the worshippers of Nanak (the Sikhs), wherever they were found. These were the orders for genocide. A massive Mughal Force of over 60,000 marched on Sirhind and drove out the Sikhs. They now took up positions in their Fort of Lohgarh in the Shivalik Hills. Banda was married to the daughter of one of the Hill Chiefs and had been blessed with a son. He was now surrounded in his hill capital. The Mughals laid siege and tried to starve him into surrender. Banda launched sudden raids to recapture Sadhaura and Lohgarh. The Mughals now increased their massive force to a 100,000 and surrounded Banda Bahadur with his force of just 4,000 at the village of Gurdas Nangal about 6 kms from Gurdaspur.

They were now besieged by some 100,000 Mughal soldiers and starved for eight months. Banda's deputy Binod Singh advised him to break out of this siege and escape to the hills to carry out guerilla warfare. Banda, however, wanted to fight in the style of a regular army. Pride had now replaced his earlier cunning. He let Binod Singh and his men charge out of the fortress and escape. Banda Singh held on and was reduced to abject starvation. They were forced to survive on boiled leaves and the bark of trees. On 17 December 1715, Abdus Samad Khan, one of the Mughal Commanders asked Banda to surrender. He promised that their lives would be spared. Banda opened the gate of his fortress. His decision to stand up and fight in the manner of a regular army was a tragic mistake. The odds were so heavily against him. Binod Singh's advice had been correct but having tasted victory in conventional battles, he had lost his early guerilla flair and cunning.

The Terrible End

The pitiful and starved band of some 740 Sikh soldiers were taken prisoners. Banda was put up in a cage atop an elephant and marched to Delhi in a triumphant procession. One by one, his men were tortured and killed. Banda was made to watch. His commanders were tortured horribly to find out where they had hidden the looted treasures. Finally on 9 June 1716, Banda's cage was again hoisted atop an elephant and he was taken to the mausoleum of Bahadur Shah near the Qutab Minar. His four year old son was placed in his lap. His 20 badly tortured chiefs were forced to march behind. His 20 commanders were once again offered the choice to conversion to Islam or death by torture. They all chose death and were killed horribly before the eyes of Banda Bairagi. Amazingly, this iron man remained stoic and calm.

Now he was ordered to kill his own son. He refused. A Mughal executioner then cut his son in half and forced his liver into the father's mouth. Banda's eyes were now gouged out. Then his limbs were cut off one by one and his flesh torn off by red hot pincers. The man refused to even cry. It was satanic madness – this choreographed rite of macabre, public torture and depravity. Failing to hear his cries, the Mughals cut Banda's body into a hundred pieces. The Mughals had hoped to terrify the people of India into shocked submission. Each ghoulish act of torture only steeled the resolve of the Indians to throw off the terrible yolk of this rabid tyranny. Torture and extreme sadism failed to save the Mughal Empire. Within just 90 years, it had been uprooted and confined to the Red Fort of Delhi – a pathetic caricature of its heydays.

Legacy

After Banda Bahadur's martyrdom, the Khalsa leadership was taken over by new warriors like Baba Deep Singh, Nawab Kapur Singh, Chaffer Singh, Bhuma Singh, Hari Singh Dhillon, Jassa Singh Raingarhia, Jarsa Singh Ahluwalia, Budh Singh, Naudh Singh and Chant Singh Sukerchakia and others. The valiant Sikhs just refused to be cowed down. The greater the torture and tyranny, the more fierce became their resolve to be free. Nadir Shah of Iran now attacked the weakened Mughal Empire. He looted Delhi of all its treasures and piled the city high with mounds of skulls, In the wake of this invasion, the enfeebled Mughal Empire simple unravelled. Maharaja Ranjit Singh now united the Sikh Misls of Punjab and made them into a formidable military power. He employed French officers to train his Infantry and Cavalry Regiments and for the first time, Indian Armies employed Field Artillery and Muskets.

With this modernized military force, the Sikhs exterminated the Mughals and Pathans from the Punjab. In fact, Ranjit Singh now crossed the Indus and captured the Pathan areas of present day North West Frontier Province (NWFP) ,Federally Administered Tribal Areas (FATA) and Swat. He then attacked Afghanistan proper and reached Jalalabad. Hari Singh Nalwa, a gigantic Sikh warrior, was made governor of this region. The Pathans were terrified of Nalwa and till this day, the Pathan women put their children to sleep with "Hush Nalwa comes". What a profound turn around this was in South Asia. For centuries the Pathans had looted the meek Hindus of the plains.Now Afgahnistan itself had been invaded and huge swathes of land captured.

The Sikh military brotherhood had now militarized the people of North India. They had learnt the art of war and modernized their weapons. They had given up their fixation with the elephant and routed the Mughals and Pathans in battle after battle. The Sikhs had finally uprooted and destroyed the Mughal Empire. All its tyranny and torture failed to save its ignominious end. Gen Mahan Singh Bali, a Mohyal, was a deputy of Gen Hari Singh Nalwa and assumed charge of the Sikh army after the death of Nalwa in Jalalabad. He remains one of the legends of Sikh army.

Maharaja Gulab Singh, a Dogra, was anointed King of Jammu by Maharaja Ranjit Singh. His famous Dogra General, Gen Zorawar Singh launched fascinating operations into the Himalayas. He captured Ladakh and quelled five rebellions there. In 1840, he captured Baltistan and occupied Gilgit and Skardu. In 1841 he mounted a breathtaking invasion of Tibet and routed a combined Chinese-Tibetan Force on the banks of the Mansarovar. He was beaten in the end only by Gen Winter.

What India had witnessed in just one century was the historical process of an Indian Military Revival. This was led in the North by Guru Gobind Singh, who had converted the Sikhs into a Military Brotherhood. Despite all savagery and torture, they simply refused to bow or bend. Finally they uprooted and overthrew the morally rotten and depraved Mughal Empire. The Sikhs became a mighty military force that created a strong empire in North India, drove out the Mughals and Pathans and pursued them across the Indus into their own homeland in Afghanistan. It was indeed an astonishing and heartwarming reversal of history. *Most Indian historians have completely missed out this phenomenon of the Indian Military Revival that happened with the Sikhs and Marathas and revived the Indian tradition of arms.*

Between them, the Sikhs and Marathas had destroyed the Mughal Empire and ended the Muslim Rule in India, well before the advent of the British Empire. What is most gratifying is the seminal role played by the Mohyals in this process of Indian military revival. Like Lord Parshuram they led the initial revolts against the tyrannical Mughals. They suffered terribly but stoically refused to break or wilt under extreme pain and torture. They provided the shining inspiration to the Hindus and Sikhs of Punjab to rise up and overthrow the bestial tyranny of Mughal rule. Despite all Mughal attempts to crush the Sikh uprising with each revolt they grew stronger and more tenacious. By the time of Maharaja Ranjit Singh, they had reduced the Mughal Empire to a pitiful caricature of its former self. They had freed the Punjab and went on to invade Afghanistan, Ladakh and Tibet. Instead of merely defending themselves they were now launching military expeditions and campaigns of conquest in the world's most difficult terrain.

Mohyals in the Sikh Military

The Mohyals played a stellar ole in the rise of the Sikhs as a formidable military power. The role of three Mohyal pioneers who were the trusted Dewans of the Sikh Gurus has been recounted in detail. Baba Paraga, Bhai Mati Das, Sati Das and Durga Das; and Banda Bairagi – all Mohyals- played a stellar role in the rise of the Sikhs.

Mohyals in Ranjit Singh's Army

One of Maharaja Ranjit Singh's most famous generals was Gen Mahan Singh Bali, the deputy of Hari Singh Nalwa and held the Sikh outpost of Jalalabad in Eastern Afghanistan. There were a total of Five Mohyal Army Commanders in the Sikh Army. They were Diwan Bhimsen Dutt, Diwan Jawaharmal Dutt, Sardar Mahan Singh Bali, Bhai Wazir Singh Chhibber, Bhai Gabir Singh Chhibber.

Apart from these General rank officers, many other Mohyals held key positions in the Khalsa Army:

- **Diwan Gokul Chand:** served in the Military Department at Jammu
- **Sardar Karam Singh Dutt:** was the commander of Maharaja Ranjit Singh's Royal Body Guard
- **Bakshi Gurunain Dutt:** He was a very high Sikh official and holder of the Choti Mohar(seal) of the Maharaja.

Governors (Kirdars)

One of the highest positions in the Khalsa Army was that of Governor (or Kirdar) who combined the military and administrative authority in his person. There were 22 Mohyals who rose to this exalted post of Governor in the Sikh administration. A list of these Mohyal Governors is given below to give an indication of the trust and high positions that were conferred upon the Mohyals in the Sikh dispensation. This had been earned by the valour displayed in the field and the tangible results achieved on ground.

Names	Designation
Mehta Kishan Chand Chhibber	Kirdar of area between Ravi and Indus
Bakshi Hari Singh Bhimwal	Kirdar of Gilgit
Mehta Sukha Nand	Kirdar Darya and Chak Durbar
Bakshi Radha Kishan Chhibber	Kirdar Gilgit
Bhai Raja Singh Chhibber	Kirdar Jhangar
Mehta Radha Kishan Bhimwal	Kirdar Kushada
Bakshi Kahan Singh Datt	Sikh Kirdar

Names	Designation
Bakshi Balwan Singh Chhibber	Sikh Kirdar
Bakshi Ram Datt	Sikh Kirdar
Mehta Deva Singh Datt	Sikh Kirdar
Bakshi Sewa Singh Bali	Sikh Kirdar
Bakshi Dewa Singh Datt	Sikh Kirdar Khanpur
Raizada Anup Singh Bali	Sikh Kirdar Hazara
Bakshi Ram Karan Chhibber	Sikh Kirdar
Bakshi Kishan Ram Chhibber	Sikh Kirdar
Bakshi Ganesh Das Chhibber	Sikh Kirdar
Bakshi Jawaharmal Vaid	Sikh Kirdar Peshawar
Bhai Reva Singh Datt	Sikh Kirdar Mial
Bakshi Kishan Kaur Chhibber	Sikh Kirdar Jammu
Raizada Hushnaq Rai	Sikh Kirdar Jindal
Mehta Larakchand Datt	Sikh Kirdar
Bakshi Lachhman Das Chhibber	Sikh Kirdar Shadra

The high positions held by the Mohyals in the Khalsa Army and administration, testify to their skill as combat leaders and commanders and their valour and acumen displayed in the battlefields. Truly the Mohyals had played a stellar and heroic role in bringing about an Indian Military Revival – a renaissance of Indian arms after almost six to seven centuries of defeats and humiliation at the hands of invaders and looters. Not only did the Mohyals and Sikhs overthrew the tyranny of the Mughal Empire, they chased the Pathans out of the Punjab and what is more – invaded Afghanistan itself and captured all areas till Jalalabad in Eastern Afghanistan. It was a remarkable turnaround – a resounding tale of defeat into victory. It was a vindication of India's honour. It began a historic process of the revival of Indian Arms that finally culminated in Indian historic victory in Bangladesh in 1971.

History had come a full cycle.

12

The British Empire: Mohyals as a Martial Class

Fighting Brahmins of the Cavalry

It must be understood that the Mughal Empire had been destroyed and torn asunder by the revolts of the Sikhs and Marathas – even as the British had made their advent on the scene. It was not the British who overwhelmed the Mughal Empire but the indigenous people of India who were outraged by the persecution and tyranny unleashed by Aurangzeb and his successors. The unleashing of extreme cruelty and public torture and executions, led to widespread revolts and uprisings. These began the process of an Indian Military Revival and renaissance under the Sikhs and the Marathas.

The Mohyals played a major role in the rise of the Sikhs, and the Peshwa Brahmin warriors in the rise of Maratha military power. However, this widespread turbulence created a power vacuum in India, which the British exploited fully to make major inroads. The end of the Mughal Empire was bound to lead to chaos and instability. India had fragmented once again into several competing power centres – especially the Sikhs, Dogras, Marathas and Jats as also the Nizam and other Muslim kingdoms in South India, which were at war with one another and just not able to confront another foreign invader from far off Europe.

These were a set of invaders who refused to get Indianised. They had come to trade but exploited the climate of collapse and anarchy at the end of the Mughal Empire to impose their own colonial and exploitative rule. There is a tendency to believe that the indigenous Hindu population of India had been freed from Mughal tyranny by the onset of British rule. This is completely false and untrue. The indigenous population of India had risen in revolt against a Mughal empire that had turned extremely tyrannical and wanted to perpetuate its rule by carrying out large scale reprisals and state-terrorism. The People of India – in specific the Sikhs, Marathas and Mohyals had arisen and uprooted the Mughal Empire. It had been reduced to a pitiful caricature of its former self – and confined to what is now the parts of the Union Territory of Delhi.

The British initially came as traders when the Mughal Empire was at its zenith of power and glory. The Mughals were land power centric and relied primarily on their cavalry. They never dreamed that vast armies would sail in from Europe and conquer India. The British never did anything of this sort. As revolts began to weaken the Mughal Empire they began to recruit local guards to protect their factories and trading posts. As the chaos increased, and the central authority of the Delhi Durbar crumbled, they gradually increased the size of these armies. India itself had a huge military manpower pool with a purely mercenary orientation. It generally flocked to the banner of whichever local ruler who paid the best. The European success lay in *nativisation*. They built up their military contingents in India by drilling local infantry troops, who were far less expensive to maintain but in the end proved fatal to the Indian cavalry. Since there were largely "all Infantry armies" to begin with, hence the Mughals and other local powers never took them seriously till it was too late. It was the French General Dupleix who first hit upon the idea of training Indian soldiers on European lines to raise effective fighting regiments. The British soon followed suit.

The Infantry-based Revolution in Military Affairs (RMA)

The secret of the British military success lay in transforming the disorganized hosts and rabble of the Indian infantry, that merely followed the thundering cavalry into battle, into highly disciplined and skilled troopers through drill and proven military organizations that had been evolved in the battlefields of Europe. Babur had introduced Muskets and *Toofanchis* into India. However these men fought individually and were not capable of shooting in a disciplined rhythm. That is where the British and the French brought about a quiet miracle – a local RMA that shocked the Indian armies based largely on the First Wave Warfare – of well-drilled columns of infantry that could march and execute elaborate manoeuvres on shouted drill square words of command and bugle calls.

The European-style Infantry was highly disciplined and regimented and trained to stand firm in the face of cavalry charges. They would fire in disciplined and controlled rhythms. The first line of the column would take lying positions, the second kneeling positions and the last standing positions. They would now let the enemy cavalry close in. Discipline and training enabled them to hold their fire till almost the last few minutes. Then they would fire by lines on shouted words of command. While the first line was reloading, the second and then the third discharged their muskets in deadly aimed fire. An Infantry Battalion could thus generate a sustained rate of fire of almost one thousand shots per minute. In concert with rapid firing artillery – such lethal rates of fire proved to be devastating for the Moghul style cavalry in India.

This new RMA generated by European-style Infantry simply had decimated the Cavalry from the battlefields of India. India had paid the price for the second time, for failing to keep pace with the RMA of that era. The use of field artillery had destroyed the Elephant-based Indian armies and made the Cavalry supreme on the battlefields of India. The British RMA made the well-drilled Infantry the new masters of battlefields. The simple fact was that such Infantry Formations were far less expensive than huge hosts of Cavalry horses imported from Arabia. The British and French did not bring in huge armies from the continent of Europe. They simply recruited the cheap Indian military manpower and transformed them via drill and training, into skilled European-style Infantry that simply wiped out the Cavalry from the battlefields of India. That was the secret of the British success. It cost them very little to recruit from the vast military manpower pool of India. The Indian soldiers were inherently excellent soldiers – loyal to their salt. The fact is the Britain treated India as a vast reservoir of military manpower.

The Coastal Bridgeheads

The Indian economy was agrarian and rural-based. Its economic centres were the '*Ganjs*' or market towns of the Indo-Gangetic plains and other

maharaja ranjeet singh

the sikh army

river systems. The British initially formed three bridgeheads in terms of Trading Posts in the sea ports of Bombay (Mumbai), Calcutta (Kolkata) and Madras (Chennai). These trading posts were initially established to carry out the lucrative trade in spices. They then recruited local sepoys to guard these posts. It was the special achievement of French General Dupleix to introduce the European Infantry Warfare model in India. The British were quick to learn this lesson and soon native Indian troops of the two East India companies were shooting at each other and a variety of Indian adversaries in a disciplined manner. The British gradually extended their control of India from the peripheral bridgeheads established on the coast of India in Bombay, Calcutta and Madras (present day Mumbai, Kolkata and Chennai). This led to the establishment of Three Presidency Armies of the East India Company – the Bengal Presidency Army, Bombay Presidency Army and the Madras Presidency Army.

The initial militarization of the trading corporations was triggered by the wars between Britain and France in Europe. The first breakthrough for the British came at the Battle of Plassey in 1757 in Bengal. *The key to British success was a masterly understanding of the human terrain in India.* They had taken the trouble to study the languages, the people and the local politics. Most of their early military successes were due to their excellent intelligence about the court intrigues of their enemies. Thus in the battle with the vast hosts of Nawab Siraj ud-Daulah in Bengal, they subverted his minister Mir Jafar with huge bribes. He turned sides and the British started their conquest of India with a pyrrhic military victory gained purely by subversion. It made them masters of huge tracts of fertile and productive lands in Bengal. From mere traders the British became masters of highly productive lands that generated huge revenues for them. Thus was the foundation of the British Empire laid.

The British gradually extended their control of India from these peripheral bridgeheads on the coast. They captured a vast land revenue base of the fertile regions which had provided the foundation of the First Indian Empire of the Mauryans – some 2,000 years ago. Curiously, the spread of the British Empire from this eastern bridgehead, followed the pattern of the Eastward expansion of the Mauryan Empire. As their control of territory expanded – the British fully exploited the excellent Indian military manpower resources to raise sturdy Indian Infantry Regiments. The bulk recruitments initially were from the *Poorbiya* or eastern peasantry of U.P, Oudh, Bihar and Bengal. The British took the most cynical advantage of personality feuds and dissonances amongst and within the princely states of India.

The Bhumihar Brahmin Basis of the Presidency Armies

The surprising fact is that almost 60% of the Poorbiya (Eastern Troops) recruited from the provinces of U.P., Oudh, Bihar and Bengal were Bhumihar Brahmins. The third unification of India was thus effected from virtually the same manpower base that had fuelled the establishment of the Mauryan dynasty. Sixty percent of the strength of the Bengal Presidency Army comprised of Bhumihar Brahmins. Even the Presidency Armies of Bombay and Madras had a fair share of Bhumihars in their ranks. It was with this military manpower base that the British rapidly advanced into the Indo-Gangetic plains as also into Maharashtra and the inland areas of South India. What drove them was a quest for land revenue (for which they rapaciously exploited the peasants through Zamindars) and an efficient civilian bureaucracy (that would later become the steel frame of the Raj). It was largely with these Bhumihar Brahmin-based Regiments of Poorbiyas (Easterners) that the British conquered the bulk of their Indian Empire. In a series of wars they defeated the Marathas, the Nizam (who turned sides), Hyder Ali and Tipu Sultan in the South, and finally the mighty Sikh power in North India. These were the same Presidency Armies that also marched into Afghanistan.

Unfortunately, having conquered the bulk of India with surprising ease – the British turned culturally arrogant and intrusive. The early efforts at proselytization also angered the Indian subjects. They had just overthrown Mughal tyrants who were trying to convert them by the sword. The British invaders refused to Indianise. Their arrogant attitude of racial superiority soon became insufferable. Issues of religious identity have always been explosive in the Indian context. There were rumblings of discontent in the Presidency Army instigated by this veneer of British racial arrogance and superiority. The greased cartridge issue was merely symptomatic of the volatile race relations between the rulers and the ruled in India. The British had introduced a new greased cartridge in the Infantry. Soldiers were required to chew off its base to load. Rumours spread in the Indian Regiments that these cartridges had been dipped in the fat of cows and pigs. It was, they felt, a ploy to proselytize them and convert them to Christianity, by subverting their faith surreptitiously by making them bite the tainted bullets.

1857: The First War of Independence

This cumulative anger generated by British racial arrogance and subtle attempts at proselytization, led to the explosion of First War of Independence in 1857. The first to raise the banner of revolt was Mangal Pandey – a Bhumihar Brahmin in the Bengal Native Infantry. It was this spark that spread like a wildfire in the Bengal Presidency Army. It soon metamorphosed into a widespread revolt against the British.

Despite their anthropological studies – the British failed to judge the intensity of emotion raised by issues of religious identity in India. The revolt against the Mughal Empire was driven by the brutal methods employed for mass conversion by Aurangzeb. It threatened basic identities and led to an explosion that had destroyed the Mughal Empire. It was a nationalist upsurge that affected all communities and was a result of the clash of two distinct cultures and civilizational values.

The revolt against the East India Company was spontaneous but sporadic and erratic. Had all the Indian sepoys revolted together, the British Empire in India would have been finished. The revolting sepoys failed to generate an overall leadership. A number of local rulers and nobles who had been deposed by the British, joined this rebellion. Peshwa Nana Sahib, Tantya Tope, Veer Kunwar Singh and Maharani Laxmi Bai of Jhansi, assumed local command of the rebel forces. The revolting sepoys made a political statement by forcibly reinstating the luckless Mughal Emperor Bahadur Shah Zafar on the throne of Delhi. He was a helpless puppet but he was also the last scion of the Mughal Empire and concomitant political legitimacy in India. The British East India Company was so far ruling in his name.

The Sikhs however, had just recently been beaten by the Poorbiya troops of the British Presidency Armies in very hard fought battles. They deeply resented it and as such refused to join the revolt sparked off by the Bhumihar Brahmins and the deposed Maratha rulers. The Sikhs therefore joined the British based upon their local animosities and antipathy to the eastern troops.

The British were brutal in the suppression of this sporadic and uncoordinated rebellion. After a year of fighting, they were able to stabilize the situation, based upon the support of the Sikhs and an abject lack of unity in the Indians ranks. There were mass hangings and summary executions. The revolting sepoys were hung from the trees and the entire North India witnessed a nightmare of public hangings and executions. The British regained control of their empire but were badly shaken by this explosive revolt. This did call a halt to any further attempts at proselytization. The British Crown now took direct control of the Colony of India. Their first attempt was to sanitise the British Indian army, which had won for them their empire.

The Punjabisation of the Indian Army

The British were truly shaken by the large scale and widespread revolt in their Presidency Armies – especially the Bengal army. This spelt the end of the rule by the British East India Company. To ensure a semblance of governance in their acquired territories in India, the British crown assumed direct control of the empire. Its first step was to sanitise the British Indian army against such future rebellions. The Bhumiar Brahmins – the descendants of Pushyamitra Sunga, had formed the bulk of the Bengal Presidency Army (60 %). These local Poorbiya troops had helped the British conquer virtually the whole of India. Now the British called them non-martial castes and stopped their further recruitment into the Indian army. They now turned to those ethnicities which had stood by them during the revolt of 1857. As stated, the Sikhs greatly resented their military defeat at the hands of the Poorbiyas (Easterners) and refused to join the First War of Independence, out of sheer angst at their recent defeat. They in fact, sided with the British out of pique. After 1857, Lord Roberts of Kandhar took charge of the British Indian Army and propagated the martial race theory. The soldiers of Bengal ,Oudh,UP, Maharashatra and the South – who had all helped them to conquer most of India were now classed as non-martial. The entire recruitment base of the British Indian Army was now shifted to the Punjab. The Sikhs and the Punjabi Musalmans (PMs) were now recruited in very large numbers. The Mohyals, who were largely part of the Sikh armies were also declared a martial class and a farming community and recruited in large numbers. Besides the Hill tribes – the Gurkhas, Gharwalis, Kumaonis etc were also recruited in very large numbers in separate ethnicity based Regiments. The entire recruitment bias of the British Indian Army was therefore shifted to North India. The British were terrified by the 1857 revolt and how it had cut across the caste and creed faultlines to throw up the idea of India as a unified entity. The revolting sepoys had reinstated the luckless Bahadur Shah Zafar, the last Mughal Emperor on the throne of Delhi – to signify the end of British rule. To destroy the very idea of India – the British now took a series of steps :-

They imprisoned Bahadur Shah Zafar in Burma and ended the last source of legitimacy of Indian self-rule in terms of the Mughal Empire. It is noteworthy that the East India Company had so far been ruling in the name of the Mughal Emperor.

They now set about with rare determination to accentuate every single faultline in Indian Society – so that the Indian people would never again rise up as one nation. They systematically tried to destroy the very idea of India.

Caste. The primary tool they used to destroy the idea of India was the multiple faultlines of caste. They sharply accentuated the caste faultlines. Caste, gotra ,Jati etc. had now to be registered with the Collectorates and made part of the official discourse. In 1872- Sir John Risely held the first caste based census in India. The aim was to legitimize and deeply entrench the caste faultlines. As Sir John Risely famously said, "As long as there is caste – there will be no India". The caste card worked remarkably well in India to splinter Indian society into thousands of competing and squabbling social groups. The British made a major attempt to sow disaffection amongst the Scheduled Castes and Tribes and even seek their conversion enmasse.

Caste today is the bane of Indian society. Post Independence politics have only served to deepen the caste faultlines by putting economic tags on caste identities by way of reservations for education and jobs.

- **Religion and Creed.** Beyond caste – the British moved to make the religious denominations of India fly at one anothers throat. They gave separate electorates to the Muslims, Christians, Sikhs and the Scheduled Castes and Tribes. These accentuations of religious identities have led to post Independence insurgencies and terrorist movements in India – seeking to break away from the Union on the basis of religious identities.

- **The Concept of Imperial Justice .** The British virtually destroyed Indian society by accentuating every caste/creed faultline to legitimize their foreign colonial rule under the idea of "Imperial Justice". India ,they said, was such a competing cauldron of castes and creeds forever at war with one another – that it required an Imperial, non-local, foreign power to rule India and ensure "Imperial Justice" between the perpetually warring segments of its own population. The British amazingly used their foreign-ness to justify their divide and rule enterprise in India.

Thus in 200 years of colonial rule, the British so thoroughly destroyed the idea of India, that even 70 years after Independence, we have not been fully able to revive it. Our politics still relies upon the pathetic arithmetic of caste and creed. If anything, we have only deepened the idea of caste in a post-modern society by pandering to caste identities through reservations and making them a tool for political mobilisation during elections. The Indian Constitution was largely a replication of the British Indian Act of 1935 and replaced the concept of Imperial Justice with that of "Social Justice" as its cornerstone. British rule was exploitative and for the first time in Indian History – India experienced large scale famines. The last one in 1942-43 cost 3 million lives in Bengal, even as grain continued to be callously exported to Europe for building up British buffer stocks! In the 16th-17th Century, India was producing 40% of the world's GDP. By the time the British left it was reduced to just 2%.Worst of all the colonial narrative induced a deep sense of inferiority in the Indian subjects of the empire.

However there were some positives. Macauley created an Indian educational system designed to produce clerks. However to an extent it did introduce Indians to modern scientific thought and knowledge. The railway infrastructure served to unite India physically and in the two World Wars, India contributed massive armies to fight in various theatres of the world. Paradoxically these mass armies revived the idea of India for the divisions raised fought overseas as 'Indian Divisions'.

Mohyals in British India

The Mohyals, as stated earlier, were designated a martial race by the British and recruited extensively in the British Indian Army. Mohyals took to modern education with gusto and their traditional knowledge of Persian also made them indispensable for administrative posts. They became very influential in the British administration by virtue of their intelligence, language abilities and their sterling soldiering qualities. Russell Tracy was commissioned to write the first history of the Mohyals in 1911. He has left behind an exhaustive account of the Mohyal participation and recruitment in the various regiments of the British Indian Army:

Cavalry We learn from his accounts that mostly the Mohyal Brahmins were recruited into the Cavalry Regiments. The Mohyals served with great distinction in the 2nd,9th,11th,13th,16th and 19th Lancers Regiments. They also served in the 3rd,4th and 15th Cavalry Regiments. Mohyals also served in the famous Guides Cavalry and the 30th Horse.

Infantry Besides the Cavalry Regiments- the Mohyals also served in the 112th Infantry, the 124th Punjabis and also extensively in the J&K State Forces and their Imperial Service Troops. Besides, the Mohyal Brahmins also served in the 52nd and 56th Camel Corps.

Artillery The Mughals and then the British had jealously guarded their artillery. No locals or natives were permitted to serve in the Royal Artillery – which was deemed a war winning factor and the technical knowledge of these field guns was sought to be denied to the Indians. However World War I and II called for massive expansion of the British Indian Army to 1.3 million and 2.5 million men respectively. Despite the miniscule size of the Mohyal community, its men were recruited also in the Royal Artillery by virtue of their intelligence. Mohyal Battries formed part of many British Indian Artillery Regiments and one complete Artillery Regiment was manned by Mohyals.

As stated, despite the small size of this community, by 1911- the Mohyals had produced one Brigade Major, 4 Captains, 6 Risaldar Majors, 17 Risaldars, 11 Jamadars,1 Subedar Major and 5 Subedars. These 45 officers and Junior Commissioned Officers (JCOs- then Viceroy Commissioned Officers- VCOs) won between them an impressive total of 22 awards from the British. Russell Tracey's history lists these as :-

- 10 Orders of British India (ClassI&II)-(OB1)
- 3 Orders of Merit (class II)- (OOM)
- 9 Orders of Merit (Class III)-(OOM)

These are indeed impressive figures for so miniscule a community.

A pillar of the community in that era was Bakshi Ram Das Chibber, Mir Munshi of the Viceroy and Commander-in-Chief of the British Army in India. He used to teach Persian to the Viceroys and their ladies as also to the Commanders in Chief and other very senior Generals of the British Indian Army. He was highly influential and got many Mohyals appointed to high positions. In 1911 he commissioned Mr Russell Tracey to write the First History of the Mohyals. In that era he had donated Rs 30,000 to the Arya Samaj, Rs 20,000 to the General Mohyal Sabaha for scholarships to deserving Mohyal students as also Rs18,000 to the GMS for the construction of the Mohyal Ashram in Lahore. These were princely sums for that era and helped lay the foundation of these institutions. Bakshi Ram Das Chibber was indeed the founder member of the Mohyal Mitter Sabha and had laid its keel on 24 May 1891 in Lahore. In 1902 it was renamed as the General Mohyal Sabha.

World War I. In 1895 – the erstwhile Presidency armies were merged. In 1904 Lord Kitchner began the process of the modernization of the British Indian Army. Having amalgamated the three Presidency Armies, he created two closely supervised commands and a modern organizational structure of Divisions and Brigades with proper staff.

He also created the Staff College. In 1914 the strength of the British Army was 23,500 British and 78,000 Indian soldiers. It was rapidly expanded to a massive size of 1.3 million men. At the outset of the war India sent following contingents for the War-

- **France**
  2x Infantry Divisions
  2x Cavalry Divisions
  4x Artillery Brigades
- **Persian Gulf**
  1x Infantry Division
- **Egypt**
  6x Infantry Brigades
  1x Cavalry Brigade
- **East Africa**
  A Division sized Force

By the end of the War the British Indian Army had deployed:

- France – 1,38,000 men
- Mesopotamia – 6,75,000 men
- Egypt- 1,44, 000 men

Indian soldiers fought with great distinction and won 11 Victoria Crosses. The Mohyals played a stellar role – especially in the Cavalry campaigns in Mesopotamia under Gen Allenby. Many also served in France – with honour and distinction. This sudden expansion of the British Indian Army served to deepen the lost idea of India. Our soldiers fought in Europe on slogans of liberty, fraternity and equality "as men of the Indian Divisions".They expected the British to be grateful. What they got instead at the end of the War, was the horrific massacre at Jalianwala Bagh in 1919. This was in the heartland of Punjab – now the massive recruitment area of the British Indian Army. This massacre actually sounded the death knell of the empire which thereafter lost whatever legitimacy it once had to rule. It was a turning point in race relations in India. It triggered the Freedom Movement in India in earnest.

Second World War

In World War II the Indian Army was expanded to 12 times its pre-war size and at 2.5 million men became the largest all volunteer Force in the history of the world. It suffered a total of 24,338 killed, 64,354 wounded and 11,754 missing. Some 79,484 were taken prisoners. Once again Indian troops served in Europe (Italy, France, Germany), North Africa and most massively in Burma, Malaya, Singapore etc against the Japanese. Indian Prisoners of War formed the kernel of the Indesche Legion raised in Germany by Netaji Subhash Bose. Later he moved east via submarine and took charge of the INA that had been raised from Indian POWs with the Japanese Army. With Japanese help they played a crucial role in India finally becoming free. World War II had hastened the process of the Indianisation of the officer cadre. The strength of Indian officers rose from just 400 before the War to over 8,300 by the end of the war. A massive Indian Army of 2.5 million men strongly revived the very idea of India that the British had tried so hard to suppress. Once again this war was also fought on slogans of Liberty, Fraternity and Equality. The British performance against the Japanese was pathetic to begin with and the Indian soldiers were deeply disenchanted by their British Officers who had simply deserted them at Singapore. The 60,000 strong INA acted as a major catalyst and hastened the Independence of India. At its core were some 40,000 Indian Prisoners of War who had been captured by the Japanese. Mohyals played a stellar role in the INA of Subhash Bose and 30 of them were officers in this Army. Though the INA lost the battles of Kohima and Imphal it won the war for India's independence. India, in fact got its Independence merely two years after the Second World War ended. The INA trials at the Red Fort triggered a wave of outrage and violence over all the cities of India in November-December 1945. The full story of the INA tumbled out now from the war time closet of secrets and censorship. It enraged the nation. In February 1946 what the British feared the most happened. Twenty thousand sailors on 89 Ships of the Royal Indian Navy rose up in revolt. They were followed by the Royal Indian Air Force. By the end of February 1946 British Indian Army units in Jabalpur had also mutinied. The Director Military Intelligence (DMI) had clearly reported that Indian troops could no longer be relied upon to obey their British officers. Lt Gen Sinha, one of the first Indian officers to be posted to the Military Operations Directorate, saw the files of Operation Gondola – the contingency plan to withdraw some 40,000 British officers and families in case of a widespread revolt by the Indian armed forces. In February 1946- when revolts actually broke out in the Indian Armed Forces the British saw the writing on the wall. Mountbatten pre-poned withdrawal plans by one year.

In August 1947- the British left unceremoniously. The British Empire was now history. The Sun had set on the British Empire with a finality that was irrevocable.

13

Arya Samaj, Freedom Struggle and the Holocaust of Partition

Perhaps no other country in the world has been subjected to such a concerted effort to efface its national identity and destroy the very idea of India. After the First War of Independence in 1857, the British were shaken and resolved to never let the Indians ever unite again. Towards this end they consciously sought to identify and deepen every faultline in the Indian body politik. They went out of their way to exploit the faultlines of caste, jati and biradari. They then made a conscious effort to divide and rule on the basis of religion. They gave separate electorates to the Muslims, Christians, Sikhs and Dalits. The whole project was to efface and destroy the very idea of India. They exerted themselves hard to impose their colonial narrative of Imperial Justice on the native population and justify the foreignness of their rule.

India they claimed, was such a competing cauldron of castes and creeds and communities forever at war with each other, that it needed a foreign power to impose imperial justice on these warring groups, because it was external and extrinsic to this society. "India", said Churchill, "could never be a nation – even as the Equator could not serve as the basis of a nation state." It was a preposterous idea. The colonial attempt to ridicule the Idea of India flew in the face of facts. India has always been a vibrant civilizational entity. Every Indian ritual affirms the idea of a manifest geographical space as destiny and begins with 'Jambu Dweepe' – world of island of Jambu (Asia) and 'Bharat Khande' – the subcontinent of Bharat.

The *Atharv Veda* speaks of the concept of Rashtra or nation. By the epic period India was divided into 16 Mahajanapadas – with each ruler of these major states seeking to become a '*Chakravartin*' – supreme

mohyals of the cavalry

hony capt. ganda singh datt

adc to the viceroy

monarch or emperor, who ruled all the directions. A ruler was enjoined to maximize his power and territory and unite 'all under heaven'. Thus the Indian civilization was unified thrice by three empires – the Mauryan Empire, the Mughal Empire and the British Empire – each of which lasted for some two centuries and more.

So the idea of India and nationhood was not a gift of the British. Nor for that matter was democracy. India had a vibrant tradition of cultural unity and the more the British tried to suppress it – the more it flared up in revolt as it were. A large number of revivalist missions and organizations arose in India. The Ramakrishna Mission and its fiery monk Swami Vivekananda were the most effective of these Hindu organizations. Vivekananda made a mark as an eloquent speaker on matters mystical in America and Europe. The western press eulogized the Indian monk and he emerged as an iconic and charismatic figure in India – who epitomized in his being the idea of an Indian civilizational revival.

Dharma is that which is a constant in all ages. It is universal and true – but it has to be reinterpreted in the language and ideas of each age as the Yuga Dharma. Vivekananda reinterpreted Vedantic and Upanishadic philosophy in the English language and reinterpreted the same in terms of scientific and technical language of the modern era. It was the most significant attempt of an Indian civilizational renewal and revival. Rishi Aurobindo – a revolutionary turned mystic advocated a similar revivalist concept to reinterpret the ancient Vedic knowledge and wisdom in the language of the modern era and realign it with science and technology.

The Arya Samaj of Swami Dayananda

Vivekananda was an icon created by the western press and media. He worked more in the tradition of intellectual *'Digvijay'* – a campaign to conquer the hearts and minds in different lands and spread the values of Indian Sanatan Dharma. But a far more localized and revivalist conception was that of Arya Samaj. Swami Dayananda campaigned widely in North India from 1870 onwards to revive the Vedic values of the ancient Indian civilization. He opposed idol worship and sought to take Hinduism back to its original roots in the Vedas. It was a deeply revivalist conception. The more the British tried to efface and destroy the idea of India and deny a pan-Indian identity – the greater was the reaction and ferment in the Indian society. Bengal and Gujarat – in the east and west respectively became the citadels of an Indian conception of revivalism.

Swami Dayananda came from Gujarat. His Guru Swami Vrijananada Saraswati was a Mohyal Brahmin. He was blind and extremely short tempered. But he was a great scholar of the Vedas. Once, it is said that while teaching the Vedas to his disciple , he grew furious at his mispronounciation of certain texts and began to beat him with a stick. In between the stick fell from his hands and the blind saint began to grope for it. His dutiful and dedicated disciple himself picked up the fallen stick and gave it to his master. The guru was touched by his disciples dedication and devotion. Actually the fact that he was blind had perhaps sharpened his acoustic sensibilities and his sensitivity to *mantric* sounds on which vedic poetry is based. He was the greatest scholar of the Vedas in his time and gave to his disciple the keys to understanding the hidden meaning of the Vedic texts. The Sanskrit language has many synonyms and the same word can have several different meanings depending on the context it is used in. As such one needs the keys to unlock many levels of meaning in the same stanzas. A large number of European scholars were now studying the Vedas and had undertaken translations into English and German. Mostly these translations had in-built colonial biases and tended to trvialize the deeply mystic content of these revealed scriptures. These translations were divorced from the philosophical context and mystic roots of the Vedas and tended to be far too literal and simplistic interpretations designed to depict the Aryans as a backward and unsophisticated nomadic people hankering for the pastoral wealth of cows and horses. The colonial project of translation also had the barely hidden agenda of instilling a sense of inferiority in the colonized people- the natives, about their own culture and heritage. It was these distortions and hidden agendas that Swami Dayananda had to contest. Having completed his studies, Dayananda asked his Guru what would be his *guru-dakshina*(fees).

"Just spread the knowledge of the Vedas to this country. Give it back its lost Vedic heritage and restore Hinduism to its prestine glory and purity," he had said.

Dayanada had bowed at his teacher's feet and left. He energetically set about spreading the knowledge and rituals of the Vedas. It was a deeply revivalistic civilizational mission and most timely. In the wake of the terrible suppression of the First War of Independence and consequent British attempts to destroy the very idea of India,the Arya Samaj helped majorly to restore a lost sense of self- respect and pride in being Indian and in fact stirred those deep seated forces that would later manifest in India's freedom struggle. Rishi Dayananda did more than any man to revive India's interest in the lost Vedic tradition and lore. He relied upon the classical method of *shastrartha* or scholarly debate to win over his opponents. He was a most formidable scholar and skilled debater in an Indian environment where such skills are highly prized. The Adi Guru Shankracharya was the most formidable debater and scholar and had become a civilisational icon. He had done more than any man to deepen the idea of India as a civilisational entity. He had established four *Maths* or monasteries in the four corners of India and had ensured that the abbot of the monastery in the South came from the North and that of the monastery in the East came from the West and vice- versa. The British were then energetically trying to destroy the very idea of India. Caste was the primary faultline they were exploiting. Dayananda energetically attacked the caste system as the greatest weakness of Hinduism and degrader of its unity. He was equally vigourous in attacking idol worship. This did create a storm of protest from the entrenched Brahmanical elite who managed the wealthy temples but Dayananda was relentless. Soon Arya Samajees sprang up all over the country and the *yajna* (fire sacrifice ritual) was revived in a big way. Swami Dayananda soon became a civilisational icon of revivalism. Swami Dayananda emerged as a prophetic figure in India and as a savior and redeemer of the Hindu community. In his magnum opus The *Satyarth Prakash* (The Light of Truth), he carried out a comparative study of the prevailing religions in South Asia and tried to counter the insidious missionary propaganda against Hinduism.

He established the grass roots organisation of local Arya Samajees that congregated every Sunday like the Christian Churches and made the study of the Vedas open to all castes and denominations.He opposed untouchability and opened his church to all castes and even creeds. He took to prosletyzation and even began to seek reconverts to Hinduism from Islam and Christianity. In sum, he studied the organizational methodology of the Muslim mosques and Christian Churches with their set dogma and enforced norms of behaviour and conformity in conduct. Many Hindus felt that in many ways Dayananda was imitating the organisation and conformity rituals of the semetic religions- especially Islam- with his attacks on idol worship and emphasis on caste- less egalitarianism. In this he was perhaps going against the open- ended architecture of Hinduism and by and large its absence of dogmatic assertions. Dayananda however,had intuitively sensed that the primary British tool of devide and rule was based on the faultlines of caste. Hence Dayananda struck at the deeply entrenched Indian notions of caste and Jati and the endo- gamous rules of marriage. He sought to take Indian society back to the simplicity and lofty thought of the Vedic era and strengthen its unifying impulses over its entropic impulses of caste and jati faultlines. He worked hard to weld Indian society into an egalitarian whole, sans the stratification of caste hierarchies. Considering the ravages of the British colonial project, these were revolutionary insights about engendering an Indian civilisational renewal and revival and it soon caught the imagination of the people- especially in Northern and Western India. Soon the Arya Samaj was amazingly successful in its revivalist mission and made great inroads in Gujarat, Haryana, Punjab and parts of UP, Rajastahn and MP. In time , these revivalist impulses morphed into the freedom struggle. Once again , the Mohyals were at the forefront of this grass roots revivalist movement in India. Swami Dayananda's guru himself was a Mohyal Brahimin and that itself was a motivating factor.

Mohyals in the Arya Samaj Movement. Mehta Hari Chand Chibber, the tehsildar of Miani, invited Swami Dayananda to the Punjab to propogate the Vedic gospel. Hari Chand's son, Deen Dayal Shastri, became a great Vedic scholar and spent 40 years in the service of the Gurukul Kangri- which had been established to revive the Vedic system of education. Pandit Brijlal Chibber of Rawlpindi worked for the Arya Samaj under the direct guidance of Swamiji.Mehta Sawan Mall Datt was a very fiery orater and Pracharak (propogater) of the Arya Samaj. The devotional songs of Mehta Amin Chand Lau were soon being chanted in all the Arya Samaj units all over North India. Mehta Lekh Ram Bhimwal was the editor of the Arya Samaj Gazette for many years. He was a great protagonist of the *shuddhi* (purification) cult- trying to reclaim Hindus who had converted to Islam back to the fold. He was later assassinated by fanatics. Mohyals like Mehta Mohan of Amritsar and Dr G L Datt of Lahore and many others played a stellar role in propogating the teachings of the Arya Samaj and establishing DAV (Dayananda Anglo-Vedic) teaching institutions in the Punjab. This foray into the educational sector was important for it sought to reach out to the youth. The DAV movement in the Punjab was inaugurated by Mahatma Hans Raj. Four eminent Mohyal educationists pledged their services as life members of the DAV college Lahore at a pittance of just Rs 75 per month. They were Bhai Permanand, Bakshi Ram Rattan Chibber, Dr G N Datta and Prof A N Bali. The founding father of the GMS, Bakshi Ram Das Chibber was also one of the pillars of the Arya Samaj and contributed very generously to its various projects (Rs 30,000 in that era). Bakshi Gokul Chand Chibber was a contemporary of Swami Dayananda and a co-founder of the DAV college Lahore. Pandit Lakhpat Rai Datt was a great and dedicated functionary of the Arya Samaj. The Arya Samaj established many girls and boys schools for educating the youth and reaching out to them. Thus the Arya Samaj, because of its massive outreach programs ,proved to be a very successful revivalist movement in North India and tried to restore a sense of pride in our intrinsic culture. This intrinsic revivalist movement soon became a bridgehead for the upsurge of nationalism in India. The teachings and motivation provided by the Arya Samaj morphed seamlessly into the freedom movement of India and it is no surprise that a large number of the Arya Samaj stalwarts became the natural icons of the freedom struggle. A large number of revolutionaries and freedom fighters came from the ranks of the Arya Samaj. Lala Lajpat Rai- the lion of the Punjab, was one of the most fiery orators of the freedom struggle in North India. He had his roots in the Arya Samaj. Dr Lachman Das Chibber was also one of the ardent followers of the Arya Samaj and a great personal devotee of Swami Dayananda. He left his lucrative job as a surgeon to care for Swamiji and was at his bed side when he was poisoned by his cook and he passed away. Thus ended an era. In more ways than one Swami Dayanand's revivalist movement helped restore Indian pride and self- respect and hence was instrumental in paving the way for the rise of nationalism in India. It provided the leadership and also the very rank and file for waging the freedom struggle in India. The relationship between the Arya Samaj and the freedom movement in India was therefore symbiotic. The Arya Samaj in fact was part of the strong reaction in Indian society to the British colonial efforts to exploit its caste and creed fautlines and ridicule the very idea of India. The Mohyal fighting Brahmins played a very prominent role in the rise and spread of the Arya Samaj movement in North India even as they had earlier played a pivotal role in the rise of the Sikh panth and the Indian military revival after centuries of subjugation and humiliation. The Mohyals had risen then against the tyranny of Aurangzeb and his cruel persecution. In less than a century the Mughal empire was uprooted and overthrown and Sikh rule extended all over the Punjab, J&K and in parts of Afghanistan. The Mohyals now rose against the British colonial attempts to denigrate the Indian civilization and culture and joined the revivalist movement of the Arya Samaj. That lead seamlessly to the launch of the freedom movement in India.

The Indian Freedom Struggle

Dr Mithi Mukherjee writes- "the revolt of 1857 had started as a mutiny but soon mutated into a popular uprising spreading across much of North India-dramatically exposing the vulnerability of the Company's rule over India and the carefully maintained facade that the company ruled on behalf of the Mughal Emperor". After the First war of Independence, the luckless Emperor Bahadur Shah Zafar, was tried in the Red Fort and sent into exile in Burma, where he languished away and died – a lonely and homesick old man. The British crown now took direct charge of the Indian colony and went about sanitizing the

Indian army against any further mutinies and took pains to thoroughly fragment and fracture Indian society along every expoitable faultline of caste, creed, ethnicity, language and religion.

"The revolt, "Mukherjee writes, "had brought home to the British that significant parts of the Indian population, though seemingly hostile to each other, were capable of uniting against the colonial government."

Hence the concerted British assault against the very idea of India. The British now set about to comprehensively destroy the very idea of India and fragment its people along the faultlines of caste and creed. One of the most successful British instruments of subjugation (apart from the Indian Army) was the British Intelligence Bureau (IB). They were so thoroughly able to penetrate all freedom movements in India so as to render them dysfunctional and useless. The prime example is the Ghadar movement before and during World War I, which failed dismally simply because it had been so thoroughly penetrated.

" The British, " writes Dr Mukherjee, "set about to dismantle all sources of Indian national unity and identity-cultural, political and historical and thus render the very idea of India as meaning less." The colonial construct of Imperial Justice was propagated to justify the idea of British rule. Torn by internal conflict it was claimed, India was in desperate need of a neutral and impartial power at the helm to secure justice and order. Given that Indian society was divided into communities forever in conflict with each other, only an alien foreign power could be trusted to be neutral and impartial."

In other words, for India to have any order and unity, the state would have to be exterior to India. This was the strangest justification for foreign rule and subjugation of its people. The core of this colonial construct was the stark need to divide and fragment Indian society. That was so thoroughly accomplished by 200 years of foreign rule-that Indian society is still struggling to unify and re- integrate itself and re-discover its identity.

Formation of Indian National Congress. To act as a pressure release valve of sorts and channelize native anger into harmless channels – the British encouraged the formation of the Congress to introduce the natives to the ideas of a guided democracy. It was the

Swami Vrijyanand
guru of
Swami Dayanand

first representative organisation of Indians. Its first founder was Lord Hume, a Britisher, and it was largely an effete debating society to start with.

Not surprisingly, writes Dr Mithi Mukherjee, the discourse of the Congress was not addressed to the people of India but to the Queen Empress of India. It was as loyal subjects of the Queen that the Congress pleaded for freedom and hoped to receive it as a gift". The Congress thus hoped to receive freedom as a gift from a monarchy that was foreign. The Congress therefore, thought of freedom as a privilege and not a right. This also determined the precise mode of its pursuit by the Congress in the form of pleading and petitioning the British monarchy.

Vakil Raj: Thus almost all the leading lights of the Congress were lawyers who took upon themselves the role of pleading on behalf of the Indian subjects of the empire – with the Queen. The Congress mode of politics, writes Dr Mukherjee, took the form of pleading and petitioning by a small group of the educated elite led by the Lawyers of India. An overwhelming majority of the top political leadership of the anti-colonial movement (including M G Rande, B G Tilak, C R Das, M K Gandhi, M A Jinnah, Motilal Nehru and Jawahar Lal Nehru) were lawyers – a fact whose significance has been totally missed in the historiography of India.

Home Rule: The Congress was unable to envision complete national Independence, outside the empire. The Congress dismally failed to articulate a discourse of political freedom. The goal of "Home Rule" that the Congress articulated before Gandhi took over the movement, was not the same as a demand for National Freedom. Most of the Congress activism took the form of petitions to her majesty, in terms that were so slavish, obsequious and full of flattery that they would leave many of us red faced today at the abject tone of ingratiation.

The Ghadar Movement

This effete tone of the Congress was not liked by many spirited Indians who wanted 'Freedom' and not 'home rule'. Many of them were prepared to fight and die. The Ghadar movement was an outgrowth of the cultural mobilisation of the Arya Samaj and the renaissance in Bengal. It was a strong reaction to colonial racism and slurs and the outrageous attempts to humiliate divide and disintegrate Indian society. The Ghadarites believed in violent struggle. The Ghadar movement was highly successful in this mobilisation. By and large it was fuelled by Non-Resident Indians of the time who had settled down in USA, Europe and other colonised countries. They were prepared for a violent struggle and took the help of the German intelligence to obtain arms and ammunition for a violent struggle to overthrow the British. Unfortunately, the British Intelligence Bureau was able to penetrate the Ghadar movement most successfully. They tried to stage a violent rebellion in India during the course of the First World War but failed dismally. It was a tragic failure.

Jallianwala Bagh Massacre

The colonial empire was able to neutralise and nullify all attempts of the Ghadarites to stage an armed revolt in India during World War I. The British expanded the Indian Army to a mammoth size of 1.3 million men and sent large expeditionary forces outside to Europe, Middle East and Africa- without endangering internal security within India. It was a tragic failure to exploit a historic opportunity provided by the First World War. Indian soldier's however had seen the empire in dire straits in Europe. They had fought world class armies like the Germans and Turks, and earned fame and renown as Indian warriors. They had heard the slogans of Liberty, Fraternity and Equality. When they came home, they expected at least a measure of gratitude from the British. The massacre of peaceful protestors at Jallianwala Bagh however, was an outrage that shook the nation. It was a real turning point in race-relations and the Freedom Struggle in India.

Mahatma Gandhi

Only with the emergence of Gandhi did a political breakthrough occur, both in the form of demand for complete national independence, rather than home rule within the ambit of imperial justice and in the launching of a mass movement as opposed to the policies of elite pleading and petitioning. Mahatma Gandhi's singular contribution to the freedom struggle was to carry out a mass mobilisation, especially one that went beyond its cities and towns and involved the peasantry of India in a way. In 1920 he launched his non-cooperation movement and banned practising lawyers from taking leadership in the Congress. The British were initially stumped by this mass mobilisation on a pan-India level.

This non-cooperation movement involved the boycott of British goods and the creation of a pan-Indian identity. However the British calculated that its non- violent nature and psychological pressure tactics were manageable. They were worried about a violent freedom struggle breaking out and the potentially non-violent and persuasive nature of the Gandhian movement seemed to reassure the British that this perhaps would be manageable. There is a view that they tacitly encouraged this non-violent movement as a vent for release of dangerous pressures that could otherwise lead to violent upheaval. The second aspect that denied success to this mass movement was its execution in fits and starts. Mahatma Gandhi was insistent that it would be kept non-violent. Hence once the incident of Chauri Chaura occurred, Gandhiji called off his movement to the great consternation of his followers. Perhaps this fits and starts nature of this freedom movement prevented the psychological pressure from reaching a crescendo that would force the British to leave. Revolutionaries like Bhagat Singh, Azad and Aurobindo differed strongly with Gandhiji's method and became national icons and heroes as they captured the nation's imagination with their self-sacrifice and courage. Calendar art made them into household heroes and was a prime propaganda tool of the freedom struggle.

Bose and Gandhi

Bose became the president of the National Congress just before the start of the Second World War. He clearly foresaw the coming war as a historical opportunity to free India from British rule by the use of force. He was a votary of real politik and sensed that the non- violent freedom struggle would never be able to mount pressure of a level as would force the British to leave. He was the only man to question Gandhi's unchallenged position in the Congress. Despite Gandhi's objections, he won the Congress Presidentship for a second term but then was forced to leave the Congress itself. Bose escaped from India and pursued the military path to India's freedom with a rare grit and determination. He reached Germany and raised the Indesche Legion to liberate India. When the German military drive towards India via the Middle East faltered and failed , he left by submarine to Japan and took charge of the INA. He raised a Provisional Government of India in exile and it was recognised by nine countries.

He raised the INA to a strength of 60,000 and declared war against Great Britain. Meanwhile Gandhi had virtually veered towards Bose's view that it was now or never. In August 1942 he launched the Quit India movement with the slogan 'karo ya maro'. Unfortunately the British used 58 battalions (or eight brigades) worth of white troops to crush this uprising and jail the entire Congress leadership. Churchill wanted Gandhi to die fasting. Sadly, the non-violent struggle had failed. Had the Japanese attacked India in 1942, their armies would have gone through like a knife through butter. The British forces were in total disarray. In panic, the British had burned all boats in the area of what is now Bangladesh to impede a Japanese invasion via the sea. This led to massive famine in which some 3 million Indians died. The British Rule had lost its last vestige of legitimacy and decency. The Japanese attack that finally came in 1944 with some 20,000 INA soldiers was too little too late. Despite this they almost pulled it off . Though they lost the tactical battles of Imphal and Kohima, it nevertheless won the war for India's independence . At the end of the war -the secret of the INA tumbled out of the wartime closet and electrified India. The INA trials at the Red Fort in November-December 1945 inflamed the entire nation and lead to riots. In February 1946 the inevitable happened and 20,000 sailors of the Royal Indian Navy revolted. This was followed by revolts in the RIAF and then in some units of the British Indian Army. That was the last straw that broke the camels back. Just a year later in August 1947 – The British left.

Mohyals in the Freedom Struggle

Once again the Mohysls played a significant role in the freedom struggle. The freedom struggle was fuelled by the wave of nationalism and patriotic upsurge caused by the ideological revival of the Arya Samaj in North India and the Rama Krishna mission and Aurobindo in Eastern India. Mohyals played a great role in the rise of the Arya Samaj and thus many of them graduated from there to the freedom movement. The most famous of these were:

- **Bhai Parmananda**: He was a noted freedom fighter and was transported to the Cellular Jail in Andamans for life.
- **Bhai Balmukund:** He was another famous Mohyal Freedom fighter who was hanged in the central jail of Delhi on 8 May 1915.
- **Pandit Amir Chand Bhimwal:** He was an associate of Khan Abdul Ghaffar Khan (The Frontier Gandhi) and comrade in arms of great revolutionaries like Raja Mohinder Pratap, Sufi Amba Prasad ,Sardar Ajit Singh and Lala Lajpat Rai. Bhimwal was the founder secretary of the Congress in NWFP. He was condemned to transportation for life but the order was finally quashed. He went to jail over four times.
- **Bakshi Lall Chand Chibber:** He was another spirited freedom fighter and went to jail many times. He was poisoned in the Shah Kadar Fort prison by a British agent.

Mohyals in the Gadhar Party

Raizada Ram Rakha Bali was an active member of the Gadhar Party formed in America and Canada in 1913 by Baba Sohan Singh Bhakna, Baba Gurumukh Singh and Baba Kartar Singh of Kamagata Maru fame (a Japanese ship chartered in 1914 by a Punjabi businessman to take 376 Sikhs to Canada. Its people were not allowed to land and were turned back). He later migrated to Burma and joined the police. He surreptitiously began to procure and dispatch ammunition to India to supply the liberation movement. In 1919 he was discovered and lodged in Mandalay jail. He was badly tortured in jail. In protest he went on hunger strike and after 93 days of starvation he died.

Choudhary Ram Bhaj Dutt: He was a pillar of the Brahma Samaj- a revivalist organisation in northern India. He was a great orator and an activist of the Gadhar Party. Mahatama Gandhi had stayed with him in Lahore in December 1919. His wife Sarla Devi Chandwani was a scion of the celebrated Tagore family. They had been married at Shantiniketan. Sarla Devi had set to music the famous song of the freedom struggle- Vande Matram composed by Bankim Chandra Chatterjee which became the anthem of the freedom fighters.

Kaviraj Om Prakash Dutt: Was a colleague of the great martyr Bhagat Singh and ran the printing press which published vicious material against the British to rouse the people of India.

Choudhary Ram Singh Datt: He hailed from Gurdaspur and was a great revolutionary. He was sent by the Ghadar Party to Moscow in 1931 for education. He went on to Afghanistan where British agents tried to frame him in a bomb plot. The Soviets rescued him and a year later he was in Moscow. On his return voyage in 1935 he was deported from Turkey, Greece and Saudi Arabia for his political antecedents. In 1936 he reached India and was arrested and tortured. After being released he was confined to his village. He ran two propaganda organs - Kirti and Lal Jhanda. He worked with Subhas Chandra Bose to draw up plans to throw the British out by force. He was involved in instigating the mutiny of Indian troops in Ben Ghazi in Lybia. He was arrested and was to be shot dead when the Germans invaded Russia. The USSR were now allies with the British and pleaded with them to have his death sentence set aside. He was imprisoned for 10 years but that never broke his fiery spirit. A public hall in Gurdaspur now celebrates the memory of this great revolutionary.

There were a host of other Mohyal Freedom fighters like Deen Dayal Shastri (Chhibber) of Haridwar. The veteran journalist Chandra Bali who was private secretary to Lala Lajpat Rai. Subhadra Joshi Datt was a fiery youth leader of Lahore. There was Swami Omkeshwarnanda who was given the task of generating funds to purchase arms from Burma. He raised a Banar Sena of children to act as couriers during the Freedom Struggle.

Mohyals in INA

Nearly 30 Mohyal officers who had been taken prisoner by the Japanese responded to Netaji's clarion call and joined the INA. These included 2 majors (Bhai Madan Gopal and Deep Chand Datt) 10 captains and 8 lieutenants and 2 second lieutenants. Besides these officers, Mohyals from Burma also joined the INA. They fought in the bitter battles of the

Burma campaign and suffered great hardship. Capt JD Datt who was an officer of the Battalion Azad Hind in Rome, used to make regular propaganda broadcasts. Capt ML Mehta was ADC to Col Habibur Rehman, Deputy Chief of Staff to the Azad Hind Fauj and custodian of all records of the INA. Capt Mehta was tasked to smuggle 7 top secret files through enemy lines and this he managed successfully. Capt Mehta and Col Habibur Rehman were the last people to see Netaji alive on 18 August 1945 when he disappeared. Capt Harbans Lal Mehta was a member of the Netaji celebration committee. Mehta Inder Sen Vaid had property and farm near Maymyo in Burma. He provided excellent logistics support to the INA during the Burma Campaign. His nephew Mehta Girdhari Lal was also an INA veteran. The Mohyals made a solid contribution to the Freedom Struggle of the INA which was the primary catalyst for India's Independence.

The Holocaust of Partition

The 1946 mutiny in the British India Armed Forces completely panicked the British. Their original plan was to vacate India by 1948 but now they panicked completely and forwarded the date of Independence by a year. The whimsical Mountbatten chose 15 August 1947 as the date for independence - simply because it was the day that his South East Asia Command had won the war against Japan in Burma. Even while leaving - the British had their revenge. They partitioned India into two countries - India and Pakistan to reward Jinnah and his turncoats for helping them during the Freedom Struggle. The Radcliff Commission had hardly completed its job of drawing up the boundary between the two nations when the two countries were rent asunder. It led to a blood bath- one of the greatest holocausts in recent memory. Some 10 million refugees from both sides were forced to flee. It was the year of the vulture. Hundreds of refugee trains with panic stricken civilians from both sides fled for their lives. These trains were attacked by armed mobs - all men, women and children were killed and the women raped repeatedly. Many were sold into brothels. On 24 Sept a train from Pind Dadar Khan carrying some 500 Mohyals was slaughtered. In Mirpur some 40,000 Hindus and Sikhs were slaughtered. From, Panipat some 58 refugees trains were sent into Pakistan and some 37 trains were brought here. Most of these were attacked- willfully stopped at stations inside Pakistan - so that the mobs could be collected to loot, rape and kill the helpless refugees. It was a monumental tragedy. The Mohyal Community which had entire towns and villages of its own in Punjab and NWFP were now scattered all over India. It was a tragic Mohyal diaspora. An entire community was uprooted from its ancestral lands and forced to flee. After the dust of the holocaust settled down- the Mohyals found themselves scattered as under:

- New Delhi - 20%
- Punjab and Haryana - 10%
- Uttar Pradesh and Himachal Pradesh - 30%
- Rest of India - 40%

For most people it looked like the end. Most families had lost their lands, property, and had their relations slaughtered. They came homeless and penniless to India to suffer in packed refugee camps. The fact however is, none of them chose to beg. They all worked hard to resettle themselves and pick up the broken pieces of their lives. Did they manage to survive, to retain their culture, customs and traditions? Or was this diaspora the beginning of a sad end of a brave community that had defended the borders of India for so many millenniums?

14

Resurrection

The Role of the General Mohyal Sabah

The Mohyal diaspora was a monumental tragedy that had dislocated these clans from their ancestral lands. They had lived there as a close knit community with entire towns and villages solely populated by the Mohyals. The holocaust of partition uprooted them cruelly from their roots and scattered them across the length and breadth of India – largely as penniless refugees, forced to pick up the pieces of their shattered lives all over again. Despite this, if they managed to survive and prosper and rebuild their ravaged lives – a great amount of the credit for this must go to an organisation the Mohyals had created for themselves around the end of the 18th century. This was the General Mohyal Sabha, popularly known by its acronym of GMS. This is today the apex body of the Mohyal Community. It was virtually the Vatican of the Mohyals and every Mohyal was at one time obligated to pay a kind of an impost called *Muin* and *Chuti* (at Rs 5 and Rs 2 respectively). Besides this the Mohyals used to donate money on all occasions of well and woe in the family. More affluent members used to bequeath sums for various endowments and trusts in memory of their departed relatives etc. This served as a basis for creating organisations and structures to support the community and its collective works/activities.

The GMS in fact was founded on 24 May 1891. It was originally called the Mohyal Mitter Sabah. It was born in an era of great churning that arose as a reaction to British racism and its divide and rule agendas. Two organisations that rose to counter the threat to our Indian identity and culture were the Arya Samaj and the Indian National Congress. Mohyals played a significant role in the rise of these nationalist/ revivalist organisations. The need for greater unity and concerted action at the level of the community was also felt keenly at this time and led to the advent of the GMS.

The founding fathers of the GMS were:
- Bakshi Ram Das Chibber of Behara
- Bakshi Jog Dhian Bali of Lahore
- Bakshi Gokul Chand Chibber of Abottabad
- Choudhury Ganesh Das Datt of Lahore
- Mehta Dehra Mal Datt of Miani
- Raizada Maharaj Kishan Vaid of Jehur Kotli
- Mehta Lal Chand Mohan of Hardorwal
- Choudhary Ram Bhaj Datt of Kanjrur
- Choudhary Hira Singh Datt (also of Kanjrur)
- Raizada Barkat Ram Vaid

Most of these stalwarts were also staunch followers of the revivalist Arya Samaj Movement.

The first meeting of the Mohyal Mitter Sabah was convened on 20 September 1891 at the residence of Mehta Amir Chand Bali of Lahore and it was attended by some 29 veterans. The moving spirit of this organisation was Bakshi Ram Das Chibber who was then the Mir Munshi of the Viceroy and the Britsh Army Chief (Commander in Chief). He used to teach Urdu and Farsi to the Viceroy and his family members as also to the Commander in Chief and his household. He was thus one of the most influential Indians of the colonial era and was highly regarded by the Viceroys and the Commanders in Chief. He had contributed most generously to the Arya Samaj and the GMS as also for the Mohyal Ashram Fund. In 1902, the Mohyal Mitter Sabha was renamed as the General Mohyal Sabha and the name has stuck since then. In 1905 it issued an outline Mohyal Constitution in the form of a *Dastur-ul-Amal Mohyali* – or a code of conduct that emphasized sweeping reforms. It led the crusade against female infanticide – the cult of *Dehra-dari* and in favour of widow re-marriage. It also raised its voice against the practice of child marriage. Its work was extolled by the All India social Conference in Madras in 1915. One of its foremost contributions was to take up strongly with the British administration a case to declare the Mohyals as an agriculturists class. This meant better opportunities for recruitment in the army and govt services.

The Land Revenue Act of 1852 had in fact been enforced in Gurdaspur district immediately after its annexation in 1847. A demographic survey had then been conducted and the Mohyals and Datts living there were described as very brave people in the Revenue Book. As a result, Mohyals had been put in Category II of agriculturists. The GMS campaigned for its acceptance across the board in the Punjab. Thus Punjab Government Gazzette dated 8 October 1909 and No P/1600 dated 19 February 1935 – declared the Brahmins of Tehsil Una (Hoshiarpur), the Brahmins of Rawalpindi and the Mohyals of Jhelum, Gujarat and Gurdaspur districts as agriculturists. The District Gazetteer of Jhelum district clearly recorded this on pages 78-79 as far back as 1880. This had authorized them to buy and sell land and property amongst their own community members and no other community could purchase the same. This was perhaps the greatest service of GMS for the community and paved the way for the large scale recruitment of Mohyals in the Army.

The GMS was registered as a society in 1924 and after the partition, when it was shifted to Delhi – it was re-registered on 16 August 1955 under the Indian Society Act XXI of 1881. The GMS, despite the limited funds at its disposal, had commenced charitable activities like providing financial assistance to orphans, destitute widows and the elderly people. It began to offer limited scholarships to deserving students. Of course the sums it could afford then were in paltry single or double digits only. In the pre-partition days there was a network of some 40 local Mohyal Sabhas in various towns of Punjab and NWFP that were affiliated to the GMS. In fact local Sabhas had started springing up immediately in the wake of the formation of the GMS. The pioneer Mohyal Sabhas were:

- Abbotabad (established 15 August 1891)
- Jhelum (20 September 1891)
- Gujarat (04 October 1891)
- Pind Dadar Khan (November 1891)
- Jammu (12 January 1892)
- Shahpur (17 January 1892)
- Quetta (24 January 1892)
- Sri Nagar (December 1892)
- Ambala (January 1893)

In Lahore itself there were three Mohyal Sabhas. The Mohyal Sabha in Rawalpindi grew so much in stature that in 1907 they advocated shifting of GMS to Rawalpindi from Lahore. A Sahayak Mohyal Sabha had been formed by the youth who considered the GMS as old fashioned and not radical enough. They started their own Patrika.

Mohyal Constitution In 1891 – itself the GMS had drafted a prodigious constitution for itself. Its main authors were

- Choudhary Ganesh Das Dutt
- Bhai Parma Nanda Chibber
- Ch Ram Bhaj Datt.

This constitution was adopted in parts in 1925, 1930 and 1934. It was finally registered on 16 August 1955. It has generally stood the test of times. However it was reviewed and the final version published in 1966. The earlier version of *Dastur-e-Amal Mohyali* had been adopted as far back as 1905 itself. A need has been felt to revise the Constitution and give far greater role to women. The GMS had 40 members in its Managing Committee (governing body).Out of them 35 are gentlemen and 5 ladies. These five seats in fact are reserved for ladies.

Mohyal History Bakshi Ram Das Chibber had engaged TP Russell Tracey, a former Deputy Accountant General Posts and Telegraph, to write the First Mohyal History – that was published on 30 June 1911. Chibber Sahib paid for its publication. Since then many Mohyal histories have been done- the most exhaustive and notable being the one done by PN Bali in 1986. Its third edition was taken out in 2006

The Mohyal Mitter The Mohyal Mitter has the distinction of being India's oldest journal and found a place in Limca Book of Records. In fact, its first incarnation was Miratul Mohyal started in mid 1880's by the peerless Bakshi Ram Das Chibber – the Mir Munshi of the Viceroy of India. The First issue of the Mohyal Mitter of 16 pages was published in September 1891 and carried an annual subscription of Rs 2.50 which was a respectable sum in those days. It was published in Urdu. Bakshi Tara Chand Chibber put up a press in Lahore- called the Mohyal Mitter Printing Press and it was decided that the community organ would be printed here. Its fortunes waxed and waned but it was revived with the energetic efforts of Bhai Parma Nand in 1901. Its first editor was

Master Barkat Ram Vaid of Mission High School Wazirabad. Vol I Issue No 8 recorded that 18 Mohyal boys had appeared (16 in Persian and two in Sanskrit) in the Middle Exam of Punjab University held in 1892 and had all passed. Jog Raj Bali of Mirani had topped the University.

The circulation of the magazine grew steadily

- It was 350 in 1909
- 484 in 1910
- 1500 in September 1990 during the Centenary Celebrations of GMS.
- Its circulation today is over 3600.

The journal suffered a near-disaster during partition but its then editor and staff struggled to bring out its copies from Lahore even as they left personal belongings behind. They revived the journal and till 1970 it was published in Urdu alone. Only thereafter did the Hindi and English editions commence. One of its legendary editors was Sqn Leader J S Bhimwal who began the concept of life membership subscriptions to make the journal financially viable. He served till 28 May 2005 when he expired. He was succeeded by Mehta O P Mohan and the executive editor was Bakshi N D Datta, a seasoned journalist from Hindustan Times. The Mohyal mitter journal has rendered yeoman service in keeping the community together and informed of what its various members and sabhas were doing. It also served its purpose of match making. Most important it had some very useful articles and snippets about Mohyal history. All who have been charged with the task of compiling the history of the community have found it to be an invaluable source.

Mohyal Conferences The Mohyal Constitution had called for conferences to deliberate upon the issues facing the Community. The first such Conference was held on 03 November 1902 at Lahore and coincided with the annual session of the Arya Samaj. It was presided over by Sardar Bahadur Capt Ganda Singh Datt and Bhai Parmanand Chibber was its first Secretary.

Fifty-two eminent Mohyals were elected on 29 November 1902 to administer the working of the GMS. Generally one of the local Mohyal Sabha hosts this on behalf of the GMS. In 1927 senior leaders of the Bhumiar and Tyagi Brahmin Communities also attended the Conference. On 28 September 1930 an all-women Mohyal Conference was held in Rawalpindi.

The Lahore Mohyal Ashram Lahore was a famous University town in pre-partition Punjab and was called the Oxford of the East. It had a vibrant literary atmosphere. To help aspiring Mohyal students to avail of the excellent education facilities in the University town, it was decided to establish a hostel for Mohyal youth. Bakshi Ram Das Chibber donated Rs 20,000 for this project. Many other Mohyals like Moti Ram Chibber, Mrs Teka Devi and others also made hefty contributions. As a result an impressive structure was created. The land was purchased at a very reasonable price in 1921 and the Contractor Mr Ram Lal Datt gave his services free to construct the building. Prof A N Bali was appointed its first Suprintendent. The administrative office of the GMS was located on the roof of the building and a large hall served to accommodate out station guests. It had a huge open terrace – where people slept outside in the hot summer months. When the tragedy of Partition struck in 1947 two intrepid Mohyals went back to Lahore to retrieve the records of the GMS in November 1947 at grave personal risk .After partition claim of Rs 1,57,000 was proffered for this building but it was not entertained by the government on technical grounds that compensation would only be paid to individuals and not institutions.

Post Partition Partition therefore was a major blow to the community. Its primary organisation – the GMS itself was in disarray and had lost the financial resources to help the community in any meaningful way at this critical juncture. The entire community was now scattered all over India. It was a grim struggle for survival and few people had the energy or resources to look or act beyond their immediate family and survival needs. The amazing fact is that despite these major constraints – the GMS struggled manfully to re-establish itself. After partition the GMS was re-established at Amritsar. It had sought compensation for the Mohyal Ashram based in Lahore- in the hope that this would provide a corpus of funds to restart our charitable activities and alleviate distress. As stated before, this was turned down on technical grounds. In 1955, it was decided to establish the GMS in the national Capital of New Delhi. One of the largest concentration of Mohyals was here (about 20% of the Biradari had settled in Delhi). A plan was mooted to establish Mohyal colonies in many cities to meet the needs of the diaspora and try and keep the community together. A new Mohyal Ashram was built at Inderpuri in New Delhi. However due to lack of resources this was a rather modest construction and paled before the grandeur of the Mohyal Bhawan at Lahore. There were problems galore. The most pressing was the need to educate and settle our children and get jobs for the displaced, help the parents find suitable matches for their children within the community, restart the system of Mohyal annual conferences, meetings and melas. All this needed huge resources but they were simply not available. It was a sad period of helplessness and anxiety. Despite the constraints the community elders struggled manfully to keep their flock together and went out of the way to effect the outreach to their community members –now scattered all over India. No Mohyal conferences could be held from 1943-1952 due to these unsettled conditions and the upheaval of partition. Even after a manful start was made these could be held only intermittently. In fact, in the post-Independence period – only 11 Mohyal Conferences could be held over a period of 55 years. The 46th All India Mohyal Conference was held in Jammu in October 1977. This proved to be a watershed of sorts. The next Mohyal Conference was held in New Delhi in April 1982 under the Chairmanship of Bakshi S K Chibber(IAS) who had been the illustrious Lt Governor of Mizoram.

Financial Tipping Point One of the major constraints was the lack of financial resources available with the GMS. A fortunate turn of events however, now saw Raizada B D Bali assume the Presidentship of the GMS. He was a scion of the famous Mohan Meakins industrial family and now brought to bear the considerable resources of the Meakins Brewery to the service of the community. He recalls a stroke of good luck at the very outset of his tenure. There was an old Mohyal lady of considerable means – Brij Rani Vaid. Unfortunately she was old, alone and rather sick. She felt abandoned by her relatives as also by the GMS. She wrote a scathing letter to Raizada B D Bali. In response he rushed to her residence. He ensured thereafter that the old lady was properly cared for till the end of her days. The grateful lady

great mohyal commanders

Lt Gen Kulwant Singh

LT. GEN. B.K.N. CHHIBBER(RETD.)
FORMER GOVERNER, PUNJAB

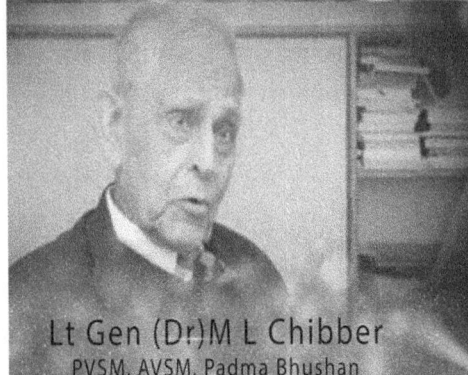

Lt Gen (Dr)M L Chibber
PVSM, AVSM, Padma Bhushan

Lt Gen HC Dutt
PVSM

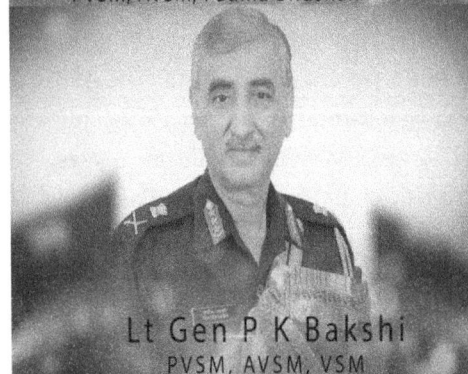

Lt Gen P K Bakshi
PVSM, AVSM, VSM

Air Marshal B M Bali

Air Marshal S D Mohan

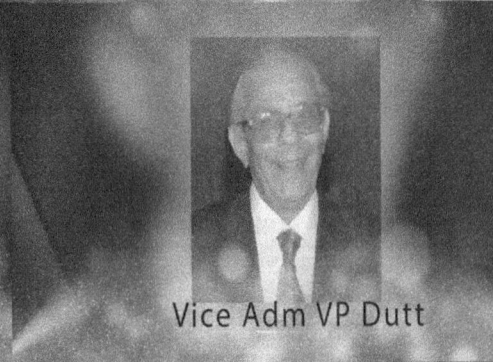

Vice Adm VP Dutt

willed her entire property to the GMS. This included a three storied house in New Delhi. The sale of this property now provided the GMS a considerable sum of money which served as seed capital. After ages the GMS could at last breathe easy and had acquired the resources to do some meaningful work for the Community. Things really began to look up thereafter in terms of concrete and visible action on the ground.

To begin with in 1982 the dilapidated structure of the Mohyal Ashram at New Delhi was pulled down and the construction of a grand new building was commenced. This was to be the new Mohyal Bhawan. Concurrently work was also commenced on construction of Mohyal Bhawan in Chandigarh, Jalandhar, Karnal, Ambala, Saharanpur, Agra, Hyderabad, Secundarabad and Mumbai. The GMS gave financial help for the construction of these. The only Mohyal Bhawan that had survived the tragedy of partition was the one located at Jammu.

Mohyal Foundation Phase I Lt Governor Shri S K Chibber informed Raizada B D Bali that land was available in the New Qutub Industrial Area in New Delhi. The seed money contributed by Brij Lal Vaid was used to acquire this. Work on the Mohyal Foundation Phase I was commenced and in March 1991, the foundation stone was laid by Bakshi S KChibber (former Lt Governor Mizoram). This now houses the Assembly Hall, Library, Archives and Seminary. To earn revenue a part of it was leased to the ITC Company.

Mohyal Foundation Phase 2 The foundation stone for this was laid in April 1996 by Lt Gen B K Chibber then Governor of Punjab. This was inaugurated in March 2001. The ceremonial inauguration of the second wing of the foundation complex was done on 13 April 2003 by Lt Gen Z C Bakshi MVC. Sunil Dutt, Member of Parliament was also present. The Foundation Complex had cost Rs 3.5 crores. GMS offices were established here in 2003. The wheel had come full circle from the beginnings made in Lahore. MERIT (Mohyal Educational and Research Institute of Technology)was set up here in September 1999. Maj Gen K K Mehta was its first Chairman. Today MERIT has 50 computers and its Computer Training Program is considered on par with the IIT program. This building has a conference room and basement and now offers job oriented computer courses.

Mohyal Ashram Haridwar Every Hindu has sometime or the other to visit Haridwar to carry out the death ceremonies and last rites of his ancestors. The ashes are required to be scattered in the sacred Ganga River. To facilitate these ceremonies it was decided to construct a three storied Mohyal Ashram there. Haridwar is also a major pilgrimage centre and the grand Ganga Arti here is a ritual which all wish to see at least once in their life time. Today the community is proud to have a truly grand, three storied Mohyal Ashram with 8 suites, 32 rooms and two dormitories with attached bathrooms. Food is served here free as per the langar tradition for which various members of the community have donated for a corpus fund. This is truly one of the most visible and imposing accomplishments of the GMS and testifies to the turn around in its fortunes and its ability to support the welfare activities for the community. The total cost of this complex was Rs 3.5 crores approximately.

Mohyal Ashram Vrindavan Shilanayas was done on 12 September 1999 by Lt Gen BK Chibber and it was inaugurated on 28 October 2001 by Bhai Mahavir Governor of Madhya Pradesh. Another centre of pilgrimage is the holy city of Vrindavan, where Krishna played as a child. Here another Mohyal Ashram was constructed for our pilgrims with 4 suites and 34 rooms (with attached bathrooms).

Mohyal Ashram Govardhan A third Mohyal Ashram has come up at Govardhan with some 8 rooms and one common kitchen. This also facilitates the Mohyal pilgrims.

Primary School Dehradun The GMS runs a primary school with some 120 students in two buildings in Dehradun.

Meerut Bungalow GMS has a fine bungalow property in Meerut.

Agra Guest House Agra is famous for the Taj Mahal- one of the seven wonders of the world. GMS owns a plot here on which a Guest House is planned to be constructed.

Baba Thakkars Samadhi, Gurudaspur A Samadhi of the Mohyal saint, Baba Thakkar is being constructed at Gurudaspur.

Thus the GMS soon created a whole range of assets for the common use of the Community.

Financial Status It was heart warming to see the major turnaround in the financial status of the GMS. In 1901 the corpus fund had a sum of just Rs 238. By 1978 this had gone up to Rs 2.38 lakhs and now in 2017 the value of the corpus fund stands at a staggering Rs 7.38 crores. In 1978 it had 31 Trusts worth Rs 2.26 lakhs worth of property. Today it has 3000 trusts with a combined value of Rs 5.16 crores. This vast improvement in its financial position has enabled it to undertake a whole range of community service activities and the construction of Mohyal Ashrams/ Bhavans and educational institutions.

Mohyal Conferences. Chief amongst the community service activities are the revival of the annual Mohyal conferences. The first one had been held on 03 November 1902 in Lahore under the Chairmanship of Sardar Bahadur Ganda Singh Dutt. Till date over 50 such conferences have been held. The first Women Mohyal Conference was held on 28 September 1930 at Rawalpindi.

- **100th Foundation Day of GMS** The 48th Mohyal Conference and the Centanary of GMS were celebrated concurrently.This celebration was held with great pomp and show on 14-15 September 1991 at Talkatora indoor stadium in New Delhi. It was presided over by Ch Harnam Das Datt who was then 96 and one of the oldest surviving Mohyals.

- **Our 50th Golden Jubilee Conference** Held at Bhopal on 18-19 January 2003 was the golden jubilee session of this series of conferences. The President then was Lt Gen (Dr) M L Chibber PVSM,AVSM. Seventy-two Mohyals were awarded the Gaurav Samman.

All India Mohyal Youth Forum This was established in October 1985 to mark the International year of Youth. Rajinder Kumar Vaid was its first founder President. They organised the first All India Mohyal Youth Conference on 25-26 January 1986 at the JNU City Centre at New Delhi.

Shadi Melas One of the significant support services is the organisation of Shadi Melas or marriage fairs where the parents could locate suitable matches for their children within the community. These were recommenced in 2006 as annual features.

Scholarships With the vast improvement in its financial situation the GMS has now been providing meaningful financial assistance to good students in schools and colleges. It is also giving financial assistance to widows.

The 125th Foundation Day Celebrations of GMS. Even as we go to press, these are scheduled to be held on 12 March 2017 at the Talkotara Indoor Stadium in New Delhi . Highlights will be screening of two documentaries – one on the History of the Mohyals and the other on the History of the GMS. The Mohyal Ratna will be awarded posthumously to Mr Sunil Datt actor and MP.

Summation : Some Eminent Mohyals

In numerical terms the Mohyals number just 6-7 lakhs. They are a miniscule community but have distinguished themselves in India's Military history as the guardians of our gates. From times immemorial they have barred the path of each and every invader of India- whether he came via the Khyber Pass or the Bolan Pass or via the sea coast in Sindh. They stopped and turned back Alexander the Great's all conquering Greek armies. They took part in the Karbala War on the side of the grandsons of the Prophet. Later the Shahi Mohyal dynasty of Afghanistan stopped the world conquering Arab armies in their tracks on the ramparts of the Hindu Kush. The Arab armies were decisively beaten and turned back for the first time in global military history. It was only three centuries later that the recently converted Muslims of Central Asia and Afghanistan (Ghaznavi and Ghauri) who knew the terrain, took adavantage of the disarray and infighting in North India and launched a series of raids for loot and plunder. Then came the wars of conquest. The Mughals of Uzbeikistan finally established an empire in India under Babur with the help of the technological revolution of field artillery and muskets. It was Akbar however, who with his secular and liberal policies, actually consolidated and expanded the Mughal empire. He took Hindus into senior positions in his armies and as court officials and economic advisors. The Mohyals rose to exalted ranks in his empire. Under Aurangzeb however the Mughal empire undid the secular consensus and turned tyrannical. This led to the revolts of the Sikhs and the Marathas which finally overthrew the Mughal empire. The Mohyals played a stellar role in the Indian military revival led by Guru Gobind Singh. The British then conquered India and relied heavily on the Sikhs and Mohyals for recruitment in their post-1857 army. The Mohyals were declared a martial caste and served with distinction on many battlefields. They also played a significant role in the revivalist movement of the Arya Samaj and then the Freedom Movement and INA.

Post Independence Achievements

Post 1947, the miniscule Mohyal community recovered from the shattering impact of the Mohyal diaspora and the holocaust of partition and has performed spectacularly. Mohyals have excelled in diverse fields such as soldiering, administrative and police services, education, industry, performing arts and sciences. Here we will record just a few of them who have truly excelled in the post-Independence era. There are so many more who have done well – here we are just putting across a representative sample of Mohyal high achievers to give an idea of their accomplisments.

Governors: This is one of the highest ranking positions in the post independence era hierarchy and is listed just below the President, Vice President and PM. There have been three Mohyals who have held gubernatorial posts as under:

- **Shri S K Chibber** was appointed Lieutenant Governor of Mizoram in 1974. He was an IAS officer of great scholarship and distinction and had commendable administrative experience and acumen.
- **Lt Gen B K N Chibber** was the corps commander who ultimately played a great role in the pacification of the Punjab. As chief of Staff Western Command, he was appointed Security Advisor to the governor. In 1996 he was appointed Governor of Punjab and administrator of Union Territory of Chandigarh. Since he comes from the martyr family of Bhai Mati Das himself, he was a hugely popular Governor and contributed a great deal to the restoration of peace in the Punjab.
- **Dr Bhai Mahavir** In 1998, Dr Bhai Mahavir was appointed the Governor of Madhya Pradesh, the biggest state of the Union.

Armed Forces

The Mohyals have been renowned soldiers of Indian history and many regard them as the Samurais of the Indian tradition. This great tradition of soldiering has continued in the post-Independence period and many Mohyals have distinguished themselves on the battlefields and risen to high ranks. Only very few are being mentioned here due to lack of space. The highest rank in the Army (just below that of the Chief) is the Army Commander. The Mohyals have produced 6 officers who reached this exalted rank in the Army and the Air Force.

Army Commanders and Equivalents

- **Lt Gen Kulwant Singh (Western Army Commander):** He was commissioned from Sandhurst and served with the Dogra Regiment. He led the Indian Forces in J&K in 1947-48 and stopped and rolled back the Pakistani advance. He was later Chief of the General Staff and finally the Western Army Commander.

- **Lt Gen H C Datta PVSM (Central Army Commander, Commissioned in Gurkhas):** He had passed his staff college from Canada and had been Commandant of the College of Combat, Deputy Chief of Army Staff and finally Army Commander Central Command.

- **Lt Gen (Dr) M L Chibber Padma Bhushan, PVSM, AVSM (Northern Army Commander):** A scholar-warrior par excellence, Gen Chibber was from the Gurkhas. He had served in Korea and had commanded a brigade in the 1971 operations. He was Director Military Operations, Adjutant General and finally Army Commander Northern Command in whose tenure the army secured the formidable Siachen Glacier.

- **Lt Gen P K Bakshi PVSM, AVSM, VSM (Eastern Army Commander):** He is from the armoured corps and commanded an Armoured Division,the 9 Corps and is now commanding the Eastern Army. Sadly he was overlooked for promotion to the post of the Army Chief, which looked very certain at one time.

- **Air Mshl S D Mohan PVSM, AVSM (AOC-in-C- Southern Air Command):** A fighter pilot of great distinction he was the first Mohyal to reach the coveted rank of Air Marshal. He had commanded a Gnat Squadron in the 1971 war and had been Joint Director Intelligence at Air HQs. He did an instructional stint with the Iraqi Air Force and retired as the Air Officer in Chief Southern Air Command

- **Air Mshl B M Bali AVSM, VM (AOC-in-C Central Air Command):** He was also a fighter pilot and took part in the 1971 war. He also did a stint as instructor with the Iraqi Air Force and commanded Jaffna air base in the IPKF operations in Sri Lanka. He was director of Air Force Plans and Deputy Chief of Air Staff and finally AOC-in- C Central Air Command.

Corps Commanders and Equivalents

- **Lt Gen Zorawar Chand Bakshi:** He is one of the most decorated officers of the Indian Army. He won a VRC in the 1947-48 J&K operations, MVC for the capture of the strategic Hajjipir Pass in 1965 war and led his division for the capture of Chicken's Neck in 1971 war. Later he commanded the 11 Corps. A truly legendary combat soldier, he epitomizes the fighting spirit of this community
- **Lt Gen B K N Chibber** He was from the Gurkha Rifles. He took part in the 1962 war and in the 1971 war in the DBN sector. He served as corps commander in the Punjab during the turbulent days of Khalistani terrorism, then as security advisor to Governor of Punjab and later as Governor of Punjab itself.
- **Lt Gen G L Bakshi** A colonel of the J&K Rifles he led a company in the 1965 war, commanded a division against the Chinese in Arunachal Pradesh and later raised and commanded the 21 Strike Corps
- **Lt Gen O P Datt** He was from the Engineers.
- **Lt Gen Yuvraj Mehta** He was from the Engineers and was Military Secretary.
- **Lt Gen R S Mehta** He hailed from the Paras and commanded the 7th Para in Manipur and the 11th Brigade in CI operations in Assam and 29 Division in Op Parakram. He was Military Advisor to the UN Secretary General in New York.
- **Lt Gen J C Vaid** He was the Director General Medical Services of Ministry of Defence.
- **Lt Gen O P Chibber** He was Commandant Armed Forces Medical College.

- **Lt Gen R K Bali:** He was Director General Perspective Planning and is currently Commanding a Corps. He hails from the Punjab Regiment.
- **Vice Admiral N P Datt:** He commanded the Cruiser Mysore and the Western Fleet in 1974-75. He was Chairman and Managing Director Mazagon Docks and also Deputy Chief of the Naval Staff.

Apart from this some 15 Mohyals reached the rank of Major General and some 23 were Brigadiers in the Army. The Air Force has had five officers who became Air Vice Marshals and two who became Air Commodores. These are indeed impressive figures for such a miniscule community.

Notable Gallantry Award Winners
Ashok Chakra This is the highest gallantry award in peace time. Second Lieutenant Puneet Nath Datt of the 1/11 Gurkha Rifles, was the only son of Maj P N Datt of the same regiment. In 1997 his unit was serving in J&K at Shaura village 7 kms North East of Srinagar. On 20 July 1997 he got in to a major encounter with a group of terrorists. He killed three foreign terrorists before he laid down his life heroically at the young age of 24. He got the Ashok Chakra posthumously for his great bravery and supreme sacrifice and brought great glory to his community.

Maha Vir Chakras: The community is proud to have four MVCs. These include:

- **Lt Gen Z C Bakshi PVSM,MVC,AVSM,Vrc,VSM:** He is the interepid hero who captured the Hajji Pir Pass in the 1965 war and was awarded the MVC for this gallant action. He is one of the most decorated combat heroes of this army and has taken part in all its wars since independence and won laurels in each of them.
- **Maj Gen M M S Bakshi MVC:** He commanded his armoured regiment with great dash and bravery in the Sialkot sector in the 1965 war and was awarded the MVC for his gallantry and leadership.
- **Lt Col Harbans Lal Mehta MVC:** He bravely led his battalion in the Sialkot sector through some very heavy fighting and was killed in action. For his inspiring leadership he was awarded the MVC posthumously.

- **Maj V R Choudhury MVC:** He was tasked to clear a path for tanks through an enemy minefield in the Shakargarh sector in the 1971 war. He completed his task despite heavy shelling. Even as he cleared the last mines he was killed by an enemy shell. He was awarded the MVC posthumously.

Vir Chakras The community has four officers who won the Vir Chakras on various battlefields. Besides we have 6 Sena medals and 10 VSMs. The Vrcs include:

- Lt Gen Z C Bakshi, PVSM, MVC, AVSM, VrC, VSM
- Maj R K Bali, VrC
- Capt Rakesh Bakshi, VrC
- Capt Ramesh Chandra Bakshi, VrC

Our Martyrs: A Sense of Loss. So many brave Mohyals have laid down their lives fighting on various battlefields of the country. I was keen to compile a roll of honour but in view of the limited time available for completion of this book in time for the 125th anniversary of the GMS ,I will have to undertake that task in the next edition. The saga of bravery and sacrifice of this community is unparalleled. Some names that come to mind are recorded below.

1965 War. Lt Col Harbans Lal Mehta was commanding his battalion in the Sialkot sector in the 1965 war . He led his battalion bravely in the fierce fighting and was awarded the MVC posthumously. Capt Ramesh Chandra Bakshi was killed fighting bravely in the 1965 war and was awarded the VrC posthumously for his gallant action. Capt Rakesh Bakshi fought very bravely in the Lahore sector in that war and was also awarded the VRC posthumously. My own elder brother Capt SR Bakshi of the 11th Battalion of the J&K Rifles was martyred in the 1965 war. He was then just 23 years old. The road where we lived in Jabalpur has been named after him.

1971 War. A real great story of courage and sacrifice is that of Maj Vijay Rattan Choudhury (Datt) of the Madras Engineer Regiment.In the 1971 war his unit was tasked to clear mines in the Shakargarh sector to clear a path for our tanks to attack. The enemy heavily shelled the minefield. Unmindful of the grave risk, Maj Choudhary cleared the mines. He was killed by an enemy shell but had opened a path. He was awarded the MVC posthumously for this brave action.Then there is the brave 2Lt Pushpinder Singh Vaid who laid down his life fighting in the Punch sector in the 1971 war. Another hero of that war was the 24 year old Capt Hitesh Mehta of the Gurkhas. He was ADC to Maj Gen Gandharv Nagra who was leading the advance from the North on Dacca. The GOC sent this brave young man with a message for the Pakistani Army Commander, Gen Niazi- it said – "Abdulla I am here- the game is up- you surrender to me and I will look after you". Gen Niazi led the largest surrender of forces after the Second World War. Some 93,000 Pakistanis laid down their arms. The young hero was sent again to tell the Pakistani troops still holding out in Dacca to surrender as the war was over. They opened fire and killed the intrepid soldier on the spot. He was awarded the Sena Medal posthumously.

Kargil Conflict. Maj Nitin Bali, Capt Kamal Bakshi, Flt Lt Gaurav Chibber and Hav Navin Kumar Vaid were martyred in the Kargil war. Second Lieutenant Puneet Datt displayed great courage and determination in fighting the terrorists in J&K. He killed 3 foreign terrorists before laying down his life. He was awarded the highest gallantry award of Ashok Chakra posthumously. The Mohyal tradition of courage and sacrifice continuous unabated. We would like to salute our martyrs and humbly acknowledge their great sacrifice.

Police

Many Mohyals have earned laurels in the Police. A few of them are:

- J K Vaid DG Police J &K. He is heroically leading the police counter-terrorist operations in J&K.
- R S Mehta – I G BSF
- Brig Udai Chand Datt – IG Police (J&K)
- Rai Bahadur Ishan Das Mohan – I G Police (Nahan)
- Raizada Gian Chand Bali – DIG CID (J&K)
- Mehta Dharam Vir Bhimwal IG Police (Lucknow)
- P Bali – Commisioner Police (Nagpur)
- Rajan Bakshi – IGP (J&K)

Cinema

Mohyals are great actors and have done very well in the field of cinema and T.V. Notable Mohyal artists are –

- Sunil Dutt (Member of Parliament) Padma Shri
- Nargis Dutt Padma Shri
- Om Prakash
- Anand Bakshi (Lyricist)
- Sanjay Dutt
- Lara Datta
- Divya Dutta
- J P Dutta (Director)

Medicine

- Dr Baldev Vaid-Padma Bhushan
- Dr R K Bali-Padma Shri

Science And Technology

- Rakesh Bakshi (Scientist) Padma Shri
- Krishna Dev Bali (Engineer) Padma Shri

Industry

- Mehta N N Mohan-Padma Shri
- Col V R Mohan-Padma Shri
- Rz B D Bali

Literature

- Chaudhury Brahm Datt-Padma Shri
- Dr Ashok Lav International Peace foundation Award (UNESCO)

Social Activist

M S Gaurav Devi Datt Winner 7 th Jamna Lal Bajaj Award (1984)

Conclusion

This book is primarily a military history of the fighting Brahmin clans of India. Besides the Mohyals – these include the allied Bhumiars and Tyagis who are closely related. Social upheavals perpetrated by tyrannical rulers forced the scholarly Brahmins to take up weapons in the era of sage Parshuram. He became a legendary military hero- who turned the peaceful Brahmins into a force of scholar-warriors or Indian Samurai (poet-warriors). The Saraswat Mohyal Brahmins primarily dwelt along the tract of the ancient Saraswati river. This put them squarely in the path of all invaders. The Mohyal fighting Brahmins thus became the guardians of Indian gates and battled heroically with each and every invader. They fought the Greeks of Alexander, the Sakas, the Huns and Scythians and then the Arabs, the Turk tribes of Central Asia and Afghanistan, the Mongols and then the Uzbeks. The Mohyals had played a major role in the rise of the Sikhs and the overthrow of the Mughal rule that had turned unbearably tyrannical. The Mohyals thus played a major role in the Indian military revival. The British recognized them as a martial race and recruited them extensively in the British Indian Army.

The Mohyals once again played a leading role in the revivalist movement of the Arya Samaj and the freedom movement. A brief look at the post Independence accomplishments of just a few Mohyals indicates that their strong marital traditions are very much alive and vibrant. Six of them reached the rank of Army commanders and equivalent in the Air Force, 10 became Lt Generals in the Army and one equivalent rank in the Navy. Fifteen have attained the rank of Major Generals and 23 became Brigadiers. Five Mohyals became Air Vice Marshals and two reached the rank of Commodores in the Air Force. This is indeed an impressive tally for a community which is just 6 -7 lakhs strong today and scattered far from their original ancestral lands along the tracts of the Saraswati and Indus river systems.

This military history of the Mohyal Fighting Brahmins also incidentally, covers the entire history of the foreign invasions of India – especially by the Greeks, Arabs, Turko-Mongols, Pathans and Uzbeks. A lot of new facts have come to light from the study of the Muslim invasions of India. For the first time, the heroic resistance put up against the all conquering Arab armies by the Hindu kings of Afghanistan (the Rutbils and Hindu Shahi- Mohyals) has been recounted in detail. For the first time the Arab armies had been checkmated and thrown back from the ramparts of the Hindu Kush. The Arab invasions were brought to a grinding halt only in India and much later on the French borders in Europe. This ranks as a remarkable feat in the annals of the world's military history.

What is also surprising is that despite 800 years of Muslim rule – some 80% of the Indian population remained Hindu. Contrast this with what happened to the ancient civilizations of Egypt, Iran, and Central Asia. India proved to be a weak state but a strong society. Once the political institutions of the Hindu State collapsed due to military defeat, the society fragmented itself into tightly knit local Jatis and biradaries that kept their flocks together by the dire threat of ex-communicating all those who weakened and converted. Despite large scale and horrific massacres, the Hindus retained their identity as a distinct civilization. They refused to convert under duress and held on to their faith even in the face of abject military defeat. This defeat was not sudden. The Hindu kingdoms in Afghanistan put up such fierce resistance that the Arab armies were thrown back for the first time anywhere and when pushed to attack again, simply mutinied. The same had happened to the Greek armies. The Indian civilization has a lot of inherent strength and tenacity. Even though Hindu states had been weakened by constant infighting – the Hindu society has shown amazing strength and resilience in the face of adversity. It was able to close ranks against the foreign invaders and did not convert en masse. The caste system helped to save Hindu Society by providing local support networks and identity preservation mechanisms. The Caste system however is now an anachronism. The Indian State has now been revived and the caste faultlines have become a weakness adversaries can exploit. Today we need to strengthen the State and the very idea of India. We need to do away with the divisions of the caste system – which the British had exploited with great efficiency and thoroughness. They had well studied and understood the human terrain in India (even as they mapped the geo-physical terrain). With industrialisation – and consequent urbanization – Caste and Jati must loose their relevance. They are more relevant to an agricultural society. As we urbanise, Caste must become an agricultural era anachronism. The pity is the very pettiness of our post- Independence politics. These have put economic tags on caste identities and helped preserve and deepen the idea of caste instead of letting it atrophy and die out. Today we need to strengthen the idea of India and stress a pan-Indian identity to strengthen a national awareness and unity. We are far too fragmented a state and must focus on factors that strengthen our unity and the very idea of India. The British Colonial regime had attacked this idea of India very viciously – in the post 1857 scenario. They had exploited every caste, creed, language and race faultline to divide and rule our society. They had imposed a congenital sense of deep-rooted inferiority upon our people. The colonial experience was deeply dislocating. We now need to grow beyond this psychological slavery and rediscover our lost self respect. The idea of India needs to be revived. India's nationalism is in urgent need of resusication. To do that, we must take a deeper look at our own history and especially focus on the Muslim and British invasions of India. Given the weakness of State institutions in India – the survival of the Indian identity presents a paradox. How did this society resist outside penetration and mass scale conversions even in the aftermath of abject military defeat and in the face of great persecutions and mass killings? We need to ingest the lessons of the Hindu holocaust which was far worse than the Jewish holocaust. The problem is that where as the Jews make it a point to remember their past, we seek to forget about what happened and not recount the traumatic details. That is escapism. An ostrich does not become safe by burying its head in the sand. Today the Indian civilization needs to take a very close look at its past of invasions and slaughters and learn to defend itself. It is no point generating fabulous wealth if foreigners will simply come and loot it. Traditionally Indians have given low weightage to matters military. They have tended not to think strategically. Not being unified is our biggest curse.Remembering our recent history will help us overcome this failing. That precisely is the purpose of this military – historical exercise. For me personally, this book has also been a quest for my own roots and identity. It is above all a tribute to my parents and my ancestors. It is tribute to that tradition of courage and valour which has been our ancient inheritance. Today the very eco-system that sustained the ethic of courage, self-transcendence and sacrifice is gone. We need more historical narratives like this one to study and learn the lessons of our history.

"Those who don't learn from history', said George Santanya," are condemned to repeat it". We must understand the tenacity of our enemies. Pre-Medieval India had held off the invaders for 300 years. But they persisted till we grew complacent. Then they routed our armies and slaughtered our people- simply because we failed to keep pace with RMAs of our era. We failed to keep pace with the technology of warfighting and we failed to evolve new organisations, tactics and techniques to match the changes the enemies had introduced. We held on to the War Elephant for a thousand years because we refused to change the way we fought wars. To defend ourselves we need to militarise our mind sets and also our ethics. Pacifism in the face of such trenchant and tenacious foes can be an invitation to a dire civilisational disaster. Let us hope we have learnt our lessons. That was the express purpose of this military historical exercise. It also informs us that we have emerged from the dregs of defeat to a new Indian Military revival that saw its apogee in the 1971 War for the liberation of Bangladesh. Our armed forces then broke Pakistan in two and that war saw the emergence of a new nation state based upon the force of arms. It also saw the mass surrender of 93,000 prisoners of war-the largest after the Second World War. It has been a magnificent saga of defeat into victory in which the Mohyal Fighting Brahmins have made a notable and magnificent contribution.

2/Lt Puneet Nath Dutt
AC

Lt Gen Z C bakshi
PVSM, MVC, Vrc, VSM

Maj Gen MMS Bakshi
MVC, AVSM

Lt Col. Mehta, Harbans Lal,
MVC

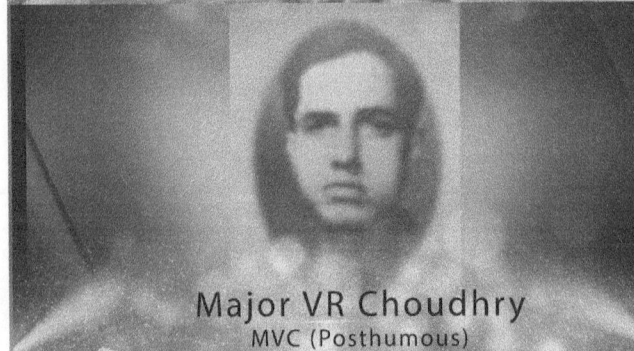

Major VR Choudhry
MVC (Posthumous)

mohyal military heroes

mohyals who became governors of state

shri sk chibber
lt. governor mizoram

lt. gen bkn chibber
governor punjab

bhai mahavir
governor mp

Select Bibliography

1. Al Biladuri, Ahmad, *Kitab Futuh al Buldan*, Murgotten F.C., *The Origins of Islamic State*, Translation, Pt. II, New York; Extracts in *The History of India as Told by its Own Historians* by Elliot H.M. and Dowson J, Vol. I.

2. Ali Muhammad, *Chach-nama or Tarikh-i-Hind wa Sind*, trans. By Mirza Kalich Beg Fredunbeg, Two Vols., Karachi, 1900; Delhi reprint, 1979.

3. Azraqi, Abu Al-Walid Muhammad, *Akhbar Makka*, ed. Wustenfield, Leipzig, 1858.

4. Badaoni, *Muntakhabu-t-Twarikh*, translation by George S.A. Ranking, Patna, 1973 ed.

5. Bahar, Malik Ash Shura, ed., *Tarikh-i-Sistan*, Tehran.

6. Baihaqi, Abual-Fadl Muhammad, *Tarikh-i-Baihaqi*, ed. Q. Ghani and Fayyad, Tehran, 1946.

7. Bakshi Pawan, Umar Khalid Bin & Mehta Narinder, *Mohyal Chhibbers in Indian History*, Hindustan Publishers, Lucknow, 2011.

8. Bali P. N., *The History of the Mohyals: A Legendary People*, Published by GMS New Delhi, Third Ed., 2006.

9. Basham A.L., *The Wonder that was India*, Delhi, reprint, 1988.

10. Bosworth C.E., *The Ghaznavids: Their Empire in Afghanistan and Eastern Iran 994-1040*, Edinburg, 1963.
    - 'Notes on the Pre-Ghaznavid History of Eastern Afghanistan', *Islamic Quarterly*, Vol. IX, 1965, pp.12-24.
    - 'Early Sources for the History of the First Four Ghaznavid Sultans', *IHQ*, Vol. XII, 1965, pp.12-24.
    - *Sistan under the Arabs: From the Islamic Conquest to the Rise of the Saffarids (651-684 A.D.)*, Rome, 1968.
    - Ubaidullah B, 'Abi Bakra and the 'Army of Destruction' in Zabulistan (698 A.D.)', *Der Islam*, Vol. 50, 1973.

11. Bakshi G D, *The Rise Of Indian Military Power: Evolution of an Indian Strategic Culture*, KW publishers , New Delhi 2010(reprint 2015)

12. Ibid, *Bose an Indian Samurai: A Military Assessment of Netaji and The INA*,KW Publishers, New Delhi 2016.

13. Ibid, *The Indian Military Revival,* Lancers New Delhi 1987

14. Ibid, *Footprints in the Snow: the Saga of General Zorawar Singh,* Lancers , New Delhi , 2002

15. Briggs John, English translation of *History of the Rise of the Mahomedan Power in India* from the original Persian of Mahomed Kasim Ferishta, Vol. 1, Indian ed., Calcutta.

16. Brockelmann Carl, *History of the Islamic People,* London, 1949.

17. Buhlar G., *The Laws of Manu (Manusmriti),* Delhi, reprint, 1990.

18. Bykov A.A., 'finds of Indian Medieval Coins in East Europe', *Jouranl of the Numismatic Society of India,* XXVII, 1965.

19. Caroe Olaf, *the Pathans,* Oxford University Press, Karachi, reprint, 1988.

20. Chatterjee C.D., 'Unique Gold and Brass Coins o the Imperial Guptas', *bulletin of the U.P. historical Society,* No. 2.

21. Collected Papers, *International Seminar on How Deep are the Roots of Indian Civilization? An Archeological & historical Perspective,* November 25-27, 2010, New Delhi.

22. Cunningham Alexander, *Coins of Medieval India from the Seventh Century down to the Muhammadan Conquest,* Varanasi, reprint, 1963.

23. Dani A.H., 'Mazar-i-Sharif Inscription of the Time of Shahi ruler Veka', *Journal of Asian Civilisations,* vol. XXIV, No. 1, July 2001, pp.81-86.

24. Drake H., *The Book of Government Rules for Kings,* trans. Of *Siyasat Namah,* London, 1960.

25. Elliot H.M., and Dowson John,*The History of India as Told by its Own Historians,* Vols. I and II, Indian ed., Kitab Mahal.

26. Fauja Singh, 'Sita Ram Kohli' in *Historians and historiography in Modern India,* ed. S.P. Sen, Calcutta, 1973.

27. Feuerstein Georg, Subhash Kak and David Frawley, *In Search of the Cradle of Civilization: New Light on Ancient India,* Motilal Banarsidas Publishers, Delhi, 1997 (First Indian Ed.).

28. Gafurov B.G., *Central Asia – Pre-Historic to Pre-Modern Times,* Delhi, 2005, English trans. of *Tahziki* in Russian language, Dushanbe, 1989.

29. Gardizi Abd al-Hayy, *Kitab Zain-ul-Akhbar,* ed. By Muhammad Nazim, trans. of extracts by S.R. Sharma in *Medieval Indian History,* see Sharma.

30. Ghose Ajit, 'A Uniqu Gold Coin of the Hindu Kings of Kabul', *The Numismatic Chronicle,* Sixth Series, Vol. XII, 1952, pp. 133-35.

31. Gopal L., *the Economic Life of Northern India (700-1200 A.D.),* Delhi, 1989 ed.

32. Haig Wolseley, *The Cambridge History of India*, Vol. III, Delhi, reprint 1987.

33. Haukal Ibn, *Kitab-ul-Masalik-wal-Mamalik*, trans. of extracts in *The History of India as Told by its Own Historians*, Elliot and Dowson, Vol. I. Also, De Goeje M.J. (ed.), *Kitab al-masalik wa'l mamalik of Abu-l-Qasin ibn Hauqal* (Leiden, 1873).

34. Ibn al-Athir, Abu al Hasan Ali, *Al Kami Fi al-Tarikh*, ed. C.J. Tornberg, London, 1867-71.

35. Idrisi Al, *Nuzhat-al Mushtak fi Ikhtirak-ul Afak (The Delight of those who Seek to Wander through the Regions of the World*, trans. of extracts in *The History of India as Told by its Own Historians*, Elliot and Dowson, Vol. I.

36. Istakhri Al, Ishak Abu, *Kitab-l Akalim (Book of Climes)*, trans. of extracts in *The History of India as Told by its Own Historians*, Elliot and Dowson, Vol. I.

37. Ikram S.M., *Muslim Civilisation in India*, New York, 1964.

38. Jenkins G.K. and Narain A.K., 'The Coin Types of the Shaka-Pahlva Kings of India', *Numismatic Notes and Monograph No. 4* of the Numismatic Society of India, Varanasi, 1957.

39. Khuda Buksh S., *A History of the Islamic People*, trans. from the German of Dr. Well's *Geschichte der Islamitischen Volker*, Delhi.

40. Lal B. B., *Saraswati Flows On: The Continuity of Indian Culture*, Aryan Books International, New Delhi, 2002.

41. Macdowall David W., 'The shahis of Kabulo and Gandhar', *Numismatic Chronicle*, Seventh Series, Vol. VIII, pp. 182-224, London, 1968.

42. Mas'udi Al, Hasan Abu-l, 'Abi, *Muruj-ul Zahab (Meadows of Gold)*, trans. Of extracts in *The History of India as Told by its Own Historians*, by Elliot and Dowson, Vol. I.

43. Majumdar R. C., and others, eds., *The Age of Imperial Kanauj* Vol. IV of *The History and Culture of the Indian People,*, Bombay, 1993 edn.
    - *The Struggle for Empire*, Vol. V of *The History and Culture of the Indian People*.
    - *The Classical Age*

44. Mazumdar A. K., *Early Hindu India, A Dynamic Study*, Dacca, 1917, New Delhi, 1981 edn.

45. Mazumdar Bhakat Prasad, *Socio Economic History of Northern India (1030-1194 A.D.)*, Calcutta, 1960.

46. M'crindle J. W., *The Invasion of India by Alexander The Great – As Described by Arrian, Q. Curlius, Diodoros, Plutarch and Justin.*

47. Mehta J. L., *Advanced Study in the History of Medieval India,* Sterling Publishers.

48. Mishra S. M., *Yasovarman of Kanauj,* New Delhi, 1978.

49. Mishra Vibhuti Bhushan, *The Gurjara Pratiharas and Their Times,* Delhi, 1966.

50. Mishra Yogendra, *The Hindu Sahis of Afghanistan and the Punjab A.D. 865-1026 (A Phase of Islamic Advance into India,* Patna, 1972.

51. Mohan Mehta Vashisstha Deva, *The North-West India of the Second Century B.C.,* Ludhiana, 1974.

52. Mukherjee Dr. Mithi, *India in the Shadow of Empire: A Legal and Political History 1774-1950,* Oxford University Press, New Delhi, 2010.

53. Domino Michael, *The Lost River: On the Trail of the Saraswati,* Penguin Books, Delhi, 2010.

54. Mohan RT, *Afghanistan Revisited: The Brahman Hindu Shahis of Afghanistan and the Punjab (840-1028 CE),* General Mohyal Sabha (Regd.), Delhi, 2003.

Mohyal History

55. Bali P. N., *The History of Mohyals – A Legendary People,* General Mohyal Sabha, Mohyal Foundation, A-9, Qutab Institutional Area, USO Road, Jeet Singh Marg, New Delhi-110067, E-mail: gmsoffice@yahoo.co.in; gms_delhi@india.com.

56. Chopra P. N., *Religions and Communities of India,* Vision Books, 1982.

57. Datt Gauri Shankar 'Sagar' Chaudhari, *Mohyal History,* Urdu.

58. Datt Chunilal, *Mohyal History,* Urdu, Delhi, 1955.

59. Gazetteer of Jhelum District of 1904, pp. 120-121.

60. Gazetteer of Rawalpindi District of 1894, pp. 80 & 83.

61. Gazetteer of Sialkot District of 1907, pp. 78-79.

62. Griffin L., *The Chiefs and Families of Note in the Punjab,* Vol. II, 1910, p. 254.

63. Imperial Gazetteer of India, Vol. III, Behrampur to Bombay, p. 100.

64. Rose H. A., *A Glossary of the Tribes and Castes of the Punjab and North-West Frontier Province,* see Rose.

65. Russel Stracey T. P., *The History of the Mohyals – The Militant Brahman Race of India,* Lahore, 1911, reprint Chandigarh.

66. Vaid Harichand Raizada, *Gulshan-e-Mohyali,* Urdu, Lahore, 1923.

67. Jonraja, *Rajatarangini Dvitiya*, Hindi trans. and commentary by Raghunath Singh, Varanasi, 1972.

68. Naipaul V. S., *Among the Believers*, New York, Vintage Books, 1982.

69. Nazim M., *The Life and Times of Sultan Mahmud of Ghazna*, New Delhi, reprint 1971.

70. Nizam-ud-Din Ahmad Bakshi, *Tahakat-I Akbari*, ed. & trans. By B. Dey, Calcutta, 1913.

71. Owen Sydney, *From Mahmud Ghazni to the Disintegration of Mughal Empire*, Delhi, Kanishka Publishing House, 1987.

72. Pandey D. B., *The Shahis of Afghanistan and the Punjab*, Delhi, 1973.

73. Pandit Kalhana, *Rajatarangini*, English trans. and commentary by R. S. Pandit, New Delhi, reprint.

74. Pandit Kalhana, *Rajatarangini*, English trans. see Stein.

75. Prakash Budha, *Rigveda and the Indus Valley Civilisation*, Hoshiarpur, 1966.

76. Rahman Abdur, *The Last Two Dynamites of the Shahis*, Islamabad, 1979, Delhi, reprint 1988.
    - 'Date of the Overthrow of Lagaturman – The Last Turk Shahi Ruler of Kabul', *Lahore Museum Bulletin*, Vol. VI, No. 1 & 2, January-December, 1993, pp. 29-31.
    - 'The Zalamkot Bilingual Inscription', *East & West*, Vol. 48, Nos. 3-4 December 1998, pp. 469-73.
    - 'Ethnicity of Hindu Shahis', *Quarterly Journal of Pakistan Historical Society*, July-Sptember 2003, Vol. L1, No.3.
    - 'New Light on the Khingal, Turk and the Hindu Shahis.

77. Rashid Ahmad, *TALIBAN – The story of Afghan War Lords*, Pan Books, 2001.

78. Raverty H. G., *Notes on Afghanistan, Geographical, Ethnological and Historical*, London, 1880.
    - *Tabaqat-i-Nasiri (of Minhaj ud-Din)*, English trans., Delhi, reprint 1970.

79. Ray H. C., *The Dynastic History of Northern India (Early Medieval Period)*, Vol. I, New Delhi, reprint 1973.

80. Raya Panchana, *A Historical Review of Hindu India*, Delhi, 1939.

81. Raychaudhuri Hemchandra, *Political History of Ancient India*, Delhi, 1997.

82. Rose H. A., *A Glossary of the Tribes and Castes of the Punjab and North-*

West Frontier Province, Census Reports 1883 and 1892, Lahore, 1911-15, reprint Delhi, 1982.

83. Sachau E. C., *Alberuni's India*, trans. of the book *Tehqiq ma li't-Hind* (Arabic) written byt Abu Rihan Muhammad al-Biruni, Indian ed., New Delhi, reprint 1981.

84. Sahni D. R., 'Six Inscriptions in the Lahore Museum', *Epigraphia Indica*, Vol. XXI, No.44, 1938, pp.298-99.

85. Satya Shrava, *The Kushana Numismatics*, New Delhi, 1985.

86. Sen Amulya Bhusan, 'A Neglected Chapter of Indian History – The Shahis of Udbhandapur', *The Modern Review*, Vol. CX, No.6, 1961, pp.476-84.

87. Sen S. P., ed., *Historians and Histography in Modern India*, Calcutta, 1973.

88. Sharma R. S., *Indian Feudalism*, Macmillan, Delhi.

89. Sharma S. R., *Studies in Medieval Indian History*, Sholapur, 1956.

90. Singh Bhajan Singh, *Aryon Ka Adi Niwas: Madhya Himalaya* (Hindi), Tehri, 1986.

91. Singh Mahendra Pratap, *Life in Ancient India 9800-1200 A.D.).*

92. Singh D. C., *Studies in Indain Coins*, Delhi, 1968.

93. Smith V. A., *Early History of India from 600 B.C. to the Muhammadan Conquest*, Oxford, 1962.
     • Oxford History of India

94. Stein M. A., *Kalhana's Rajatarangini*, English trans., Delhi, reprint 1989, Vols. I & II.
     • *Kalhana's Rajatarangini*, Sanskrit text with critical notes, ed. By M. A. Stein, Delhi, reprint 1988.

95. Tabri Abu Ja'afar Muhammad, *Tarikhar-Rasul wa al-Muluk*, ed. M de Goeje and others, 1964, E. J. Brill reprint.

96. Thakur U., *History of Suicides in India*, Delhi, 1962.

97. Tod James, *Annals and Antiquities of Rajasthan*, London, 1832, Delhi, reprint 2002.

98. Upadhyay Vasudev, *The Socio-Religious Conditions of North India (700-1200 A.D.)*, Varansi, 1964.

99. Utbi Abu Nasr Muhammad, *Kitab al-Yamini* or *Tarikh al-Yamini*, trans. of extracts by H. M. Elliot, *The History of India as Told by its Own Historians*, Vol. II, trans. by J. Reynolds, London.

100. Vaidya C. V., *History of Medieval Hindu India*, Poona, Vols. I, II and III, Poona, 1921-26.

101. Walker J., 'Islamic Coins with Hindu Types', *The Numismatic chronicle*, Vol. VI, 1946, pp. 121-28.

102. Watters Thomas, *On Yuan Chwang's Travels in India (629-645 A.D.)*, London, 1904.

103. Wink Andre, *Al Hind: The Making of the Indo-Islamic World*, Vol. I, *Early Medieval India and the Expansion of Islam 7th-11th Centuries*, New Delhi, reprint 1999.

104. Yaqut Aby Abd Allal Yaqub, *Kitab Mu-jam al-Baldan*, ed. F. Wustenfeld, Leipzig, 1866-73.

Index

www.ingramcontent.com/pod-product-compliance
Lightning Source LLC
Chambersburg PA
CBHW021815270326
41932CB00007B/192